Texts in Compu

Volume 22

Languages, Machines, and Classical Computation

Texts in Computing Series Editor
Ian Mackie   mackie@lix.polytechnique

Languages, Machines, and Classical Computation

Third Edition

Luis M. Augusto

© Individual author and College Publications 2019. Second edition 2020, Third edition 2021.
All rights reserved.

ISBN 978-1-84890-300-5

College Publications
Scientific Director: Dov Gabbay
Managing Director: Jane Spurr

http://www.collegepublications.co.uk

Cover produced by Laraine Welch

Contents

Contents

Contents

List of Figures

List of Tables

List of Algorithms

Preface to the 1st edition

Teachers tend to be picky with the material they use in teaching contexts. This may be for personality reasons, but the variety of contexts and students also plays a role in this pickiness. Be it as it may, it often is the case that students end up with teaching material in many formats and from many different sources, creating often a lack of uniformity, both in notation and terminology. Because I am picky for all the reasons above, I typically feel that my teaching task is substantially facilitated and optimized when I have gone to the great lengths of putting all the material for a particular academic subject together in a single manual or textbook. This guarantees not only conceptional and notational uniformity, but also a selection of approaches that I feel work well, or better, for particular topics or problems.

This book is not about discovering the wheel; that is, possibly no novel contents are to be found in it. The objective when writing it was that of "putting together" a textbook on the classical theory of computing. If there is any novel aspect in this textbook, it may well be the fact that I insist on preceding the terms "(theory of) computation" and "(theory of) computing" with the adjective "classical" to collect under the same label the Chomsky hierarchy and the Turing-von Neumann paradigm of computing. The former comprises three closely associated central topics, to wit, formal grammars, formal languages, and models of computation (a.k.a machines, or automata), and the latter gives to these, namely via the Turing machine, measures of the spatial and temporal costs of computation. I say that this collection constitutes *(the)* classical (theory of) computation, because many, often newer, other forms of computing have emerged or become (more) popular since the Turing "revolution," many of which today may be said to constitute *the* non-classical (theory of) computation. This is, for the initiated, more immediately the field of quantum computing, but other forms of computation such as artificial neural networks and evolutionary computing may be seen as also non-classical versions of computing.

It is arguably possible to produce a textbook on formal languages, grammars, and automata with no emphasis on computing, let alone with any specific computational concerns. One such approach might be with linguists in mind, though contemporary linguistics is not averse to computation. On the extreme pole of this position, formal grammars, languages, and automata are often reduced to *the* theory of computation, namely as it serves the theoretical foundations of the digital computer. Without taking a reductive view, I discuss formal languages and grammars from the viewpoint of computation, and consider the associated automata as models thereof. This said, readers with other foci will find that the computational perspective taken here does not hinder–and may even facilitate–their particular interests and concerns.

The backbone of this book is undoubtedly the Chomsky hierarchy. Although much computing has run in the digital computer since N. Chomsky first conceived it, it still works well for combining the mostly linguistic approach with the computational one. In particular, it keeps reminding us that we are linguistic beings to the point that one of our most interesting creations–the digital computer–is language-based through and through, a feature well-patent in the famous Turing Test, a "test" conceived by the creator of the Turing machine to distinguish a human computer from a non-human one. Indeed, it seems to have been the rationale in Turing (1950) that language is sufficient to distinguish the human from the non-human computer or reasoner. More than anything, it might have been this insistence on the verbal behavior of computers that motivated the can-of-worms idea of AI (artificial intelligence) as ultimately aiming at human-like machines, at least from the viewpoint of intelligence, if not of emotion.

There is no way to go around this and it requires emphasis: (Classical) computing is a mathematical subject. Although the presence of automata, of which the most famous is the Turing machine, lends it a flavor of engineering, these are not physical machines nor can they be; they are mathematical objects. To be sure, the digital computer is based on the Turing machine, but this has a feature–an infinite tape–that makes of the former a mere approximation of the latter. The mathematical nature of this subject accounts for the clearly mathematical approach in this book: I distinguish statements into definitions and propositions, and provide proofs (or sketches thereof) to further distinguished–if not distinct–statements, to wit, theorems and their companion lemmas and corollaries. The numbering of such statements finds its utility in internal referencing, if it gives a more high-brow quality to the main text. I reserve the status of theoremhood for statements of higher importance than propositions, but the reader is free to consider (most) propositions in this text as *de-facto* theorems; the fact that proofs are provided (or left as exercises) for propositions supports this view.

This mathematical nature of the subject also justifies the large selection of exercises here provided. Indeed, only few students are gifted with mathematical skills that free them from the arduous and time-consuming practice of doing exercises. On the other hand, some may find this a pleasant activity. Between these fall most mortals, one should think. But the selection of exercises in this book was also guided by the belief that one should be confronted with novel material and problems, in order to develop research, as well as creative, skills.

Still with regard to the mathematical nature of this text, there are throughout it a few algorithms for the computation of specific functions (e.g., computing the Chomsky normal form of a given grammar). I chose not to stick to a single pseudo-code or to a single algorithm format in the belief that different algorithms can be better grasped in distinct ways. Yet another advantage of this might be the familiarity with diverse pseudo-codes and algorithm formats. Importantly, too, no programming language or software plays any role whatsoever in this book. This is so deliberately to keep the subject matter as general as possible, untied to specific implementations or applications.

As said above, the aim for this book is not (re)inventing the wheel. Although classical computing and its theory are in a current state of development, with many a problem as focus of research–notably so the **P=?NP** problem–, the subject of the theory of classical computing has attained a certain fixed form that is historically justified. In the second half of last century, when this subject emerged, an abundance of text-books and monographs were published, and a few of these established themselves as standard references in the field. As such, it is only natural that in pedagogical pursuits one should resort to them as sources. This I do with two such classics in particular, to wit, Davis & Weyuker (1983) and Hopcroft & Ullman (1979), the latter of which has evolved into the more undergraduate-friendly Hopcroft, Motwani, & Ullman (2013). A further source is Du & Ko (2001), a thoroughly mathematical approach. Readers can greatly benefit from a direct use of all these referenced works. Texts and manuals on this subject matter directed at under-graduate audiences abound, with many a good one to further assist readers in their academic pursuits. Referencing them all is of course impossible, but interested readers know where to find them. More specific, often more advanced, literature is cited throughout this text in the appropriate places; in particular, I cite the works in which important results (e.g., theorems) were first published.

Lastly, this textbook is a further elaboration on what was originally a chapter in a book of mine first published by College Publications, to wit, Augusto (2018).[1] In this book, a chapter on the theory of comput-

---

[1] Now Augusto (2020a).

ing appeared to be relevant, because issues such as Turing-completeness of logic programming and the complexity of the satisfiability problem (a.k.a SAT) required a minimal grasp of, among other topics, the Turing machine. Having resorted to this chapter to teach topics in automata, formal languages, and the classical theory of computation, and having obtained satisfactory results, I decided to expand it to what is now the present textbook. The main guideline for this expansion was the inclusion of topics that were left out in the mentioned chapter for spatial and temporal reasons, but which are essential for a fuller treatment of this subject. Some of these new topics–e.g., characteristic equations of finite automata, grammar cleaning algorithm–may appear quite inessential from an Anglo-Saxon perspective, but my individual work with Spanish students preparing themselves to take exams on the above-mentioned topics made me realize the need to be as encompassing and comprehensive as possible, namely with the large diversity of readers of this subject in mind.

I wish to thank Dov M. Gabbay, the scientific director of College Publications, and Ian Mackie, the editor for the Texts in Computing series, for publishing this book. My thanks go also to Jane Spurr, the managing director, for a smooth publication process.

Madrid, February 2019

Luis M. S. Augusto

Preface to the 2nd edition

The present edition corrects identified addenda and errata, and has both improved and new figures. It also includes the odd minor change in the main text of the first edition. The major changes are as follows:

- Figures 4.1.11 and 4.3.7 were replaced by more adequate ones: In the case of Figure 4.1.11, the union of languages was rather opaque, and the original finite automaton was replaced by a clearer illustration; as for Figure 4.3.7, the original Turing machine, which was too simple, was replaced by a more complex one.

- Exercise 4.1.9 (originally 4.1.14) has now five items, an increase aiming at providing more practice of a complex algorithm.

- An additional algorithm for the conversion of a context-free grammar into a pushdown automaton (Algorithm 4.5) is now included and, based on it, Example 4.2.3 was greatly revised and extended. This change entailed a new Figure (4.2.7),[1] to be found in Exercise 4.2.8, which was completely redesigned.

These changes are now made available thanks to the readiness of College Publications to publish a second edition so shortly after the first. Renewed thanks are in order.

Madrid, May 2020

Luis M. S. Augusto

---

[1]Figure 4.2.4 in this 3rd edition.

Preface to the 3rd edition

The present edition improves on the previous ones in many ways, of which a few can be specified:

- Many exercises were introduced and others were rewritten, in particular in Chapter 2. In this Chapter, the emphasis fell on functions and algorithms, two topics that were not satisfactorily–in any case not sufficiently–discussed in the previous editions. Many of the functions and algorithms involve recursion, a fundamental notion in classical computation that was also not sufficiently discussed before. In the belief that research is an essential task in the understanding of mathematical topics, a belief that had already been present in the writing of the two previous editions, many of the exercises introduced require that the student research integrally in specific topics (e.g., Ackermann functions).

- A wholly new Section on algorithms and programs (Section 2.4) was introduced.

- Further topics in regular languages and finite automata were introduced, namely the Thompson construction, product automata, and the direct sum of automata. This, in turn, motivated the introduction of two new algorithms, to wit, Algorithms 4.3 and 4.4.

- More exercises with Turing machines were added, both for function-computing and language-accepting machines.

Thanks are due to College Publications for their readiness to publish the present 3rd edition.

Madrid, October 2021

Luis M. S. Augusto

Part I.

Introduction

1. Classical computation: Turing, von Neumann, and Chomsky

1.1. Computers, information, and computations

Given some device or structure capable of receiving an input and producing an output that is more or less uniquely associated to the input, we may call it a *computer* if it goes through a series of more or less well-defined states or configurations, called a *computation*, and both the input and the output are essentially informational. (We do not say that a device or structure taking as input, say, oxygen and outputting carbon dioxide is a computer.) Typically, a computer processes information by making a decision or by solving a function. The output of a computer may thus be in the form of a "Yes/No" answer, or as a printed string of symbols, respectively.

Until recently, when speaking of computation one would take it for granted that one's audience would think of the digital computer. But then new notions of computation emerged–or became (at last) popular–that, though they might be (partly) implemented in a digital computer, diverge from this notion of computation in foundational ways. We speak here of, for instance, computation as carried out by artificial neural networks, cellular automata, quantum computers, fuzzy computers, etc.

This variety is directly connected to the equivocal definition of *information* (Augusto, 2020d). While there are many faces to information, which makes it approachable from a large plethora of subjects (semiotics, linguistics, philosophy, mathematics, engineering, etc.), we shall restrict its meaning to *(strings of) symbols* over some set called an *alphabet* (e.g., the Roman alphabet, or the 0-9 digit set) that can be measured in *bits* representable by the Boolean values 0 and 1, and we shall mean by its *processing* the sequence of well-defined states or configurations a computer goes through from an initial input to a final output. This may, and often does, involve aspects such as extraction, interpretation, and storage, but we shall be mostly interested in these insofar as they are carried out in *discrete* computation, i.e. in discrete states or configurations.

This focus segregates our notion of computation from that carried out by:

- Quantum computers, inasmuch as these use quantum bits (vs. "plain" bits) and operate by means of quantum algorithms, which are often probabilistic;

- artificial neural networks and the so-called fuzzy computers, because their computing is essentially quantitative (vs. symbolic) and approximate (vs. "Yes/No" decisions);

- computing systems operating with evolutionary algorithms inasmuch as these change/adapt during the computations, whereas the digital computer is not altered by its computations;

- etc.

By and large, the above divergences allow us to speak of *hard computing* when referring to the digital computer, by opposition to *soft computing*, or forms of computation that are approximate, probabilistic, often heuristic, largely quantitative, and adaptive–features that might be collected under the label *computational intelligence*. But, as a matter of fact, further divergences are of import; for instance, the digital computer diverges from cellular automata and many soft computers insofar as these compute in a parallel/distributed manner, whereas the computation over symbol strings as carried out by the digital computer is essentially a serial/sequential business.

1.2. Computational problems, algorithms, and decisions

We can summarize the above by saying that our notion of computation is synonymous with *algorithm*: Given an input symbol or string over some alphabet, each configuration of our computer is the result of one of a series of well-defined moves, or steps, leading to a decision or to an output string over the same or another alphabet. To be sure, there are algorithms everywhere, for a large plethora of problems (for instance, you need an algorithm to change a burnt light-bulb), and of many types (e.g., probabilistic algorithms), but in our specific case we are interested in algorithms insofar as they give us a "Yes/No" solution to (an instance of) a *computational problem*.

Say there is a large educational institution (e.g., a university) offering one thousand different courses. Large as it may physically be, it is unlikely that it has one thousand rooms, one for each course. Hence, it requires a schedule, or a distribution of courses into rooms such that there are no two different classes in the same room at the same time. This is an instance of what is known as *the scheduling problem*, and we say that this is a computational problem because it clearly requires a computer capable of receiving the input of n courses and m rooms and outputting a solution that takes into consideration the facts that classes take place only on working days, from Monday to Friday, from 9 a.m. to 6 p.m., and that in fact a course requires only a specific number (say k) of weekly classes of l hours each. Putting all these factors together in a cooking pan will not provide a solution, nor will saying "Abracadabra!"; one does need a computer, and for this reason this is called a computational problem.

Although a human computer–i.e. a human brain–can solve this problem, it can do so typically only for low n and m, so that other computers are required. But an artificial neural network, or a fuzzy computer, will not be good candidates to solving this problem, though, as said, they are also computing systems; and neither will evolutionary computing systems provide a solution. The above institution requires a solution such that on, say, Mondays, from 9 a.m. to 6 p.m., n classes of l hours can take place on m rooms. That is to say that, queried whether course A can take place on room B at time C on day D, the computing system from which we expect an answer to our query can tell us "Yes" or "No". Our computational problem thus diverges from problems computable by other computing systems in that it is a *decision problem*, and the computation carried out by our computer is in fact a *decision procedure*.

1.3. The Turing-von Neumann paradigm

This is what essentially distinguishes what we may call *classical computation*, formulated in the *classical theory of computation*, from non-classical computation, which includes all the types of soft computing above, as well as other forms of computation. Summing up, classical computation is:

- Symbolic (vs. quantitative),

- Boolean (vs. many-valued or fuzzy-valued),[1]

---

[1] Fuzzy logic can be seen as type of many-valued logic in which the truth-value set

- Discrete (vs. continuous),

- Serial (vs. parallel),

- Precise (vs. approximate, probabilistic, or uncertain in the quantum sense).

We use here the adjective "classical" in at least two senses. Firstly, because this form of computing is *classical* in the logical sense of the term, which refers to the bivalent symbolic logic according to which every proposition is either true or false. In effect, the "Yes/No" solutions to computational problems map directly into the two Boolean values 1 and 0.

Secondly, we say that it is classical, because its theory was founded on proven mathematical results that can be said to be *classical*, and this long before the other forms of computing attained the same or a comparable level of theoretical stability. For instance, fuzzy computing was founded on fuzzy set theory and fuzzy logic, which emerged only in the second half of the 1960s (e.g., Zadeh, 1965); artificial neural networks, while supported by well-established mathematical results formulated in the early 1940s (McCulloch & Pitts, 1943) and showing a strong development in the 1980s (e.g., Rumelhart et al., 1988), were not able, for many reasons, to impose themselves as the standard model of computation, though these computing systems have now many industrial and scientific applications; quantum computing, while theoretically founded on a well-established field of modern physics (quantum mechanics), is still in its infancy, with a plethora of physical realizations appearing as possible but only a single quantum computer commercially "released" (in 2019 by IBM); inspired in biological processes that can be interpreted as adaptive algorithms, evolutionary computing has yet to fully converge as a specific subject, though it emerged in the 1960s (examples of early influential texts are Fogel et al., 1966, and Holland, 1975).

But the fundamental difference is that, in these, the term *algorithm* must be used with caveats and nuances, whereas what we call here classical computation has as cornerstone the very classical definition of algorithm, and this we owe to A. Turing. In effect, we may place the emergence of classical computation in, or around, 1936-7, when this British scientist proved the celebrated negative result for the decision problem for formulas of the classical first-order predicate logic (Turing, 1937). This problem, known as *Entscheidungsproblem* due to its formu-

---

is infinite, namely the interval $[0, 1]$. See Augusto (2020b) for a comprehensive study of many-valued logics that includes the main fuzzy logics.

lation by the German mathematician D. Hilbert,[2] asked whether there was an algorithm to decide on the universal validity of an arbitrary logical sentence in a first-order theory. In giving a negative answer to the *Entscheidungsproblem*–i.e. there is no general solution to this decision problem, a result known as *Turing's theorem*–, Turing provided a mathematical definition of algorithm that, though it has equivalent contemporary conceptions (cf. Church, 1936a, b; Kleene, 1938), given its more intuitive character became the equivalent to the definition of a computable function. We speak here of the Turing machine, a theoretical simplification of the machine featuring in Turing's proof, to wit, the *universal Turing machine.*

The Turing machine is a surprisingly parsimonious abstract machine: It has a read-and-write head that can move to the left and to the right to read and write on a tape with cells that, when not blank, are occupied by single symbols. This model is not very different from other finite automata; actually, a pushdown automaton, with its stack, has a more complex mechanical behavior. But it has something of a tremendous import: Its tape is infinite. This means that the only limits to its computations are the limits of computable functions themselves. This gives to this machine a purely theoretical character, no physical machine being capable of concretizing the infinite length of its tape. This purely mathematical character entails that the Turing machine expends no energy on its computations, nor is it constrained by any form of complexity of its inputs, time and space resources being wholly irrelevant: If a function is computable, then the Turing machine can compute it.

This accounts for a core concept in classical computation, to wit, *Turing-completeness*, it being said of a computational construct that it is Turing-complete if and only if it can do whatever a Turing machine can do. For instance, the class of context-free languages, a central class in programming-language theory, can be said not to be Turing-complete, because no finite automaton, the machine associated to these languages, can recognize or accept a language with strings like *aaabbbccc*, characterized by the concatenation of three symbols exactly with the same number of occurrences; a Turing machine can easily be programmed to do this. Because every Turing machine can be simulated by the universal Turing machine, Turing-completeness is in fact the ability to simulate this central construct of classical computing.

Anyone who has programmed a Turing machine for even very simple functions must have realized how daunting the task is. So, given this,

---

[2]Cf. Hilbert & Ackermann (1928). W. Ackermann was Hilbert's assistant and he actually redacted this work, based on Hilbert's lectures.

and the fact that it is physically non-realizable, why do we still keep it as the very cornerstone of classical computation? Firstly, because though it itself does not expend any time or space resources, it provides the framework for measures of space and time expenditure on specific computations, and this in an axiomatic way. We speak here of the Blum axioms (cf. Blum, 1967) that, though somehow outdated and originally theoretically independent from the Turing machine, still provide the basic measurements for the temporal and spatial costs of computations.

Secondly, because it is theoretically behind the architecture of the digital computer, which is known as the *von Neumann architecture* in honor of its conceiver, a group of scientists led by J. von Neumann (1945). The universal Turing machine can simulate any other Turing machine by running in its infinite tape the program of each and every one of these; the von Neumann architecture provides the means to store and randomly access these programs, even if physical realization sets limits to the infinite storage capability of the universal Turing machine. This duo, universal Turing machine - von Neumann architecture, tangoes so well that we can speak of the *Turing-von Neumann paradigm of classical computation.* According to this paradigm, computations:

- Are carried out over strings over the alphabet $\{0, 1\}$;

- are series of steps taken by the computer, each step resulting in a configuration or unequivocally describable state of the machine;

- are measurable in terms of space-time costs as performed in a Turing machine and these measures dictate their realizable vs. non-realizable character;[3]

- take up physical resources (e.g., the material constituents of the computer; electrical energy) that typically involve financial costs, but these are irrelevant from the theoretical viewpoint;

- do not change the underlying program (the *software*), which is fixed;

- do not alter the physical machine (the *hardware*) itself.

This defines computation as, respectively,

- encoded in binary notation, i.e. over 0s and 1s,

---

[3]In computer science jargon, tractable vs. intractable, respectively. Incidentally, the scheduling problem above is essentially intractable. See Chapter 5.

- discrete,

- Turing-machine realizable vs. non-realizable,

- physical-cost free,

- fixed-program, and

- hardware-independent.

As the reader can readily verify, these are a refinement, as well as an extension, of the properties listed in the beginning of this Section, now taking into consideration both the theoretical costs and the physical support of computation in the classical sense.

1.4. Models of classical computation: Automata

At a time when the digital computer was still to be built there was already a variety of machines that carried out computations. Although some physical machines that assisted humans in carrying out computations had existed already for a long time (e.g., the abacus), by *machines* we more properly mean *mathematical models* of computation. Moreover, these machines were conceived as fully autonomous computers, reason why they would become known as *automata* (singular: *automaton*).

Interestingly enough, together with the Turing machine we can consider the work by W. McCulloch and W. Pitts cited above as an early propeller of automata theory. In effect, the main idea behind these machines was that of being able to model the way humans make computations in what is seemingly a wholly autonomous process: Give a piece of paper and a pencil to a schooled human, give him or her a problem to solve–say, an arithmetic problem–and an algorithm to solve it, and you can expect a written output after a shorter or longer period of time, depending on the calculator. In the early 1940s, it was already well known that human neural networks are astonishingly complex in connective terms, but both the Turing simulator (the Turing machine) and the McCulloch-Pitts artificial neural net operated on symbolic Boolean terms: Both operated over a symbolic alphabet that can be encoded in binary and the operations carried by these simulators can be mapped to the Boolean values 0 and 1, in the senses that the characteristic function computed by a Turing machine outputs one of these values, and the McCulloch-Pitts neuron has an "all-or-none" character, i.e. it is either on (= 1) or off (= 0).

Although the notion of *weights* in McCulloch & Pitts (1943) would also contribute to the conception of artificial neural nets as quantitative–rather than symbolic–computers (see above), the idea that nervous activity could be simulated by localized connected groups of neurons whose activity could be segregated into a finite number of determining and determined states that constituted a sequence (with a very limited and circumscribed memory)[4] put this work directly in relation with Turing's previous work, a relation readily seen by W. McCulloch and W. Pitts themselves:

> It is easily shown: first, that every net, if furnished with a tape, scanners connected to afferents, and suitable efferents to perform the necessary motor-operations, can compute only such numbers as can a Turing machine; second, that each of the latter numbers can be computed by such a net; and that nets with circles can be computed by such a net; and that nets with circles can compute, without scanners and a tape, some of the numbers the machine can, but no others, and not all of them. This is of interest as affording a psychological justification of computability and its equivalents, Church's λ-definability and Kleene's primitive recursiveness: If any number can be computed by an organism, it is computable by these definitions, and conversely. (McCulloch & Pitts, 1943)

Shortly later on, in the mid 1950s, two computer scientists generalized this incipient but already powerful theory of automata to models of computation capable of producing a symbolic output: These were the Mealy and Moore machines, originating in the independent papers Mealy (1955) and Moore (1956).

The fundamental concept of non-determinism in the operation of a finite automaton, and the equivalence between this and the operation of a deterministic finite automaton, were introduced and proven, respectively, in the late 1950s, namely in Rabin & Scott (1959). The pushdown

---

[4]Memory is said to be limited and circumscribed in the sense that it is *circumscribed* to the current state, inasmuch as this determines the next state, and *limited* in the sense that it is stored in a program that is a finite set of transitions from states to states. For instance, if there is an intermediate state s between states q and p, then the machine can be said to "remember" only insofar as there is a sequence of states psq; if one expects the sequence pq skipping state s, but there is no such direct transition in the program of the machine, then one expects in vain. The celebrated fact that the Turing machine has an infinite tape does not, in practical terms, equate with an infinite memory, though it does so virtually: It can store an infinite number of programs.

automaton, a specific type of finite automaton that has a stack pile in addition to the input tape, was conceived in the early 1960s (cf. Oettinger, 1961). In the 1970s, there was an explosion in the applications of these machines to a plethora of fields, but we restrict our interest in them largely as they play an important role in the Chomsky hierarchy, a theoretical construct born in the mid 1950s.

1.5. The Chomsky hierarchy

The relation between formal languages and computing machines is an idea that dates at least from as early as the 17th century, when the philosopher G. Leibniz conceived a *calculus ratiocinator* in which the solutions to arbitrary problems input in a formal language he called *lingua universalis* could be computed in a wholly mechanical way. However, real progress in computing machinery was made only in the 19th century with C. Babbage, who conceived the first automatic computing machine, named Analytical Engine, and with Augusta Ada Lovelace, a.k.a Countess of Lovelace, who is considered to have written the first program for a computing machine. More exactly, she wrote an algorithm for the Analytical Engine to compute Bernoulli numbers, but, as a matter of fact, Ada Lovelace already established a much deeper relation between this computing machine and a symbolic, formal system:

> [The Analytical Engine] might act upon other things besides *number*, were objects found whose mutual fundamental relations could be expressed by those of the abstract science of operations, and which should be also susceptible of adaptations to the action of the operating notation and mechanism of the engine. ... Supposing, for instance, that the fundamental relations of pitched sounds in the science of harmony and of musical composition were susceptible of such expression and adaptations, the engine might compose elaborate and scientific pieces of music of any degree of complexity or extent. (Lovelace, 1843).

Interesting as these developments were, they did not shed much light on the relation between languages and automatic machines. This was not so much because of this work in itself, but for historical circumstances. Contrarily to Leibniz's conception, which envisaged already an intimate relation between a symbolic, formal language and automatic computation, in the early 20th century the components of language and computing machinery developed largely independently of one another.

1. Classical computation: Turing, von Neumann, and Chomsky

By the mid 1950s, we had the conception that languages were sets of strings, or more properly portions thereof, known as *corpora* (singular: *corpus*); we had grammars that generated specific sets of strings, known as generative (but also transformational)[5] grammars; and we had models of machines operating by means of discrete changes in what was a finite set of states, the Turing machine at the head of the list. Moreover, we had an idea of how grammars and languages are associated, and how these are associated to abstract finite-state models of computation. For instance, the equivalence between the regular languages and finite automata (as modeled on the neural nets of McCulloch and Pitts) was formulated in Kleene (1956). What we did not have was an unequivocal, parsimonious, classification of types of languages, grammars, and machines, let alone a theory of their general equivalences and a hierarchy thereof. The Chomsky hierarchy established both: (i) for each grammar G_i of type $i = 0, 1, 2, 3$ there is an equivalent language $L(G_i)$ and an equivalent machine model $M(G_i)$ (see Figure 1.5.1), and (ii) there is a hierarchy defined by a relation of proper containment $3 \subset 2 \subset 1 \subset 0$.[6]

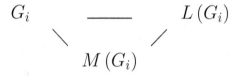

Figure 1.5.1.: The basic postulate of the Chomsky hierarchy.

Interestingly enough, it was in the quest of how from the rules of grammar and from the established *corpora*, which constitute a finite set, humans produce (or "project the *corpus* into") a virtually infinite number of correct statements in a natural language–say, English–that the North-American linguist N. Chomsky came up with what we call today the Chomsky hierarchy. As he put it:

> This paper is concerned with the formal structure of the set of grammatical sentences. ... We (...) ask what sort of linguistic theory is required as a basis for an English grammar that will describe the set of English sentences in an interesting and satisfactory manner. (Chomsky, 1956)

The importance of this paper notwithstanding, it did not completely establish what we know today as the Chomsky hierarchy. For instance, the

---

[5]To put it briefly: transformational-generative grammars. But note that the two adjectives do not necessarily co-occur.

[6]See below Sections 3.5, 4.4, 5.3, and 5.5 for a discussion of these aspects.

equivalence of one of the language classes in this hierarchy, the context-free languages, and the model of computation known as pushdown automaton was firstly realized only in Chomsky (1962). But the clear triple equivalence of a formal grammar with a formal language with a finite-state automaton was already established via finite-state Markov processes:

> The most elementary grammars which, with a finite amount of apparatus, will generate an infinite number of sentences, are those based on a familiar conception of language as a particularly simple type of information source, namely, a finite-state Markov process. Specifically, we define a *finite-state grammar* G as a system with a finite number of states $S_0, ..., S_q$, a set
>
> $$A = \{a_{ijk}|0 \leq i, j \leq q; i \leq k \leq N_{ij} \text{ for each } i, j\}$$
>
> of transition symbols, and a set $C = \{(S_i, S_j)\}$ of certain pairs of states of G that are said to be *connected*. As the system moves from state S_i to S_j, it produces a symbol $a_{ijk} \in A$ [and it ultimately] generates all sentences
>
> $$a_{a_1 \alpha_2 k_1} a_{a_2 \alpha_3 k_2} ... a_{a_{m-1} \alpha_m k_{m-1}}$$
>
> for all appropriate choices of k_i (i.e. for $k_i \leq N_{\alpha_i \alpha_{i+1}}$). The language $L(G)$ containing all and only such sentences is called the language *generated* by G. ... We say that a language L is a *finite-state language* if L is the set of sentences generated by some finite-state grammar G. (Chomsky, 1956; slightly edited)

In this seminal paper, other notions such as *phrase-structure grammar* and *context-dependency* are unequivocally formalized. Although Chomsky firstly rejects the *finite-state (grammar) model* in favor of the *phrase-structure (grammar) model*, namely because the latter is more abstract "in the sense that symbols that are not included in the vocabulary of a language enter into the description of this language" (Chomsky, 1956), he actually sees them as equivalent models.[7]

Chomsky (1956) concludes that a phrase-structure grammar alone is inadequate with respect to a natural language like English, namely because this is too complex to be generated by such a limited grammar, where by *complexity* it is meant, for instance, ambiguity. For example,

---

[7] *Phrase-structure grammar* just is an alternative label for a formal grammar.

the sentence *They are flying planes* can have two non-equivalent derivation trees (see Figures 1.5.2.1-2) given the same grammar (in this case,
the grammar of English), one in which *they* refers to pilots and another
in which *they* refers to, say, those specks on the horizon. This ambiguity
arises from the following grammar rules[8] that constitute a subset of the
grammar rules of English:

$$\left\{ \begin{array}{c} \langle VP \rangle \to \langle V \rangle \langle NP \rangle \\ \langle Verb \rangle \to are\_flying \\ \langle Verb \rangle \to are \\ \langle NP \rangle \to they \\ \langle NP \rangle \to planes \\ \langle NP \rangle \to flying\_planes \end{array} \right\}.$$

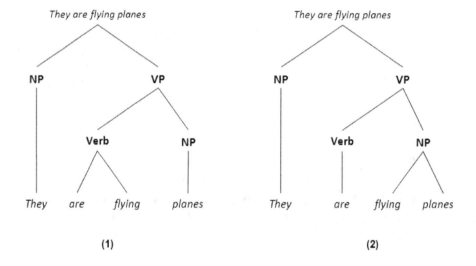

Figure 1.5.2.: Two derivation trees.

A third model is then proposed: the *transformational (grammar)
model*, as a complement to the phrase-structure model, might help us
to tackle the complex description of natural languages and improve our
understanding of their nature and use.

While the conclusion of Chomsky (1956) was cautious with respect
to natural languages, the Chomsky hierarchy had been sketched in it.
From its conception on, progress was fast with respect to this hierarchy,
and when in 1979 the first edition of Hopcroft and Ullman's *Introduction*

---

[8]VP and NP stand for "verb phrase" and "noun phrase," respectively. The symbol
→ indicates that the left side can be rewritten as the right side.

to automata theory, languages, and computation was published the relations between the Chomsky hierarchy and the theory of computation were already well established, and this in such a way that, despite many subsequent developments in the field, this textbook can still be used for a (perhaps only graduate) course. The same can be said of another of our main sources, to wit, Davis and Weyuker's *Computability, complexity, and languages*, firstly published in 1983.

Part II.

Mathematical Preliminaries

2. Mathematical and computational notions

As it is, the theory of computation, classical or other, is to a great extent (if not entirely) a field of mathematics. Mathematics in classical computing is intimately associated mostly with mathematical objects and structures, proofs of statements, and algorithms. With respect to the objects and structures, they are known as *discrete* (vs. continuous); for instance, the Boolean values 0 and 1 are discrete objects, and finite automata are discrete structures. We thus provide here the notions of discrete mathematics that are essential for our discussion of computing constructs and related results. This we do in Sections 2.1.1-2. As far as mathematical proofs are concerned, two proof techniques are ubiquitous in the theory of classical computing, to wit, structural induction and *reductio ad absurdum*, or proof by contradiction. In Section 2.1.3, we give the basics of these techniques. Finally, no text on formal languages and classical computation would be complete without some discussion on algorithmics; tightly associated to this is programming and programming languages (including pseudo-code), and in Section 2.1.4 we provide the basic notions, or suggest research exercises, on algorithms and languages that are expected to facilitate an adequate understanding of the contents of this textbook.

The present Chapter is not intended to substitute textbooks on set theory and discrete mathematics, being provided for the sake of notational and definitional uniformity, as well as self-containment. In particular, the examples and exercises in this Chapter were conceived with the contents of this book in mind; for instance, we focus on computability–with an emphasis on recursion–and countability with respect to functions and sets, respectively. For the same reason, our treatment of graphs and trees is very elementary, as in this book we shall be using these essentially for state diagrams, as well as for syntactic trees and derivation graphs.

The reader requiring further material on discrete mathematics should consult adequate textbooks. For example, Gallier (2011) provides a conventional textbook on discrete mathematics, whereas Makinson (2008) might be more accessible for the mathematically reticent reader. Between these two poles, many textbooks are to be found satisfying the individual needs of readers.

2.1. Basic notions

In this Section, we give the *sine-quibus-non* notions of mathematics from the viewpoint of classical computing. Taken collectively, they can be said to pertain to discrete mathematics; more specifically, many topics pertain to abstract mathematics, which typically includes mathematical proofs as a topic on its own (e.g., Bloch, 2011). Although we give very general definitions, the examples and exercises are directed to the typical application of these notions in the field of classical computation.

2.1.1. Sets, relations, functions, and operations

The fundamental notion of mathematics is that of set.

2.1.1. **(Def.)** A *set* is a collection of objects from a *universe* or *domain of discourse* **U**; these objects are its *members* or *elements*.[1]

1. The elements of a set can be specified *intensionally* (e.g., $A = \{x \mid x$ is an even positive integer, $x \leq 10\}$), or *extensionally* (e.g., $A = \{2, 4, 6, 8, 10\}$). The order of the elements is irrelevant (e.g., $\{2, 4, 6, 8, 10\} = \{10, 4, 2, 8, 6\}$) and repeated elements are not considered (e.g., $\{a, c, b, a, c, a\} = \{a, c, b\}$).

2. If x is an element of a set A, we write $x \in A$; otherwise, we write $x \notin A$. The *complement of* A is the set $\overline{A} = \{x \mid x \notin A\}$.

3. A set with a single element is a *singleton*. The *empty* set, i.e. the set with no elements, is denoted by $\emptyset$.

4. The *cardinality* of the set A, denoted by $|A|$, is the number of elements of A. A is finite if $|A| = n$, $n \geq 0$ is finite; otherwise, A is infinite. If A is infinite, we specify it extensionally by means of ellipses (e.g., $\{1, 2, 3, ...\}$ or $\{..., -2, -1, 0, 1, 2, ...\}$).

---

[1]Sometimes it is useful to distinguish the universe, denoted by **U**, and (its) domains, denoted by $\mathscr{D}$. For instance, for **U** = *Numbers*, we may specify $\mathscr{D}_1$ = *Integers*, $\mathscr{D}_2$ = *Even numbers*, etc.

Example 2.1.1. The following are infinite sets that play an important role in discrete mathematics:[2]

$$\mathbb{N} = \{0, 1, 2, 3, ...\} \text{ is the set of natural numbers}$$

$$\mathbb{Z} = \{..., -2, -1, 0, 1, 2, ...\} \text{ is the set of integers}$$

$$\mathbb{Z}^+ = \{1, 2, 3, ...\} \text{ is the set of positive integers}$$

$$\mathbb{Q} = \left\{ \frac{p}{q} \middle| p, q \in \mathbb{Z}, q \neq 0 \right\} \text{ is the set of rational numbers}$$

Given one or more sets, the exact relations that can be established among them are crucial for many fundamental results. We begin with the containment relations and then move on to n-ary relations.

2.1.2. (Def.) Let $\supset, \subset$ denote a *containment relation*.

1. A set B is said to be a *subset* of a set A if $B \subseteq A$ (read "the set B is contained or is equal to the set A").

2. In turn, a set A is called a *superset* of B if $A \supseteq B$ (read "the set A contains or is equal to the set B").

3. If we have $B \subsetneq A$ ("B is contained in, but is not equal to, A") and $A \supsetneq B$ ("A contains, but is not equal to, B"), then we speak of *strict containment*. B is called a *proper subset* of A and A is called a *proper superset* of B if $B \subsetneq A$ or $A \supsetneq B$, respectively.[3]

4. We have the equality $A = B$ if and only if $A \subseteq B$ and $B \subseteq A$.

5. Given a set C, the *power set* of C, denoted by 2^C, is the set of all the subsets of C. Let $C = \{x, y, z\}$; then

$$2^C = \{\emptyset, \{x\}, \{y\}, \{z\}, \{x, y\}, \{x, z\}, \{y, z\}, \{x, y, z\}\}.$$

The power set 2^C of a set C always contains $\emptyset$ and always contains C itself.

Example 2.1.2. We have the following containment relation for the sets in Example 2.1.1:

---

[2] One often sees $\mathbb{N} = \mathbb{Z}^+$, in which case the inclusion of 0 in the natural numbers is denoted by $\mathbb{N} \cup \{0\}$.

[3] Note that $B \subsetneq A$ is not necessarily equivalent to $B \subset A$, unless it is so stated. In effect, $B \subset A$ usually denotes that B is an arbitrary subset of A.

$$\mathbb{Q} \supset \mathbb{Z} \supset \mathbb{N}.$$

This strict containment relation helps us to define the set $\mathbb{R}$ of the real numbers in the following way: A real number r is rational if $r \in \mathbb{Q}$; otherwise, r is *irrational*. In effect, we have the strict containment relation

$$\mathbb{R} \supset \mathbb{Q} \supset \mathbb{Z} \supset \mathbb{N}.$$

$\sqrt{2} = 1.41421356...$ and $\pi = 3.14159265....$ are examples of irrational numbers.[4]

2.1.3. (Def.) Let A be a set. For $n \geq 1$, R is a *n-ary relation* over A if $R \subseteq A^n$, i.e. R is a subset of $\underbrace{A \times ... \times A}_{n}$. Thus, a *unary* relation R on A is a relation $R \subseteq A$, and a *binary* relation R on A is a relation $R \subseteq (A \times A)$. When $n = 0$, we may speak of a *degenerate* relation. Let A and B be sets. A relation R from A to B is a binary relation from A to B, i.e. $R \subseteq (A \times B)$.

2.1.4. (Def.) A *function* (or *mapping*) f defined on two sets A (the *domain* of f) and B (the *range* of f), denoted by $f : A \longrightarrow B$, is a subset $C \subseteq (A \times B)$ such that for each $x \in A$ there is one and only one *pair* in C of the form (x, y), $y \in B$, such that $f(x) = y$.

1. A function $f : A \longrightarrow B$ is said to be *defined at* $x \in A$, A is the *domain of definition* of f, if the value $f(x) = y \in B$ is calculable. Otherwise, f is said to be *undefined at* x.

2. Let $f : A \longrightarrow B$ be a function, $D \subseteq A$ and $E \subseteq B$. The *image of D under f* is the subset $f(D) = \{f(x) \mid x \in D\}$. The *inverse image of E under f* is the subset $f^{-1}(E) = \{x \mid f(x) \in E\}$.

3. For $n \geq 1$, we say that f is a *n-ary function* over a set A if $f : A^n \longrightarrow A$, i.e. if $f(x_1, ..., x_n) \in A$ whenever $x_1, ..., x_n \in A$. If $n = 0$, we may speak of a *degenerate* function. A 0-ary function over A denotes a fixed element of A, i.e. a *constant*.

4. We say that a function $f : A \longrightarrow B$ is *one-to-one*, or *injective*, when for all $x, y \in A$ if $x \neq y$, then $f(x) \neq f(y)$. An *injection* is also called a *monomorphism* (cf. Def. 2.2.2.2).

---

[4]The set $\mathbb{C}$ of the complex numbers contains all the other sets of numbers, but they play no role in the contents of this book, reason why we omit them above.

5. A function $f : A \longrightarrow B$ is said to be *onto*, or *surjective*, when for every $y \in B$ there is a $x \in A$ such that $f(x) = y$. A *surjection* is also called an *epimorphism* (cf. Def. 2.2.2.4).

6. A function is said to be *bijective*, or a *bijection*, if it is both one-to-one and onto. A bijection is also called a *one-to-one correspondence*, or an *isomorphism* (cf. Def. 2.2.2.5). The bijective function $\iota_A : A \longrightarrow A$ such that $\iota_A(x) = x$ for all $x \in A$ is called the *identity function*.

7. Given two sets A and B, a function f that assigns to each element $x \in A'$, $A' \subset A$, exactly one element $y \in B$ is called a *partial function on A* (and is denoted by φ). If f applies to the whole of A, then f is a *total function*. A (total) function f is said to be *computable* if there is an algorithm that, given input x, produces the value $f(x)$ in finitely many steps. A partial function φ is said to be *partially computable* if there is an algorithm that, on input x, produces the value $\varphi(x)$ in finitely many steps but produces no output if φ is not defined at x (e.g., the algorithm may not terminate).

8. Let $f : A \longrightarrow B$ and $g : B \longrightarrow C$. Then, the *composition of f and g* is the function $g \circ f : A \longrightarrow C$ defined as $(g \circ f)(x) = g(f(x))$ for all $x \in A$.

9. A function $f : A \longrightarrow A$ such that $f \circ f = f$ is said to be *idempotent*.

10. We say that a function $f : A \longrightarrow A$ is *iterated* or *iterative* if we have $f^n : A \longrightarrow A$ such that the f^n are defined recursively by $f^0(x) = \iota_A(x)$ and $f^n(x) = f \circ f^{n-1}(x)$ for some $x \in A$.

The finite or infinite cardinality of a set plays a central role in many results in the classical theory of computation. We accordingly expand on Definition 2.1.1.4.

2.1.5. (Def.) A set is *finite* if it is either empty or else it can be put in a one-to-one correspondence with the set $\{1, 2, ..., n\} \subseteq \mathbb{Z}^+$ (or the set $\{0, 1, 2, ..., n-1\} \subseteq \mathbb{N}$) such that its elements constitute the *sequence* $a_1, a_2, ..., a_n$ (or $a_0, a_1, a_2, ..., a_{n-1}$, respectively) with n *terms*. A set is *infinite* if it is not finite. A set is *denumerable*, or *countably infinite*, if its elements can be listed in a sequence indexed as $a_0, a_1, a_2, ...$ (or as $a_1, a_2, ...$), i.e. if it can be put in a one-to-one correspondence with the sets $\mathbb{N}$ or $\mathbb{Z}^+$, respectively.[5] We say that a set is *countable* if it is either

---

[5] In other words, a set is denumerable if it has the same cardinality as $|\mathbb{N}| = \aleph_0$ (or $|\mathbb{Z}^+| = \aleph_0$). The symbol $\aleph_0$ is read "aleph null."

finite or denumerable; otherwise, it is *uncountable*.

Theorem 2.1.1. *The sets $\mathbb{N}$, $\mathbb{Z}$, and $\mathbb{Q}$ are countable.*

Proof: Left as an exercise. (Hint for $\mathbb{Q}$: First list the elements p/q with $p + q = 2$, followed by those with $p + q = 3$, and so on, i.e. $1/1, 1/2, 2/1, 3/1, 2/2...$ Make each different p and q determine a table with entries a_{ij} where $i = p$ and $j = q$.)

Theorem 2.1.2. *The set $\mathbb{R}$ of the real numbers is uncountable.*

Proof: The proof is by contradiction and is known as *Cantor diagonalization argument*. Suppose that the set $\mathbb{R}$ is countable. Then, because any subset of a countable set is also countable (cf. Exercise 2.1.6.2), the subset of all real numbers in the interval $[0, 1]$ is also countable, and by Definition 2.1.5 we can list the numbers in this interval in some order, say, $r_1, r_2, ...$ Let d denote decimal representation and let d_{ij} represent the j-th number in the decimal representation of the i-th r, with $j \in \{0, 1, 2, ..., 9\}$. For instance, if $r_6 = 0.573421...$, then $d_{61} = 5$, $d_{62} = 7$, $d_{65} = 2$, etc. Then we have the list

$$r_1 = 0.d_{11}d_{12}d_{13}d_{14}d_{15}...$$

$$r_2 = 0.d_{21}d_{22}d_{23}d_{24}d_{25}...$$

$$r_3 = 0.d_{31}d_{32}d_{33}d_{34}d_{35}...$$

$$\vdots$$

Create now a real number $r = 0.d_1 d_2 d_3 d_4 d_5...$ according to the following rule for the decimal digits (choose any two different digits for α and β):

$$d_i = \begin{cases} \alpha & \text{if } d_{ii} \neq \alpha \\ \beta & \text{otherwise} \end{cases}$$

For instance, given the list

$$r_1 = 0.572819...$$

$$r_2 = 0.051689...$$

$$r_3 = 0.182543...$$

$$r_4 = 0.935164...$$

$$r_5 = 0.134638...$$

$$\vdots$$

and choosing $\alpha = 2$, $\beta = 3$, we have the number $r = 0.22322...$ But r is not in the list, as for each i it differs from the decimal expansion of r_i in the i-th place to the right of the decimal point. This shows that the assumption that every number in the interval $[0, 1]$ can be listed is false. Moreover, we have it that any set with an uncountable subset is itself uncountable. Therefore, we conclude that $\mathbb{R}$ is uncountable.[6] **QED**

2.1.6. (Def.) Let A be a set. A *n-ary operation O* on A, for $n \geq 1$, is a function f that assigns an element of A to every n-tuple of elements of A, i.e. $f : A^n \longrightarrow A$. When $n = 0$, we may speak of a *degenerate* operation.

We next give the fundamental operations on sets.

2.1.7. (Def.) Let A and B be two sets.

1. The *intersection* of A and B is the set $A \cap B = \{x | x \in A \text{ and } x \in B\}$. Now let $\{A_i | i \in I\}$ be the family of sets A_i indexed by the set I; then the intersection of the sets A_i, written

$$\bigcap_{i \in I} A_i = \{x | \forall i \in I, x \in A_i\}$$

is the set of objects that are members of every set A_i. We can further specify the intersection of n (sub)sets A_i as

$$\bigcap_{i=1}^{n} A_i.$$

A and B are *disjoint* sets if $A \cap B = \emptyset$ and a collection of sets $\{A_i | i \in I\}$ is disjoint if $\bigcap_{i \in I} A_i = \emptyset$.

2. The *union* of A and B is the set $A \cup B = \{x | x \in A \text{ or } x \in B\}$. Now let $\{A_i | i \in I\}$ be the family of sets A_i indexed by the set I; then

---

[6]We actually have $|\mathbb{R}| = 2^{|\mathbb{N}|} = 2^{\aleph_0} = \mathfrak{c}$, and $\mathfrak{c} > \aleph_0$, given that–this is a theorem stated by G. Cantor–the cardinality of a set is always less than the cardinality of its power set. Moreover, $\mathfrak{c} = \aleph_1$, and $\aleph_0 < \aleph_1$, there being no cardinal number X between $\aleph_0$ and $\aleph_1$. This celebrated hypothesis by Cantor is known as *the continuum hypothesis*.

the union of the sets A_i, written

$$\bigcup_{i \in I} A_i = \{x | \exists i \in I, x \in A_i\}$$

is the set of objects that are members of at least one set A_i in the family. We can further specify the union of n (sub)sets A_i as

$$\bigcup_{i=1}^{n} A_i.$$

3. We call the set $\{(a, b) | a \in A \text{ and } b \in B\}$, where (a, b) is an *ordered pair* or *2-tuple*, the *Cartesian product* of A and B. We denote this set operation by $A \times B$. The Cartesian product of $A_1, A_2, ..., A_n$ is the set

$$A_1 \times A_2 \times ... \times A_n = \prod_{i=1}^{n} A_i = \{(a_1, a_2, ..., a_n) | \forall i\, (a_i \in A_i)\}$$

of n-tuples whose i-th coordinate is from A_i.

4. The *set difference* is the set

$$A - B = A \backslash B = A \cap \overline{B} = \{x | x \in A \text{ and } x \notin B\}.$$

$A - B$ and $A \backslash B$ are alternative ways to write the same set operation.

2.1.8. (Prop.) Let A, B, C be arbitrary sets. Then, the following properties are satisfied with respect to the set operations of union, intersection, and complementation:

1. *Commutativity*: $A \cup B = B \cup A$ and $A \cap B = B \cap A$.

2. *Associativity*: $(A \cup B) \cup C = A \cup (B \cup C)$ and $(A \cap B) \cap C = A \cap (B \cap C)$.

3. *Idempotency*: $A \cup A = A$ and $A \cap A = A$.

4. *Absorption*: $A \cup (A \cap B) = A$ and $A \cap (A \cup B) = A$.

5. *Distributivity*: $A \cup (B \cap C) = (A \cup B) \cap (A \cup C)$ and $A \cap (B \cup C) = (A \cap B) \cup (A \cap C)$.

6. *Identity laws:*

    a) $A \cup \emptyset = A$ and $A \cap \emptyset = \emptyset$.

    b) $A \cup \mathbf{U} = \mathbf{U}$ and $A \cap \mathbf{U} = A$.

7. *Complement laws:*

    a) $A \cup \overline{A} = \mathbf{U}$ and $A \cap \overline{A} = \emptyset$.

    b) $\overline{\mathbf{U}} = \emptyset$ and $\overline{\emptyset} = \mathbf{U}$.

8. *Double complement, or involution law:* $\overline{\overline{A}} = A$.

9. *De Morgan's laws:* $\overline{A \cup B} = \overline{A} \cap \overline{B}$ and $\overline{A \cap B} = \overline{A} \cup \overline{B}$.

Proof: Left as an exercise.

2.1.9. (Def.) Let there be given a set A. If for every $a \in A$ it is the case that $a \in A_i$ for some $A_i \subseteq A$, $A_i \neq \emptyset$, then the collection $\mathscr{P}_A = \{A_1, ..., A_n\}$ such that

1.
$$\bigcup_{i=1}^{n} A_i = A$$

    and

2. $A_i \cap A_j = \emptyset$ for $i \neq j$,

is called a *partition* of A and each A_i is called a *part* (or *block*, or *cell*) of $\mathscr{P}_A$.

Example 2.1.3. Let there be given the set $\mathbb{N}$. Then, for $n \in \mathbb{N}$, the sets $A_1 = \{n | n^2 < 10\} = \{0, 1, 2, 3\}$ and $A_2 = \{n | n^2 > 10\} = \{4, 5, 6, ...\}$ constitute a partition of $\mathbb{N}$, as

$$A_1 \cup A_2 = \{0, 1, 2, 3, 4, 5, ...\} = \mathbb{N}$$

and
$$A_1 \cap A_2 = \emptyset.$$

Conditions 2.1.9.1 and 2.1.9.2 are satisfied and we write

$$\mathscr{P}_{\mathbb{N}} = \{A_1, A_2\}.$$

On the contrary, the sets $B_1 = \{n|n < 6\}$ and $B_2 = \{n|n > 6\}$ do not constitute a partition of $\mathbb{N}$, as $6 \notin B_1 \cup B_2$ and thus $B_1 \cup B_2 \neq \mathbb{N}$, and condition 2.1.9.1 is not satisfied. Let now $C_1 = \{n|n \leq 6\}$ and $C_2 = \{n|n \geq 6\}$; then, condition 2.1.9.2 is violated, and the sets C_1, C_2 do not constitute a partition of $\mathbb{N}$, either.

2.1.10. (Def.) Let $\mathscr{P} = \{C_1, ..., C_n\}$ be some partition.

1. By $|\mathscr{P}| = n$ we denote the *index* of $\mathscr{P}$.

2. If

- $\bigcup_i C_i \in \mathscr{P} = \bigcup_i C_i' \in \mathscr{P}'$
- $|\mathscr{P}'| > |\mathscr{P}|$
- for all the $C_i' \in \mathscr{P}'$ there is a $C_j \in \mathscr{P}$ such that $C_i' \subseteq C_j$

then $\mathscr{P}'$ is said to be a *refinement* of $\mathscr{P}$ (and $\mathscr{P}$ is said to be *coarser* than $\mathscr{P}'$).

For a set A or a partition $\mathscr{P}$, it is sometimes useful to index the first element thereof as 0, i.e. $A = \{A_0, A_1, ..., A_n\}$ or $\mathscr{P} = \{C_0, C_1, ..., C_m\}$, in which case we have $|A| = n + 1$ and $|\mathscr{P}| = m + 1$.

2.1.2. Binary relations and ordered sets

Given a set A, it is often important to order its elements in a specific way and to specify relations among them. Binary relations are central in classical computing.

2.1.11. (Def.) A *binary relation* R over a set A is a relation $R \subseteq A \times A$. We say that a binary relation R is

1. *reflexive* if for every $x \in A$ we have it that xRx.

2. *irreflexive* if for every $x \in A$ it is not the case that xRx.

3. *symmetric* if for every $x, y \in A$ we have it that if xRy, then yRx.

4. *antisymmetric* if for every $x, y \in A$ we have it that if xRy and yRx, then $x = y$.

5. *transitive* if for every $x, y, z \in A$ we have it that if xRy and yRz, then xRz.

6. an *equivalence relation* if it is reflexive, symmetric, and transitive.

Example 2.1.4. Let the set $\mathbb{Z}$ be given.

- For $x \in \mathbb{Z}$, the relation $=$ is reflexive, as we have $x = x$, while the relation $<$ is irreflexive, because $x \not< x$.

- For $x, y \in \mathbb{Z}$, the relation "is immediately next to" is symmetric, as for any two integers x and y we have the pairs (x, y) and (y, x) (e.g., $(1, 2)$ and $(2, 1)$), but $x \neq y$.

- Let $m \neq 0, n \in \mathbb{Z}$; we say that m divides n and n is divisible by m, denoted by $m|n$, if there is $p \in \mathbb{Z}$ such that $n = mp$, or equivalently, if $\frac{n}{m} \in \mathbb{Z}$. For $m, n \in \mathbb{Z}^+$, the relation $|$ is antisymmetric, as whenever we have $m|n$ and $n|m$, then $m = n$.

- Let us consider $m \in \mathbb{Z}, m > 1$. We say that x is congruent to y modulo m, and we write $x \approx y \,(\bmod\, m)$, if $x - y$ is divisible by m. The relation $R = x \approx y \,(\bmod\, m)$ is an equivalence relation on $\mathbb{Z}$. In effect, for every $x \in \mathbb{Z}$ we have $x \approx x \,(\bmod\, m)$, as $x - x$ is divisible by m, and thus R is reflexive. R is also symmetric, as for any $x, y \in \mathbb{Z}$, if $x - y$ is divisible by m, then $-(x - y)$ is also divisible by m. Finally, R is transitive, because if for $x, y, z \in \mathbb{Z}$ we have it that $x - y$ and $y - z$ are both divisible by m, then $x - z = (x - y) + (y - z)$ is also divisible my m.

2.1.12. (Def.) Let R be an equivalence relation on a set A. The *equivalence class* of $a \in A$, denoted by $[a]_R$, is the set

$$[a]_R = \{b \in A | aRb\}.$$

1. Any element $b \in [a]_R$ is a *representative* of $[a]_R$.

2. The set of equivalence classes of A is the *(induced) partition* of A under the relation R. Equivalently, the collection of all equivalence classes of A under the relation R, denoted by A/R, is the set

$$A/R = \{[a]_R \, | a \in A\}$$

called the *quotient set* of A by R.

We abbreviate $[a]_R$ as $[a]$ when only one relation R is under consideration.

Example 2.1.5. Let us consider the set $\mathbb{Z}$ and let R be the relation on A defined by $x \approx y(\bmod 5)$. R is an equivalence relation, and

$$A/R = \{[0], [1], [2], [3], [4]\}$$

for remainders of $0, 1, 2, 3, 4$ when division by 5 is carried out. The equivalence classes are

$$[0] = \{5n|n \in \mathbb{Z}\} = \{..., -10, -5, \underline{0}, 5, 10, ...\}$$

$$[1] = \{5n+1|n \in \mathbb{Z}\} = \{..., -9, -4, \underline{1}, 6, 11, ...\}$$

$$[2] = \{5n+2|n \in \mathbb{Z}\} = \{..., -8, -3, \underline{2}, 7, 12, ...\}$$

$$[3] = \{5n+3|n \in \mathbb{Z}\} = \{..., -7, -2, \underline{3}, 8, 13, ...\}$$

$$[4] = \{5n+4|n \in \mathbb{Z}\} = \{..., -6, -1, \underline{4}, 9, 14, ...\}$$

2.1.13. (Def) A binary relation $\leq$ on a set A that is reflexive and transitive is called a *preorder*, and $\mathcal{R} = (A, \leq)$ is correspondingly called a preorder.

1. $\mathcal{R}$ is a *partial order*, or a *poset*, if $\leq$ is reflexive, antisymmetric, and transitive.

2. If $\leq$ is irreflexive and transitive, then $\mathcal{R}$ is a *strict partial order* (often denoted by $<$ or $\lneq$). Let $\mathcal{R}$ be a strict partial order; then for $x, y, z \in A$ we say that y *covers* x in A if $x < y$ and for $x \leq z \leq y$ it is the case that $z = x$ or $z = y$.

3. A poset $\mathcal{R}$ is *totally ordered* if every two elements $x, y \in A$ are comparable, i.e. we have $x \leq y$ or $y \leq x$. We then speak of a *total* or *linear order*.

A convenient way to represent graphically a poset is a Hasse, or poset, diagram. This structure is a graph, namely a simple graph, which will be defined only in Section 2.2.2 below (cf. Def. 2.2.15.4); however, its highly intuitive character sanctions its use in examples and exercises after a brief informal definition. Essentially, the elements of a poset are depicted in a Hasse diagram both vertically and horizontally in such a way that if $a \leq b$ then a is located below b, and if $a \not\leq b$ then both a and b may be placed at the same level; additionally, neither reflexivity nor transitivity are explicitly represented, i.e. there are neither loops (edges connecting a vertex a to itself), nor edges of the form $a\_\_c$ whenever $a\_\_b$ and $b\_\_c$ are in the diagram, respectively.

Example 2.1.6. Let the set A be given whose members and partial order are those of the Hasse diagram (also: poset diagram) of Figure 2.1.1. Clearly, the pairs $(\square, \spadesuit)$ and $(\triangle, @)$ are incomparable. Comparable are, for instance, $\square < \blacklozenge$ and $\triangle > \spadesuit$.

2.1.14. (Def.) Given a poset $\mathcal{R} = (A, \leq)$ and a subset $B \subseteq A$, we have the following order relations for $x, y \in A$ and $z \in B$:

1. x is a *maximal element* of A, written $max\,(A) = x$, if there is no $y \in A$ such that $x \leq y$.

2. x is a *minimal element* of A, written $min\,(A) = x$, if there is no $y \in A$ such that $y \leq x$.

3. x is the *least element* of A if for every $y \in A$ we have $x \leq y$.

4. x is the *greatest element* of A if for every $y \in A$ we have $y \leq x$.

5. x is an *upper bound* of B if for every $z \in B$ we have $z \leq x$.

6. x is a *lower bound* of B if for every $z \in B$ we have $x \leq z$.

7. x is a *least upper bound (lub)*, or *supremum*, of B, written $lub\,(B) = x$ or $sup\,(B) = x$, if x is the upper bound of B and $x \leq x'$ for any other upper bound x' of B.

8. x is a *greatest lower bound (glb)*, or *infimum*, of B, written $glb\,(B) = x$ or $inf\,(B) = x$, if x is the lower bound of B and $x' \leq x$ for any other lower bound x' of B.

Figure 2.1.1.: A partially ordered set.

2.1.15. (Def.) Let there be given a binary relation R on a set A. If there is a sequence of elements $a, x_1, x_2, ..., x_{n-1}, b$ such that $(a, x_1) \in R$, $(x_1, x_2) \in R$, ..., and $(x_{n-1}, b) \in R$, we then say that there is a *path* from a to b of length $n \in \mathbb{Z}^+$ if and only if $(a, b) \in R^n$. For instance, the relation R^2 contains (a, b) if there is some element $c \in A$ such that $(a, c) \in R$ and $(c, b) \in R$.

1. We speak of the *connectivity relation*, denoted by R^*, as the pairs (a, b) such that there is a path of length $n \geq 1$ in R, and define it as

$$R^* = \bigcup_{i=1}^{\infty} R^n.$$

2. The *transitive closure* of R is the connectivity relation R^* associated with R such that $R^* = \bigcup_{i=1}^{\infty} R^i$ of all the positive powers of R. In other words, for a relation R, the transitive closure of R is the smallest transitive relation containing R.

2.1.16. (Def.) Let $\mathcal{R} = (A, \leq)$ be a poset. The *interval* between

$x, y \in A$ is defined as

$$[x, y] = \{z \in A | x \leq z \leq y\}$$

$$(x, y) = \{z \in A | x < z < y\}$$

$$[x, y) = \{z \in A | x \leq z < y\}$$

$$(x, y] = \{z \in A | x < z \leq y\}$$

Exercises

Exercise 2.1.1. For each of the following functions, give (a) the domain and the range, and (b) an informal account of its behavior:

1. Floor function (denoted by $\lfloor a \rfloor$ for some a in the domain).

2. Ceiling function (denoted by $\lceil a \rceil$).

3. Exponential function (denoted by a^x).

4. Logarithmic function (denoted by $\log_a x$).

5. Remainder function (denoted by $a \bmod b$).

6. Factorial function (denoted by $a!$).

7. Step function.

Exercise 2.1.2. Indicate relevant applications of the functions in Exercise 2.1.1 in classical computation.

Exercise 2.1.3. Show that:

1. Given two sets A and B, a partial function from A to B can be seen as a function $\dot{\varphi} : A \longrightarrow (B \cup \{u\})$, where $u \notin B$

$$\dot{\varphi}(a) = \begin{cases} \varphi(a) & \text{if } a \in A' \\ u & \text{if } \varphi \text{ is undefined at } a \end{cases},$$

A' is the domain of definition of φ.

2. The following functions are computable:

   a) $f(x) = x - 1$, for $x > 0$ and $f(0) = 0$.
   b) $f(x, y) = y$.

3. The set $\emptyset$ is computable.

Exercise 2.1.4. Research into *recursive functions*. After giving a precise definition of a recursive function, elaborate on the following notions and state their relation to *recursion*:

1. Ackermann function.

2. Fibonacci sequence.

3. Towers of Hanoi.

4. Wrapper function.

5. Tail-recursive function.

6. μ-recursive function.

7. Primitive recursive function.

Exercise 2.1.5. Is an iterative function the same as a recursive function? Elaborate on this topic and illustrate your elaboration with relevant examples.

Exercise 2.1.6. Prove that:

1. For every set S, (i) $\emptyset \subseteq S$, and (ii) $S \subseteq S$.

2. Every infinite set has a countably infinite subset, and every subset of a countable set is countable.

Exercise 2.1.7. Show that:

1. The set $\mathbb{N} \times \mathbb{N}$ is countable.

2. If S_i is a countable set for every $i \in \mathbb{N}$, then

$$S = \bigcup_{i=0}^{\infty} S_i$$

where ∞ denotes an infinite sequence, is also countable.

Exercise 2.1.8. Determine whether, and show why, the following sets are countable or uncountable:

1. $\{A|A \subset \mathbb{N}, A \text{ has three elements}\}$ (consider all such sets A)

2. $\{B|B \subset \mathbb{N}, B \text{ is finite}\}$ (consider all such sets B)

3. $\{C_i|C_i \subset \mathbb{N}, i = 1, ..., n, C_i \cap C_j = \emptyset \text{ for all } i \neq j, \bigcup_{i=1}^n C_i = \mathbb{N}\}$

4. $\{f|f : \mathbb{N} \longrightarrow \{0, 1\}\}$ (consider all such functions f)

5. $\{g|g : \mathbb{N} \longrightarrow \mathbb{N}\}$ (consider all such functions g)

6. $\{h|h : \mathbb{N} \longrightarrow \mathbb{N}, h \text{ is non-decreasing}\}$ (consider all such functions h)

Exercise 2.1.9. Prove that if S is a countably infinite set, then 2^S is uncountable. Apply the diagonalization method.

Exercise 2.1.10. Let there be given the set U of all the current students of a particular university.

1. Give a first, coarse, partition $\mathscr{P}_U$ and consider then progressive refinements $\mathscr{P}_U', \mathscr{P}_U'', \ldots$ of this first partition.

2. Give an example of a partition of U that cannot be further refined.

Exercise 2.1.11. Consider the set $A = \{a, b, c\}$ and the following five relations on A:

$R_1 = \{(a, a), (a, b), (a, c), (c, c)\}$
$R_2 = \{(a, a), (a, b), (b, a), (b, b), (c, c)\}$
$R_3 = \{(a, a), (a, b), (b, b), (b, c)\}$
$R_4 = A \times A$
$R_5 = \emptyset$

1. Determine which of these relations are reflexive, irreflexive, symmetric, antisymmetric, transitive.

2. Is any of them an equivalence relation?

Exercise 2.1.12. Consider the following relations on $\mathbb{Z}$:

$R_1 = \{(a, b) | a < b\}$
$R_2 = \{(a, b) | a \geq b\}$
$R_3 = \{(a, b) | a = b\}$
$R_4 = \{(a, b) | a + b > 5\}$
$R_5 = \{(a, b) | a - b \leq 0\}$

Which of these relations contain the following pairs?

1. $(3, 4)$

2. $(1, 1)$

3. $(-1, 1)$

4. $(2, 1)$

5. $(-2, -1)$

6. $(3, 3)$

Exercise 2.1.13. Show that, given a set A, if R is an equivalence relation on A, then A/R is a partition of A, and conversely, given a partition $\{A_i | i \in I\}$ of A, there is an equivalence class R that has the A_i as its equivalence classes.

Exercise 2.1.14. Let $A \neq \emptyset$ be the domain of a function f. Let there be given the following definition for $x, y \in A$:[7]

$$x R y \text{ iff } f(x) = f(y) \text{ for all ordered pairs } (x, y).$$

1. Show that R is an equivalence relation on A.

2. Give the equivalence classes of R.

Exercise 2.1.15. Consider the poset with the Hasse diagram of Figure 2.1.2. Find, if they exist,

1. the upper bounds and the lower bounds of $\{\alpha, \beta, \gamma\}$.

2. the upper bounds and the lower bounds of $\{\iota, \theta\}$.

3. the upper bounds and the lower bounds of $\{\alpha, \beta, \gamma, \varsigma\}$.

4. $glb(\{\beta, \delta, \eta\})$ and $lub(\{\beta, \delta, \eta\})$.

Exercise 2.1.16. Let S be the set of the 26 letters of the Roman alphabet and let R be a relation on S such that $a R b$ if and only if $|a| = |b|$, for $|x|$ the length of string x. Is R an equivalence relation?

Exercise 2.1.17. Let $\mathscr{C}$ be any class of sets. Show that the relation $\subseteq$ is a partial order on $\mathscr{C}$.

---

[7]We abbreviate "if and only if" as "iff."

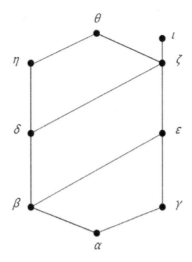

Figure 2.1.2.: Hasse diagram of a poset.

Exercise 2.1.18. Let the set of all people be given and let R be defined on it as
$$R = \{(a, b) \,|\, a \text{ has met } b\}.$$

1. Determine R^n for $n > 1$.

2. Determine R^*.

Exercise 2.1.19. Let the set of all European countries be given and let R be defined on it as

$$R = \{(a, b) \,|\, a \text{ and } b \text{ share a border}\}.$$

1. Determine R^n for $n > 0$.

2. Determine R^*.

Exercise 2.1.20. Prove Theorem 2.1.1 and Proposition 2.1.8.

2.2. Discrete structures

In this Section, we provide the basics of some so-called discrete structures that are essential for our elaboration on languages, machines, and classical computing. Our interest here falls mainly on graphs and trees, which are ubiquitous structures in our subject matter, but also on algebras. Although we shall make a very limited use of explicit algebras (e.g., Boolean algebras; semigroups and monoids), we decided for a somehow extensive algebraic approach in this Section. In particular, via Boolean algebras we can define Boolean variables and functions in such a way that we can discuss the computational problem of satisfiability, at the core of the theory of classical computation, without requiring a lengthy elaboration on classical logic (as it can be found in Augusto, 2019; 2020a). Moreover, though generalizable to simple sets, some notions, such as *homomorphism*, are formally better defined by invoking the concept of an algebra.

2.2.1. Boolean structures

The impact of the work of the 18th-century English mathematician G. Boole is to be seen everywhere in classical computation. In this textbook, we shall be mostly interested in Boolean algebras, tightly related to Boolean logic, both discrete structures that play an important role in classical computing. The reader interested in a comprehensive discussion of Boolean functions in the context of classical computing can consult, for example, Crama & Hammer (2011). Before elaborating on these structures, we review the basic notions of abstract algebra.

2.2.1.1. Algebras and morphisms

2.2.1. (Def.) An *(abstract) algebra* is a pair

$$\mathfrak{A} = (U, O) = (U, \{o_i | i \in I\})$$

where U is a non-empty set, called the *universe* or *carrier* of $\mathfrak{A}$, and for each $i \in I$, o_i is a *(basic) operation* on U.

1. If U is a singleton, then $\mathfrak{A}$ is said to be *degenerate*.

2. $\mathfrak{A}$ is a *finite* algebra if I, the *index set* of $\mathfrak{A}$, is finite; otherwise, it is *infinite*.

3. An algebra $\mathfrak{D} = (U, \{p_k | k \in K\})$ is *similar* to the algebra $\mathfrak{A}$ if and only if $I = K$ and $o_i^m = p_i^m$ for each $i \in I$ and m the arity of o_i, p_i.

Example 2.2.1. An algebra $\mathfrak{X} = (X, \star)$ such that X is a non-empty set and $\star$ is an associative binary operation is a *semigroup*. If X is a poset, then $\mathfrak{X}$ is called a *partially-ordered semigroup*. A (partially-ordered) semigroup with the distinguished element 1 (the identity or unit element), $\mathfrak{X} = (X, \star, 1)$, is a *monoid*.

2.2.2. (Def.) Let $\mathfrak{A} = (U, \{o_i | i \in I\})$ be an algebra.

1. A *homomorphism* of $\mathfrak{A}$ into a similar algebra $\mathfrak{D} = (Y, \{p_i | i \in I\})$, denoted by $Hom\,(\mathfrak{A}, \mathfrak{D})$, is a mapping

$$h : U \longrightarrow Y$$

such that for each $i \in I$ and for arbitrary $u_1, ..., u_{m(i)} \in U$ we have

$$h\left(o_i\left(u_1, ..., u_{m(i)}\right)\right) = p_i\left(h\left(u_1\right), ..., h\left(u_{m(i)}\right)\right).$$

2. A one-to-one homomorphism is a *monomorphism* or *embedding* of $\mathfrak{A}$ into $\mathfrak{D}$.

3. A homomorphism of $\mathfrak{A}$ into itself is an *endomorphism*.

4. If $h : \mathfrak{A} \longrightarrow \mathfrak{D}$ is a homomorphism such that $h\,(U) = Y$, then h is an *epimorphism*.

5. An epimorphism that is also a monomorphism is an *isomorphism* of $\mathfrak{A}$ and $\mathfrak{D}$.

2.2.1.2. Boolean algebras and Boolean logic

In this Section, the reader should be attentive to the subtle transition between Boolean algebra and Boolean logic.[8]

2.2.3. (Def.) Let $\mathfrak{B} = (A, ', \wedge, \vee, 0, 1)$ be an algebra such that $'$ denotes the unary operation of *complementation*, $\wedge$ denotes the binary operation of *meet*, and $\vee$ does so for the binary operation of *join*; moreover, 0 and 1 are distinguished elements. $\mathfrak{B}$ is called a *Boolean algebra*

---

[8]We do not discuss in detail how from Boolean algebra we obtain propositional Boolean logic; this is a topic of (abstract) algebraic logic, greatly beyond the scope of this text. For our purposes, we shall simply see propositional Boolean logic as "behaving" in a similar way to a Boolean algebra.

2. Mathematical and computational notions

if the following properties are satisfied for all $x, y, z \in A$ and for the distinguished elements 0 and 1:

a.	$x \wedge y = y \wedge x$	*Commutativity of $\wedge$*
	$x \vee y = y \vee x$	*Commutativity of $\vee$*
b.	$x \wedge (y \wedge z) = (x \wedge y) \wedge z$	*Associativity of $\wedge$*
	$x \vee (y \vee z) = (x \vee y) \vee z$	*Associativity of $\vee$*
c.	$x \wedge (y \vee z) = (x \wedge y) \vee (x \wedge z)$	*Distributivity of $\wedge$*
	$x \vee (y \wedge z) = (x \vee y) \wedge (x \vee z)$	*Distributivity of $\vee$*
d.	$0' = 1$	*Complementation*
	$1' = 0$	*Complementation*
e.	$(x')' = x$	*Complementation*
f.	$x \wedge x' = 0$	*Complementation*
	$x \vee x' = 1$	*Complementation*
g.	$x \wedge 1 = x$	*Identity element of $\wedge$*
	$x \vee 0 = x$	*Identity element of $\vee$*

1. If $|A| = 0$, then $\mathfrak{B} = (\emptyset,', \wedge, \vee, 0, 1)$ is a degenerate Boolean algebra, in which the operations of meet, join, and complementation are constant and $0 = 1$.

2. If $|A| = 2$, then we have the two-element Boolean algebra $\mathfrak{B} = (\{0, 1\},', \wedge, \vee, 0, 1)$ with elements 0 (the empty set) and 1 (the one-element set), $0 \leq 1$, such that we have the following equalities:

   a) for the unary operation of complementation ('): $0' = 1$ and $1' = 0$

   b) for the binary operations meet ($\wedge$) and join ($\vee$):

$\wedge$	1	0
1	1	0
0	0	0

$\vee$	1	0
1	1	1
0	1	0

3. Let $x, y \in A$. The operations $\wedge$ and $\vee$ are inter-definable by means of ' as the *De Morgan's laws*

$$x \wedge y = (x' \vee y')'$$

$$x \vee y = (x' \wedge y')'$$

4. For elements $x, y \in A$ we have the following equalities:

$$x \wedge y = min\,(x, y)$$

$$x \vee y = max\,(x, y)$$

$$x' = 1 - x$$

2.2.4. (Def.) Given two Boolean algebras $\mathfrak{A}$ and $\mathfrak{B}$, a *Boolean homomorphism* is a function $h : \mathfrak{A} \longrightarrow \mathfrak{B}$ such that for all $x, y \in \mathfrak{A}$ we have

$$h\,(x \wedge y) = h\,(x) \wedge h\,(y)$$

$$h\,(x \vee y) = h\,(x) \vee h\,(y)$$

and

$$h\,(x') = h\,(x)'.$$

Although in this Definition $\mathfrak{A}$ and $\mathfrak{B}$ have exactly the same operations, this need not be so. For instance, we could have the set of operations $O_{\mathfrak{B}} = \{-, \cap, \cup\}$ such that

$$h\,(x \wedge y) = h\,(x) \cap h\,(y)$$

etc., and we still have a Boolean homomorphism. This is an important remark, as we shall consider the algebraic (lattice) operations of meet, join, and complementation as the logical operations of *conjunction* (AND), *disjunction* (OR), and *negation* (NOT), respectively, by a homomorphism $h : \mathfrak{B} \longrightarrow \mathfrak{L}$ where $\mathfrak{B}$ is a Boolean algebra and $\mathfrak{L}$ is an algebra of formulas similar to $\mathfrak{B}$.

2.2.5. (Def.) Let $\mathfrak{L} = (F, ', \wedge, \vee, 0, 1)$ be an algebra of formulas, in which F is a set of formulas. A variable $x_i \in F_0 \subseteq F$ in a finite sequence $x_1, ..., x_n$ is said to be a *Boolean variable* if there is a *Boolean function of degree n*

$$f : \{0, 1\}^n \longrightarrow \{0, 1\}$$

such that we have $f\,(x_i) = 0$ or $f\,(x_i) = 1$, spoken of as *truth-value assignments*. Additionally, we have:

$$[f\,(x_i) = \neg x_i] = 1 - f\,(x_i)$$

$$\left[f\,(x_1, ..., x_n) = \bigwedge_{i=1}^{n} x_i \right] = min\,(f\,(x_1), ..., f\,(x_n))$$

2. Mathematical and computational notions

$$\left[f\left(x_1, \ldots, x_n\right) = \bigvee_{i=1}^{n} x_i \right] = max\left(f\left(x_1\right), \ldots, f\left(x_n\right)\right)$$

We often abbreviate and write simply $x_i = 1$ or $x_i = 0$, as well as:

$$\neg x = 1 - x$$

$$\bigwedge_{i=1}^{n} x_i = min\left(x_1, \ldots, x_n\right)$$

$$\bigvee_{i=1}^{n} x_i = max\left(x_1, \ldots, x_n\right)$$

2.2.6. (Def.) A *Boolean expression* ϕ in the individual variables $x_1, \ldots, x_n$, written $\phi\left(x_1, \ldots, x_n\right)$, is an expression defined inductively in the following way:

1. the constants $0, 1$, and all variables x_i are Boolean expressions in $x_1, \ldots, x_n$;

2. if ϕ and ψ are Boolean expressions in the variables $x_1, \ldots, x_n$, then so are ϕ', $\phi \wedge \psi$, and $\phi \vee \psi$.

The constants 0 and 1 are the logical constants known as *falsum* (false) and *verum* (truth), respectively, in Boolean logic. Definition 2.2.6.2 "translates" directly to the *well-formed formulas* of Boolean logic $\neg\phi$, $\phi \wedge \psi$, and $\phi \vee \psi$.[9]

Example 2.2.2. The following are examples of Boolean expressions:

- $\phi\left(p\right) = \neg p$

- $\omega\left(p, q, r\right) = \left(p \vee q\right) \wedge \left(\neg p \vee r\right)$

- $\chi\left(x, w, y, z\right) = \left(x \wedge \neg w\right) \vee \neg y \vee z$

- $\psi\left(x_1, x_2, x_3\right) = \neg x_1 \wedge \left(\neg x_2 \vee x_1\right) \wedge \left(\neg x_2 \vee \neg x_3\right)$

2.2.7. (Def.) An expression of the form

$$\phi\left(p_1, \ldots, p_n\right)$$

---

[9] For convenience, we shall write indifferently $\neg\phi$ or ϕ' in the framework of Boolean logic.

where the p_i are propositional Boolean variables, is called a *propositional Boolean formula.*

2.2.8. (Def.) An expression of the form

$$\blacklozenge_1 x_1 ... \blacklozenge x_n \left(\phi \left(x_1, ..., x_n \right) \right)$$

where the x_i are individual Boolean variables and $\blacklozenge_i \in \{\forall, \exists\}$, is called a *quantified Boolean formula* (QBF).

Both expressions, propositional and quantified, constitute the basic elements of *Boolean logic.* Quantified formulas have a higher expressive power compared to propositional formulas. For instance, a proposition like "Everybody likes some kind of pet" cannot be expressed formally in a propositional formula. However, in this book we shall not need quantified formulas, thus remaining in propositional Boolean logic.

2.2.9. (Def.) The pair $\mathcal{L} = (F_{\mathfrak{L}}, \models)$, where $F_{\mathfrak{L}}$ denotes the set of propositional formulas of the language $\mathfrak{L}$ formed according to Definition 2.2.6 and $\models$ denotes logical consequence, is a *propositional Boolean logic.*[10]

Importantly, $\mathcal{L}$ is also called *classical propositional logic.*[11] In the framework of computational logic, two normal forms for Boolean formulas are ubiquitous; any propositional Boolean formula can be in a *conjunctive normal form* or in a *disjunctive normal form,* according to the following definitions:

2.2.10. (Def.) A formula $\phi \left(x_1, ..., x_r \right) \in F$ is said to be in a *conjunctive normal form* (CNF) if and only if ϕ has the form $\phi = C_1 \wedge ... \wedge C_n$, $n \geq 1$, where each C_i has the form $x_1 \vee ... \vee x_m$ and in which each x_i may be in the form $\neg x_i$. Formally:

$$\phi = \bigwedge_{i=1}^{n} \left(\bigvee_{j=1}^{m_i} x_{i,j} \right)$$

2.2.11. (Def.) A formula $\phi \left(x_1, ..., x_r \right) \in F$ is said to be in a *disjunctive normal form* (DNF) if and only if ϕ has the form $\phi = \mathcal{E}_1 \vee ... \vee \mathcal{E}_n$, $n \geq 1$, where each of $\mathcal{E}_i$ has the form $x_1 \wedge ... \wedge x_m$ and in which each x_i

---

[10]It should be remarked that $\mathcal{L}$ is more properly a *logical system*; seen as *a logic*, then $\mathcal{L}$ is the subset of formulas of $\mathfrak{L}$ that are tautologies (or theorems), i.e. consequences of the empty set: $\mathcal{L} = \{\phi | \emptyset \models \phi\}$. The notion of logical consequence is far from trivial and beyond the scope of this book; see Augusto (2020c) for a comprehensive discussion of this central notion in formal logic.

[11]The introduction of quantification constitutes what is called *(classical) first-order predicate logic.*

may be in the form $\neg x_i$. Formally:

$$A = \bigvee_{i=1}^{n} \left(\bigwedge_{j=1}^{m_i} x_{i,j} \right)$$

Example 2.2.3. The formula

$$\phi(p, q, r, s) = (p \vee r \vee s) \wedge \neg q \wedge (\neg p \vee q)$$

is in CNF and the formula

$$\psi(p, q, r) = p \vee (q \wedge \neg r) \vee (\neg p \wedge \neg q \wedge r)$$

is in DNF.

2.2.12. (Prop.) Let $\{\phi_1, ..., \phi_n\}$ be a finite set of formulas. Then,

$$\neg \left(\bigwedge_{i=1}^{n} \phi_i \right) \equiv \left(\bigvee_{i=1}^{n} \neg \phi_i \right)$$

and

$$\neg \left(\bigvee_{i=1}^{n} \phi_i \right) \equiv \left(\bigwedge_{i=1}^{n} \neg \phi_i \right)$$

where $\equiv$ denotes logical equivalence.[12]

Proof: (Sketch) We have it that $\neg(\phi) \equiv (\neg\phi)$. Then, obviously the proposition is proved for $n = 1$ by the equivalence $\neg \left(\bigwedge_{i=1}^{1} \phi_i \right) \equiv \left(\bigvee_{i=1}^{1} \neg\phi_i \right)$. The proof then follows by induction on n. **QED**

2.2.13. (Prop.) Let ϕ be a formula in CNF and ψ be a formula in DNF. Then $\neg\phi$ is equivalent to a formula in DNF, and $\neg\psi$ is equivalent to a formula in CNF.

Proof: If ϕ is in CNF, then ϕ is the formula $\bigwedge_{i=1}^{n} \left(\bigvee_{j=1}^{m_i} x_{i,j} \right)$. By Proposition 2.2.12, we have:

$$\neg\phi = \neg \bigwedge_{i=1}^{n} \left(\bigvee_{j=1}^{m_i} x_{i,j} \right) \equiv \bigvee_{i=1}^{n} \neg \left(\bigvee_{j=1}^{m_i} x_{i,j} \right) \equiv \bigvee_{i=1}^{n} \left(\bigwedge_{j=1}^{m_i} \neg x_{i,j} \right)$$

---

[12]Two propositional formulas ϕ, ψ are said to be logically equivalent, written $\phi \equiv \psi$, if and only if they have the same truth value for every truth-value assignment.

The proof runs similarly for $\neg\psi$ being equivalent to a formula in CNF.
QED

2.2.14. (Def.) Given a (propositional) formula $\phi(x_1, ..., x_n)$ with m Boolean connectives $\neg, \wedge, \vee$, it is asked if $f^n(\phi) = 1$ for *at least one* Boolean function (a truth-value assignment) applied to all the Boolean variables x_i, $1 \leq i \leq n$.[13] We call this question *the (Boolean) satisfiability problem*, or *SAT*. Formulated as a language (see Chapter 5), we have:

$$SAT = \{\langle\phi\rangle \,|\, \phi \text{ is a satisfiable Boolean formula}\}$$

Example 2.2.4. Let there be given the following formula $\phi(x_1, x_2, x_3)$:

$$\phi = (x_1 \vee x_2) \wedge ((\neg x_1 \wedge x_2) \vee x_3)$$

The truth-value assignment $x_1 = 1$, $x_2 = 0$, $x_3 = 1$ produces $f^3(\phi) = 1$. In effect, applying the laws of Boolean algebra we have:

$$(1 \vee 0) \wedge ((0 \wedge 0) \vee 1) =$$

$$= 1 \wedge (0 \vee 1) =$$

$$= 1 \wedge 1 = 1$$

We conclude $\phi \in SAT$.

2.2.2. Graphs and trees

We now give the basic aspects of graphs and trees, two discrete structures ubiquitous in the field of formal languages and classical models of computation.

2.2.15. (Def.) *Graphs* – Let $V = \{v_0, v_1, ..., v_n\}$ be a set of vertices and $E = \{e_0, e_1, ..., e_m\}$, $e_i = \{v_j, v_k\}$, be a set of edges. A *graph* $\mathfrak{G}$ is a pair (V, E) such that all the endpoints v_j, v_k of E (i.e., nodes) are contained in V.

1. In a *directed graph* (or *digraph*) $\vec{\mathfrak{G}} = \left(V, E, \vec{f}\right)$, V is as for $\mathfrak{G}$, E is a set of arcs, i.e. directed edges ("arrows"), and $\vec{f} : E \longrightarrow \{tail, head\}$ is an incidence function assigning to each member of E a tail and a head, indicating the origin and the end of the edges,

---

[13] Do not confuse $f^n(\phi)$ for some formula ϕ with the iterative function $f^n(x)$ for some x (cf. Def. 2.1.4.10).

respectively, such that $e_i = (v_j, v_k)$ is an ordered pair where v_j is the tail and v_k is the head.

2. A *multi-edge* is a set of ≥ 2 edges with the same endpoints.

3. A *loop* is an edge or arc joining a vertex to itself.

4. A *simple* graph (digraph) is a graph $\mathfrak{G}$ with no loops or multi-edges (a digraph $\vec{\mathfrak{G}}$ with no self-loops and no pair of arcs with the same head and tail, respectively).

5. The edge (the arc) $e_i = \{v_j, v_k\}$ ($e_i = (v_j, v_k)$, respectively) *connects* the vertices v_j, v_k.

6. A *path* π in a graph $\mathfrak{G}$ is an alternating sequence of vertices and edges of the form $v_0, e_1, v_1, e_2, ..., e_{n-1}, v_{n-1}, e_n, v_n$ in which each e_i contains both v_{i-1} and v_i.

7. A graph $\mathfrak{G}$ is *connected* if each pair of vertices is joined by a path. The number of edges is the *length* of the path.

8. If $v_0 = v_n$ in a path, then the path is said to be *closed*.

9. A closed path is *directed* if $v_0, v_1, ..., v_n$ are pairwise distinct vertices of a digraph $\vec{\mathfrak{G}}$.

10. A *cycle* is a closed path of length ≥ 3.

11. A cycle is *directed* if it is a closed directed path.

12. A graph $\mathfrak{G}' = (V', E')$ is a *subgraph* of $\mathfrak{G} = (V, E)$ if $V' \subseteq V$ and $E' \subseteq E$.

Example 2.2.5. Figure 2.2.1 shows a simple graph. Figure 4.1.3 shows a labeled digraph, which is a state diagram of a finite automaton. Every automaton, including Turing machines, can be modeled by means of a labeled digraph (see Chapter 4).

2.2.16. (Def.) *Trees* – A *tree* is a connected graph containing no cycles.

1. A *subtree* is a subgraph of a graph that is also a tree.

2. A tree is said to be *finite* if it has a finite number of vertices (*nodes*) and edges (*branches*). Otherwise, it is said to be *infinite*.

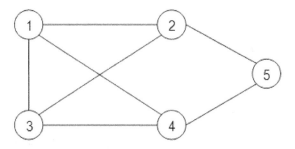

Figure 2.2.1.: A simple graph.

3. A tree is *labeled* if it has labels attached to its vertices.

4. A tree is *rooted* if it has a least node s_0.

5. In a rooted tree, the *ancestor* (the *descendant*) of a vertex v is either v itself or any vertex that is the *predecessor* (the *successor*, respectively) of v on a path from the root. A *proper ancestor* (*proper descendant*) of a vertex v is any ancestor (descendant, respectively) except v itself.

6. In a rooted tree, the *child* of a vertex v is a vertex such that v is its immediate ancestor. A vertex that is the immediate predecessor of v on the unique path from the root to v is called the *parent* of vertex v.

7. In a rooted tree, a *leaf* is a vertex that has no children. A vertex that is not a leaf is an *interior* vertex.

8. A tree is *ordered* if it is rooted and the children of each internal vertex are linearly ordered.

9. The *depth* of a vertex v in a rooted tree is the number of edges in the unique path from the root to v.

10. A tree is said to be *binary* if it is an ordered rooted tree and each of its vertices has at most two children, a right and a left child.

Example 2.2.6. Figure 3.3.1 shows a parse tree, i.e. a labeled rooted tree, and its partial trees.

Exercises

Exercise 2.2.1. Show that a Boolean algebra obeys the *duality principle: Every Boolean algebra has an isomorphic dual by interchanging* 0 *for* 1 *and* ∧ *for* ∨.

Exercise 2.2.2. Prove that a mapping between Boolean algebras that preserves join and complement is a Boolean homomorphism.

Exercise 2.2.3. Recall from Definition 2.2.3.3 the De Morgan's laws. Show that these laws hold in a Boolean algebra $\mathcal{B} = (A,', \wedge, \vee, 0, 1)$.

Exercise 2.2.4. Show that every finite Boolean algebra has 2^n elements.

Exercise 2.2.5. Show that for all Boolean functions f and g the following statements are equivalent:

1. $f \le g$.

2. $f \vee g = g$.

3. $f' \vee g = 1$.

4. $f \wedge g = f$.

5. $f \wedge g' = 0$.

Exercise 2.2.6. Determine whether the following Boolean formulas are satisfiable.

1. $(x_1 \vee x_3 \vee \neg x_4) \wedge \neg x_2 \wedge (\neg x_1 \vee x_2)$.

2. $(p_2 \vee \neg p_2 \vee p_3) \wedge p_1 \wedge (\neg p_1 \vee \neg p_3)$.

3. $p \vee (q \wedge \neg r) \vee (\neg p \wedge \neg q \wedge r)$.

4. $(x_2 \wedge \neg x_1) \vee (x_1 \vee (\neg x_2 \wedge x_3))$.

5. $x_2 \wedge x_1 \wedge (x_3 \vee \neg x_4) \wedge \neg x_2$.

6. $(p \vee \neg q) \wedge (\neg p \vee \neg q) \wedge (p \vee q) \wedge (\neg p \vee q)$.

Exercise 2.2.7. Prove the propositions in Section 2.2.1.2.

Exercise 2.2.8. Given the graph $\mathfrak{G} = (V, E)$, a $n \times n$ *adjacency matrix* $A_{\mathfrak{G}} = (a_{ij})$ is a matrix in which each a_{ij} entry satisfies

$$a_{ij} = \begin{cases} 1 & \text{if } (v_i, v_j) \in E \\ 0 & \text{otherwise} \end{cases}.$$

Draw the graphs with the following adjacency matrices:

1.

$$A_{\mathfrak{G}_1} = \begin{pmatrix} 0 & 0 & 1 & 1 \\ 0 & 0 & 1 & 0 \\ 1 & 1 & 0 & 1 \\ 1 & 1 & 1 & 0 \end{pmatrix}$$

2.

$$A_{\mathfrak{G}_2} = \begin{pmatrix} 0 & 1 & 1 \\ 1 & 0 & 0 \\ 1 & 0 & 0 \end{pmatrix}$$

3.

$$A_{\mathfrak{G}_3} = \begin{pmatrix} 1 & 1 & 0 & 1 \\ 0 & 0 & 0 & 1 \\ 1 & 1 & 0 & 1 \\ 1 & 0 & 0 & 1 \end{pmatrix}$$

Exercise 2.2.9. Describe formally the indicated graphs. (Check the Table of Figures for the page numbers.)

1. Figure 3.2.1.vi.

2. Figure 3.2.2.

3. Figure 3.4.1.

4. Figure 4.1.4.

5. Figure 4.1.9.1.

6. Figure 4.3.3.

Exercise 2.2.10. Represent by means of labeled rooted trees the following statements:

1. $\left[\left(a + \frac{b}{2}\right) \cdot c\right] - d$

2. $(\neg p \vee q) \rightarrow [\neg (r \wedge (s \leftrightarrow \neg q))]$

3. $b_{\mathrm{i}} \, [3 * [\S a]]$

4. $(6x - 5) + (2y/3)(2x)^2$

5. $\sqrt{\dfrac{a - 6b^3}{c}}$

Exercise 2.2.11. Let there be given a graph $\mathfrak{G} = (V, E)$ with $|V_{\mathfrak{G}}| = n > 1$. Show that the following statements are equivalent:

1. $\mathfrak{G}$ is a tree.

2. $\mathfrak{G}$ has no cycles and $|E_{\mathfrak{G}}| = n - 1$.

3. $\mathfrak{G}$ is connected and $|E_{\mathfrak{G}}| = n - 1$.

Exercise 2.2.12. Show that a finite tree with n vertices must have $n - 1$ edges.

Exercise 2.2.13. Describe formally the indicated trees. (Check the Table of Figures for the page numbers.)

1. Figure 1.5.2.1.

2. $\mathcal{T}_w$ in Figure 3.3.1.

3. Figure 3.3.3.

2.3. Proof techniques

Arguably, mathematical induction and proof by contradiction, often also spoken of as *reductio ad absurdum*, are the most ubiquitous proof techniques in the theory of classical computation. We duly provide the essential notions of these two techniques; a more comprehensive discussion can be found in Bloch (2011). Sometimes, constructive proofs are also called for, it being understood by such proofs that actually an object must be constructed. We use this proof technique sparingly, and it should be obvious when employed. We give some notes on further methods of mathematical proof in the appropriate places.

2.3.1. Mathematical and structural induction

In a proof by mathematical induction (abbr.: MI), two main steps are required: the *basis (step)* and the *induction step*. Say that we have a string of n symbols; the idea is that if we can prove that this string is legal for $n = 1$ (or some other $n \in \mathbb{N}^+$;[14] the basis), then we can prove (the induction step) that a string formed with arbitrarily many n symbols is equally legal by proving that if a string formed with m symbols is legal–the *induction hypothesis*–then a string with $m + 1$ symbols is also legal. MI proper is restricted to the set of natural numbers, but we can generalize it to any well-founded mathematical structure (e.g., graphs, trees), in which case we speak of *structural induction.*[15] It is this latter generalization that is of interest for mathematical logic and computer science, but it helps to understand thoroughly MI proper.

Example 2.3.1. The following is an often used example to introduce MI. We wish to prove that the following statement $P(n)$ holds for all positive natural numbers n.[16]

$$(P(n)) \qquad \sum_{i=1}^{n} i = \frac{n(n+1)}{2}.$$

Induction basis: We show that $P(1)$ holds. In effect, we have

$$1 = \frac{1(1+1)}{2}.$$

Induction step: We now show that if $P(m)$ holds, then $P(m+1)$ holds, too. We begin by assuming that $P(m)$ holds for arbitrary $m \in \mathbb{N}$ and then show that $P(m+1)$ also holds:

$$(P(m+1)) \qquad \sum_{i=1}^{m+1} i = \sum_{i=1}^{m} i + (m+1) =$$

$$= \frac{m(m+1)}{2} + (m+1) = \frac{m^2 + 3m + 2}{2} = \frac{(m+1)(m+2)}{2} =$$

$$= \frac{(m+1)((m+1)+1)}{2}$$

and what was to be proven has been proven (abbreviated **QED**, for the

---

[14]More rarely, $n = 0$ for the basis. Even more rarely, $n \in \mathbb{Z}$.

[15]Throughout this text, when we write "by induction" with respect to proofs we often mean "by structural induction."

[16]$\sum_{i=1}^{n} i$ is an abbreviation for the *summation* $1 + 2 + \ldots + n$, $1 \leq i \leq n$.

Latin expression *"quod erat demonstrandum")*.

We formalize the above:

2.3.1. (**Def.**) *Principle of mathematical induction:* Let P be a proposition defined on the set $\mathbb{N}^+$. Then, for each $n \in \mathbb{N}^+$, $P(n)$ either holds or does not hold. Suppose that $P(1)$ holds and $P(m+1)$ holds whenever $P(m)$ holds. Then, $P(n)$ holds for arbitrary $n \in \mathbb{N}^+$.

2.3.2. Proof by contradiction

Proof by contradiction is a method of mathematical proof theoretically based on the following properties of Boolean expressions (cf. Def. 2.2.3): For any (propositional) variable p, it holds that

$$(\text{LEM}) \qquad p \vee \neg p = 1$$

and

$$(\text{LC}) \qquad p \wedge \neg p = 0.$$

In logical jargon, we say that for every proposition p, either p is true or its negation (i.e. $\neg p$) is, a principle known as *law of excluded middle* (LEM), and p cannot be both true and false, known as *law of contradiction* (LC).

These two laws become the basis of a proof by contradiction in the following way: Of a given proposition p, we may assume that it is either true or false. Let us assume that p is false, so that $\neg p$ is true. If by the end of our reasoning we have reached a proposition of the form $q \wedge \neg q$, for some proposition q, then we have clearly–though indirectly[17]–reached a contradiction, and the only way out of it is to retract the truth of $\neg p$ and accept the truth of p instead.[18]

We formalize this:

2.3.2. (**Def.**) A proof by contradiction has the following structure:

---

[17] Reason why proofs by contradiction are a kind of *indirect proof.*

[18] Although proof by contradiction is often seen as equivalent to proof by *reductio ad absurdum*, it actually is a particular kind of the general form of proofs that involve an absurd, or impossible, conclusion. In fact, *reductio ad absurdum* is more properly used for argumentation, any form thereof resulting (supposedly) in absurdity qualifying as such. For example, the reasoning

If that's so, then pigs can fly.

fits into the broadest sense of *reductio ad absurdum*. This notwithstanding, it is also very frequent in mathematical reasoning to refer to a proof by contradiction as a proof by *reductio (ad absurdum)*. See Augusto (2019b) for a discussion of this topic.

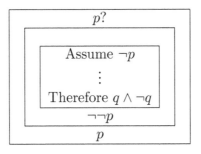

Example 2.3.2. This is a classic proof by contradiction of the irrationality of the number $\sqrt{2}$.[19] Let there be given the proposition

The number $\sqrt{2}$ is irrational.

We assume, for the sake of contradiction, that this proposition is false, i.e. we assume that $\sqrt{2}$ is rational. If $\sqrt{2}$ is rational, then there are integers a and b, $b \neq 0$, for which

$$(2.1) \qquad \sqrt{2} = \frac{a}{b}.$$

We additionally assume that $\frac{a}{b}$ is reduced to its simplest terms, which entails that not both of a and b can be even. So, one or both of a and b must be odd. From 2.1, it follows that

$$(2.2) \qquad 2 = \left(\frac{a}{b}\right)^2 = \frac{a^2}{b^2}$$

or

$$a^2 = 2b^2$$

and the square of a is an even number. Hence, a itself is an even number. Let us now replace $a = 2k$ in 2.2; we have

$$2 = \frac{(2k)^2}{b^2} = \frac{4k^2}{b^2}$$

and hence

$$2b^2 = 4k^2$$

or equivalently

$$b^2 = 2k^2$$

and we have it that b is itself even. So we have it that both of a and b are even, but we know that not both of a and b can be even, so that

---

[19]Cf. Example 2.1.2.

we have reached a contradiction. We reject the statement that $\sqrt{2}$ is a rational number, as being false, and accept the irrationality of $\sqrt{2}$. **QED**

Exercises

Exercise 2.3.1. Use MI to prove the following statements:

1. $\sum_{i=0}^{n} 2^i = 2^{n+1} - 1$ (for all $n \in \mathbb{N}$).

2. $\sum_{i=1}^{n} i = n^2$ (for all $n \in \mathbb{N}^+$, n is odd).

3. $n < 2^n$ (for all $n \in \mathbb{N}$).

4. $n^3 - n$ is divisible by 3 (for $n \in \mathbb{N}^+$).

5. If $|S| = n$ for a set S and finite n, then S has 2^n subsets.

6. For $n \geq 2$ and $A_i \in \mathbf{U}$, $\mathbf{U}$ is some universal set, $\overline{\bigcap_{i=1}^{n} A_i} = \bigcup_{i=1}^{n} \overline{A_i}$.

Exercise 2.3.2. Prove by MI that every formula ϕ has the same number of open and closed parentheses.

Exercise 2.3.3. Comment on the ubiquity of structural induction in computer science. (Hints: Parameters; infinity.)

Exercise 2.3.4. Recall from Section 2.1 the set of the reals $\mathbb{R}$. Why is it the case that in MI proofs $n \notin \mathbb{R}$?

Exercise 2.3.5. Prove the following statements by applying the method of proof by contradiction:

1. If $3n + 2$ is odd, then n is odd.

2. If A and B are sets, then $A \cap (B - A) = \emptyset$.

3. At least 4 of 22 chosen days fall on the same day of the week.

4. The sum of an irrational number and a rational number is an irrational number.

2.4. Algorithms and programs

Finally, no textbook on languages, machines, and classical computation would be complete without an introduction to algorithms and programs. We briefly introduced these notions in Section 1.2, and now provide here the basics required for the contents of this book. This being a book on formal languages, many algorithms are essentially on strings–sequences of letters or symbols from a given alphabet–or strongly string-based, constituting the subject of what has been coined *stringology*; Crochemore et al. (2007) provides a comprehensive discussion of these algorithms. Strings go on to compose programming languages, one of the central applications of formal languages. We shall not focus explicitly on programming and programming languages, of which there is a huge variety, and refer the reader to Sebesta (2012) and Scott (2009) for these foci. We refer the reader interested in a comprehensive general study of algorithms to Cormen et al. (2009).

From the short introduction in Section 1.2 we can extract the essential features of an algorithm:

2.4.1. (Def.) Given a specific input I, an *algorithm* Ψ is a finite sequence of precise instructions for a procedure Ψ leading to a solution as the output O. Formally, we have the triple $\Psi = (I, \Psi, O)$.

A procedure Ψ is said to be an *effective procedure* if, besides being an unambiguous and well-ordered set of instructions, it is carried out in a discrete, deterministic way. In general terms, the solution is a "Yes/No" answer if the effective procedure terminates. If the effective procedure (eventually) ends in a "Yes" answer, then it, together with the input and the output, is said to be an algorithm to solve a particular (class of) problem. More often than not, the "Yes" answer is actually some specific output, in particular when Ψ is a function. In any case, an algorithm is generally constituted by an *input*, an *output*, and the *procedure* between both. This is so even when the algorithm appears not to be so formally describable: For instance, a burnt light-bulb might be seen as the input to an algorithm to change a defective light-bulb, the working light-bulb as the output, and actions such as using a ladder to reach the defective light-bulb, unscrewing it, checking whether it is indeed defective (e.g., burnt), etc., are the *steps* constituting the procedure intermeadiating between the input and the output.

We shall not be concerned with such algorithms as for changing a burnt light-bulb. Specifically, the algorithms we shall be interested in are called *computational algorithms*, as they arise in the context of classical computation. In other words, they fall in the algorithmic tradition that started with D. Hilbert's *Entscheidungsproblem* and A. Turing's famous negative answer to this problem via the Turing machine. In this narrow context, a computation is formally denoted by

$$q_0, I \vdash^*_M O, q_f$$

where I and O denote the input and the output, respectively, q_0 is the initial state of computing machine M, q_f is its final state, $\vdash$ denotes a single step, and $\vdash^*_M$ denotes that M requires zero or more ($*$) individual steps to perform the computation, or carry out procedure Ψ, so that in fact we have

$$q_0, I \underbrace{\underbrace{\vdash^*_M O}_{\Psi}, q_f}_{\Psi}$$

for an algorithm Ψ_M for machine M.[20] When this computation is carried out in a classical computing device or medium (see Introduction) in such a way that the intermediate procedure does not change (say, it does not evolve), we speak of a *classical algorithm*.

In order for a computing machine like a digital computer to carry out an algorithm it requires a program, which, in turn, requires a programming language:

2.4.2. (Def.) Let L denote a precisely-defined language, i.e. a formal language. Given an algorithm $\Psi = (I, \Psi, O)$ such that $I, O \in L$ and $\Psi \subseteq L$, then L is a *programming language* and $\Psi_L = (I_L, \Psi_L, O_L) = \Pi_{M,L}$ is called a *(computer) program (written for M in L)* if there is a computing machine M that can *implement* Ψ_L so that, given input I_L, it outputs O_L by carrying out Ψ_L.

This definition entails that Ψ_L is a sequence of *instructions* rigorously formulated in a machine-readable language L, called *code*. In effect, we now have

$$q_0, I_L \underbrace{\underbrace{\underbrace{\vdash^*_M O_L}_{\Psi_L}, q_f}_{\Psi_L}}_{\Pi_{M,L}}$$

where it is evident that states q_0, q_f of machine M are considered part of the program. In effect, a computer carries out a specific computation, or algorithm, by following the instructions that amount to the correct sequence of configurations it has to realize as a–physical or ab-

---

[20]This formal representation allows for the carrying-out of algorithms to be precisely measured in terms of complexity, i.e. we can measure the temporal and/or spatial costs of an algorithmic procedure Ψ, a topic we discuss in Chapter 5.

stract–machine. This said, programmers do not in fact need to write the code for the machine, as this is an exceedingly difficult task that is better accomplished by a compiler, a piece of software that translates the high-level languages used by programmers, such as Java, C, Pascal, Prolog, etc., into the low-level, or machine, languages. For this reason, henceforth we concentrate on high-level languages, in which we include *pseudo-code*, a "programming" language that is very similar to English and whose use aims at allowing humans to read the algorithm more or less easily.[21]

Example 2.4.1. The *Euclidean algorithm* is one of the best–and oldest–algorithms known for finding the greatest common divisor of two integers a and b, denoted by $\gcd(a, b)$ and defined as

$$\gcd(a, b) = \begin{cases} a & \text{if } b = 0 \\ \gcd(b, a \bmod b) & \text{if } b > 0 \end{cases}.$$

The operation of finding $\gcd(a, b)$ is computable by means of an algorithm, because the greatest common divisor of two integers–not both zero–exists, as the set of their common divisors is finite and non-empty. Although there are other methods to compute $\gcd(a, b)$ (e.g., prime factorization), the Euclidean algorithm is a very efficient procedure. For pedagogical reasons, we restrict our example to non-negative integers. The input to the algorithm is constituted by the two integers a and b, and the output is $\gcd(a, b) = d$, d is the greatest integer such that $d|a$ and $d|b$ (see Example 2.1.4). The simplest algorithm for this computation, which is recursion-based, is as follows:

Input: integers a, b such that $a > 0$ and $b \geq 0$
Output: $\gcd(a, b)$

if $b = 0$
    return a
else return $\gcd(b, a \bmod b) = \gcd(b, r)$

This is actually a program, as the algorithm is formulated in pseudo-

---

[21] As stated in the Preface, for the sake of generality we shall not stick to any programming language, but we shall also not stick to a particular pseudo-code. The aim of the algorithms provided in this book is the carrying-out "by hand" of specific computations and our belief is that this requires a mathematical–in any case notational–understanding of the input, the output, and the intermediate procedure; for this reason, our algorithms are frequently just mathematical descriptions of these elements. This said, we use expressions such as **if** ... **then** ... **else**, **while** ... **do**, etc., which are ubiquitous in computing.

code. In other words, the computing "machine" is here a human. However, it often pays off for a programmer to write a program first in pseudo-code, and then "translate" this into real code. Note in this example how the procedure in pseudo-code corresponds to the mathematical definition (given above) of the function for the greatest common divisor. It is evident that in case $b \neq 0$ one needs to compute $\gcd(b, a \bmod b)$, which is only possible if one knows how to carry out a modulo operation. In particular, one needs to know the theoretical basis for this requirement, which is given by the result (a lemma) "if $a = bq + r$, a, b, q, r are all integers, then $\gcd(a, b) = \gcd(b, r)$." For instance, we apply the above definition to find $\gcd(723, 320)$:

$$
\begin{array}{rcl}
723 & = & (320 \times 2) + 83 \\
320 & = & (83 \times 3) + 71 \\
83 & = & (71 \times 1) + 12 \\
71 & = & (12 \times 5) + 11 \\
12 & = & (11 \times 1) + 1 \\
11 & = & (1 \times 11) + 0
\end{array}
$$

We obtain the result $\gcd(723, 320) = 1 = \gcd(1, 0)$. Because more often than not $b \neq 0$, then a more explicit algorithm is required.

Example 2.4.2. The following is a more explicit version of the Euclidean algorithm:

Input: integers a, b such that $a > 0$ and $b \geq 0$
Output: $\gcd(a, b)$

make
    $x = a$
    $y = b$
while $y \neq 0$
    $r = x \bmod y$
    $x = y$
    $y = r$
    return x

From the short discussion above, it should be clear that the following properties are required for any classical algorithm:

- *Finiteness*: No matter how large the number of steps between the input and the output might be, the set of steps constituting an algorithmic procedure is finite.

- *Generality*: The procedure should be applicable to any given values of a specific problem, not just to particular input values thereof.

- *Effectiveness*: Each step should be completable in finite time. Otherwise, the algorithm is inefficient.

While the two first properties are easily attainable when designing an algorithm, the last one depends on many factors. In particular, an algorithm Ψ_A can be classified as *more* or *less efficient* than another algorithm Ψ_B for the same input-output depending on the physical resources, namely time or space, it requires to carry out the intermediate procedure Ψ. Hence, the classification by their complexity is a fundamental one for the design and analysis of classical algorithms, and we discuss this topic in Section 5.4 below. For other types of algorithm classification (method, task, etc.), we provide some research guidelines in the Exercises.

Exercises

Exercise 2.4.1. Bézout's theorem states that if a and b are positive integers, then there exist integers s and t such that $\gcd(a,b) = sa + tb$. From this theorem, which defines $\gcd(a,b)$ as a linear combination in which s and t are the (Bézout) coefficients of a and b, respectively, an algorithm to compute $\gcd(a,b)$ can be designed. Design it using a pseudo-code similar to that in Examples 2.4.1-2.

Exercise 2.4.2. Consider this algorithm to compute $\gcd(a,b)$:

Input: integers a, b such that $a > 0$ and $b \geq 0$
Output: $\gcd(a,b)$

if $b = 0$
    return $(a, 1, 0)$
else $(d', x', y' = \gcd(b, a \bmod b))$
    $(d, x, y) = (d', y'x' - \lfloor a/b \rfloor y')$
    return (d, x, y)

---

1. Find out the mathematical result(s) it was designed upon.

2. Compare it with the Euclidean algorithm in Example 2.4.2: Which do you think is the most efficient? Account for your answer.

Exercise 2.4.3. Research into the following types of algorithms as according to a very broad classification:

1. Divide-and-conquer algorithms.

2. Greedy algorithms.

3. Dynamic programming.

4. Linear programming.

Exercise 2.4.4. A more fine-grained classification of algorithms is given below. For each type, (a) give a definition, (b) give the most important instances, and (c) indicate relevant applications in classical computing:

1. Sort algorithms.

2. Search algorithms.

3. String matching and parsing algorithms.

4. Hashing.

Part III.

Languages, Machines, and Classical Computation

3. Formal grammars and languages

It should be easy to see that there would not be a natural language, say, English, if there were not a set of rules specifying what both English words and English sentences are. We call the set of these rules the English grammar, or the grammar of English. It is possible to have a normative perspective on a grammar, even in a scientific linguistic context; then, the English language is the set of all the constructs that follow the rules of the English grammar. However, we can see this "following" in a rather distinct perspective, namely as a "generating"; in this viewpoint, then the English language is the set of all constructs generated by the English grammar.

The concept of a natural language like English cannot be effectively captured by this strictly *syntactical* approach to a grammar, as besides this one has to consider the *meaning* of the constructs of English, as well as their *appropriate use* in context, fields that are known as *semantics* and *pragmatics*, respectively. N. Chomsky, the conceiver of the hierarchy that works as the backbone of this book, gave in Chomsky (1956, 1957) a (now) famous example of a construct of English that, though syntactically correct, has no meaning and therefore no context of use (other than poetic license):[1]

Colorless green ideas sleep furiously.

Thus, although in a restricted sense English can be considered a formal language and its grammar a formal grammar, these characterizations alone are seldom of much use. As a matter of fact, this holds also for programming languages, which in addition to a formal semantics (and arguably some pragmatics) require the level of *implementation*.

However, in this book we consider *computation* to be more strictly the process of going from one (legal) string to another (legal) string. In this narrow sense, a *computer language* just is its syntax, and we reserve the expressions *formal language* and *formal grammar* for languages and

---

[1] Once the reader grasps the notion of a parse tree (see below), it will be easy to produce sentences with the same structure that not only are formally correct, but also have meaning. For example: *Resourceful little ants work diligently.*

grammars that can be specified in a purely syntactical way. The relation between these two is that grammars generate languages and languages are generated by grammars.

But computation with respect to languages and their associated grammars can be more encompassing, and we refer the reader to specific and/or more adequate literature on specific topics: Those interested in compilation can consult, for instance, Reghizzi, Breveglieri, & Morzenti (2019); for readers focusing on natural language processing in the context of computational linguistics Hausser (2014) may be of interest.

3.1. Basic notions

Classical computation is carried out over a language that is unequivocally specified.[2] Such a language is called a formal language, and this unequivocal specification is provided by a formal grammar. A formal language consists of strings of symbols of a specified alphabet that are well formed according to specified formation rules given in the grammar.

3.1.1. Strings and operations on strings

3.1.1. (Def.) Let Σ be a non-empty set of symbols. Then, a *string*, or *word*, w on the set Σ is a finite sequence of symbols over Σ. A set Σ over which strings or words are built is called an *alphabet* and the members of Σ are its *letters*.[3]

> **Example 3.1.1.** Let $\Sigma = \{a, b, c\}$. Then, $u = abba = ab^2a$ and $v = cbabbaaac = cbab^2a^3c$, where a^n is an abbreviation for $\overbrace{a...a}^{n}$, are strings on Σ. The sequence $affe$ is *not* a string on Σ, because $f, e \notin \Sigma$.

3.1.2. (Def.) Let w be a string on an alphabet Σ.

1. The *length* of w, denoted by $|w|$, is the number of letters in w. If $|w| = 0$, then we speak of the *empty string*, and we denote it by ϵ.

2. The *frequency* of a letter a in a word w, denoted by $|w|_a$, is the number of occurrences of a in w.

---

[2]This, however, does not guarantee that it is unambiguous, as we shall see.

[3]Actually, one can distinguish *word* from *string* by defining the former as a finite *or countably infinite* sequence of symbols. Unless otherwise stated, we shall not distinguish between both; moreover, henceforth we shall speak of string.

3. A *substring w'* of *w* is a sequence of consecutive letters occurring in *w*. A substring that starts (ends) at the leftmost (rightmost, respectively) letter is a *prefix* (*suffix*, respectively).

Example 3.1.2. Let v be the string in Example 3.1.1. Then, $|v| = 9$, $|v|_a = 4$, $|v|_b = 3$, and $|v|_c = 2$. We have $|v|_a + |v|_b + |v|_c = |v|$. Two substrings of v are, for instance, $v' = cbab$ and $v'' = ba^3c$, a prefix and a suffix of v, respectively. The string $cbbb$ is *not* a substring of v.

Given one or more strings, operations can be carried out on them that result in new strings.

3.1.3. (Def.) Let $u = a_1...a_n$ and $v = b_1...b_m$ be two strings on the alphabet $\Sigma = \{a, b\}$. The following are *operations on* the strings u, v:

1. The *concatenation* of u and v, written uv, is the string constituted by the string u followed by the string v, i.e. $a_1...a_nb_1...b_m$. We have $|uv| = |u| + |v|$.

2. Given a string u, we define the *i-th power* of u as follows: $u^0 = \epsilon$, $u^1 = u$ and, for $i > 1$, $u^i = u^{i-1}u$. The length of u^i is $i|u|$.

3. A string w is the *reverse* or *mirror image* of u, denoted by u^R, if $w = a_n...a_1$. A string that is identical to its reverse is a *palindrome*.

4. Let now $v = b_1...b_n$. The *shuffle* of u and v, denoted by $u \text{ ⧢ } v$, is the string $a_1b_1...a_nb_n$.

Example 3.1.3. Let Σ be the 26-letter Roman alphabet adopted for English. Then, *bookkeeper* is the concatenation of the strings *book* and *keeper*, and *says* is the concatenation of the strings *say* and *s*. $says^0 = \epsilon$, $says^1 = says$, $says^2 = sayssays$, etc. The proper nouns *Eve*, *Otto*, and *Hannah* are palindromes. The shuffle of *goat* and *milk* is *gmoialtk*.

3.1.4. (Prop.) The empty string ϵ is an identity element for concatenation, as for some string u we have $\epsilon u = u\epsilon = u$. Concatenation is generally not a commutative operation when $|\Sigma| > 1$, though it is associative:

1. Unless v and u are identical strings we have $uv \neq vu$;

2. Given strings u, v, and w, we have $(uv)\,w = u\,(vw)$.

3.1.2. Formal languages and operations thereon

The discussion above on strings and operations thereon allows for precise definitions of a formal language. We first define it as a pair constituted by an alphabet Σ and a grammar G of rules over Σ. This definition is then naturally generalized to the definition of a language as a set of strings over Σ generated by means of G.

3.1.5. (Def.) A *formal language* is a pair $L = (\Sigma, G)$ where Σ is a (possibly infinite) set of symbols called the *letters* (of Σ),[4] and G is a finite set of *rules* for making *well-formed*, or *legal*, *strings* of L. Σ is called the *alphabet* of L and G is called the *grammar* (or *syntax*) of L.

Example 3.1.4. Clearly, a natural language like English is a formal language. The English alphabet (in this formal sense) is constituted by lower- and uppercase letters of the Latin alphabet, the digits 0,1,...,9, the blank symbol, and various punctuation symbols (e.g., ; and !). The grammar of English is the set of (many!) rules to make well-formed strings. Prolog is a formal language with far fewer rules than English, but much of what can be expressed in English can be so in Prolog as well.

Thus, both natural languages and computer languages are formal languages. Definition 3.1.5 can be further specified as follows:

3.1.6. (Def.) A *(formal) language L over an alphabet Σ* is a collection of strings on Σ. Let now Σ^* denote the set of all strings (including the empty string) on Σ. Then, a (formal) language L over Σ just is a subset of Σ^* (and any subset of Σ^*, including $\emptyset$, is a language).[5] More specifically, given a string w,

$$L = \{w \in \Sigma^* | w \text{ has property } P\}.$$

Example 3.1.5. Let $\Sigma = \{a, b\}$. The following are languages over Σ:

1. $L_1 = \{w \in \Sigma^* | w = a^m b^m, m > 0\} = \{ab, a^2b^2, a^3b^3, ...\}$

2. $L_2 = \{w \in \Sigma^* | w = ab^n, n \geq 0\} = \{a, ab, ab^2, ...\}$

3. $L_3 = \{w \in \Sigma^* | w = w^R\}$, i.e. w is a palindrome

4. $L_4 = \{w \in \Sigma^* | w \text{ has an even number of } a\} = \{aa, aab, bbbaaaa, ...\}$

---

[4]In practice, alphabets are typically finite sets.
[5]We henceforth often omit the adjective "formal" and speak only of languages.

5. $L_5 = \{w \in \Sigma^* | w$ ends with $bb\} = \{bb, abb, babaabb, ...\}$

It should be obvious that if Σ contains at least one letter, then Σ^* is infinite, and because formal languages L over Σ just are subsets of Σ^*, they are in infinite number, too. However, a language L over an alphabet Σ can be finite or infinite. In effect, $|L| = n \geq 0$ for n strings.

Example 3.1.6. Let $\Sigma = \{a, b, c, ..., y, z\}$, $|\Sigma| = 26$. Then, the following are languages over Σ, L_{1-3} are infinite languages, and L_{4-7} are finite languages:

1. $L_1 = \Sigma^*$; $|L_1| = \infty$.

2. $L_2 = \{w \in \Sigma^* | w$ consists solely of vowels$\}$; $|L_2| = \infty$.

3. $L_3 = \{w \in \Sigma^* | w = w^R\}$; $|L_3| = \infty$.

4. $L_4 = \{w \in \Sigma^* | w$ is a single-letter string$\}$; $|L_4| = |\Sigma|$.

5. $L_5 = \{my, your, his, her, its, our, their\}$; $|L_5| = 7$.

6. $L_6 = \{w \in \Sigma^* | w$ occurs in Shakespeare's plays$\}$; $|L_6| = n$ for unknown finite n.

7. $L_7 = \emptyset$; $|L_7| = 0$.

Given Proposition 3.1.4 above, we have the following mathematical characterization of a language L:

3.1.7. (Def.) Let Σ be an alphabet. Then, Σ^* is a *free monoid* with domain the set of all strings over Σ and with string concatenation as the semigroup operation $\star$. The set $\Sigma^* - \{\epsilon\}$ is the *ϵ-free semigroup* Σ^+ on the alphabet Σ with string concatenation as the semigroup operation $\star$.

This allows us to reformulate Definition 3.1.6 in a more mathematical framework:

3.1.8. (Def.) A *(formal) language* on an alphabet Σ is a subset L of the free monoid Σ^*. An *ϵ-free language* on Σ is a subset of the ϵ-free semigroup Σ^+.

Just as with strings, we can carry out operations on languages that result in new languages.

3.1.9. (Def.) Let L, L_i, $i = 1, 2, ...$, be languages over an alphabet Σ. The following are *operations on L, L_i*:

1. The *reverse* or *mirror image* of a language L, denoted by L^R, is the set
$$L^R = \{w \in \Sigma^* | w^R \in L\}.$$

2. The *concatenation* L_1L_2 of L_1 and L_2 is the set
$$L_1L_2 = \{w \in \Sigma^* | w = uv, u \in L_1, v \in L_2\}.$$

3. The *shuffle* $L_1 \,\square\, L_2$ of L_1 and L_2 is the set
$$L_1 \,\square\, L_2 = \{w \in \Sigma^* | w = u \,\square\, v, u \in L_1, v \in L_2\}.$$

4. The *i-th power* of the language L is defined as follows: $L^0 = \{\epsilon\}$ for $i = 0$, $L^1 = L$ for $i = 1$, $L^{i+1} = L^iL$ for $i > 1$.

5. The *Kleene closure* (or *Kleene star*) of a language L, denoted by L^*, is the (infinite) union of all its powers, i.e. $\bigcup_{i \geq 0} L^i$. The *positive closure* of L, denoted by L^+, is the same as L^* without the empty string, i.e. $L^+ = \bigcup_{i \geq 1} L^i$.

6. The *union* of two languages L_1 and L_2 is the set operation $L_1 \cup L_2$.

7. The *intersection* of two languages L_1 and L_2 is the set operation $L_1 \cap L_2$.

8. The *complement* of a language L over an alphabet Σ is the set
$$\overline{L} = \{w \in \Sigma^* | w \notin L\}.$$

Example 3.1.7. Let $L_1 = \{yaw, czt\}$ and L_2 be the set of the English possessive adjectives, i.e. $L_2 = \{my, your, his, her, its, our, their\}$. We have the following:

1. $L_2^R = \{ym, ruoy, sih, reh, sti, ruo, rieht\}$.

2. $L_1L_2 = \{yawmy, yawyour, yawhis, ..., cztour, czttheir\}$.

3. $L_1^0 = \{\epsilon\}$, $L_1^1 = \{yaw, czt\}$, $L_1^2 = \{yawyaw, yawczt, cztczt, cztyaw\}$, ...

4. $L_1 \cup L_2 = \{yaw, czt, my, your, his, her, its, our, their\}$.

5. $L_1 \cap L_2 = \emptyset$.

3.1.10. (Def.) Let Σ be an alphabet and let $\mathscr{L}$ be the set of all the finite subsets of Σ^*. Then $\mathscr{L}$ is a *language class*. Let $\Diamond$ be some operation on languages. A language class $\mathscr{L}$ is said to be *closed under* $\Diamond$ if and only if, whenever $L_1, L_2 \in \mathscr{L}$, then $\Diamond L_{i=1,2} \in \mathscr{L}$ and $(L_1 \Diamond L_2) \in \mathscr{L}$.

3.1.3. Formal grammars

3.1.3.1. Central notions

3.1.11. (Def.) A *formal grammar* is a 4-tuple $G = (V, T, S, P)$ where $V \neq \emptyset$ is a finite set of *variables* (or *non-terminal symbols*), $T \neq \emptyset$ is a finite set of *terminal symbols*, $V \cap T = \emptyset$, $S \in V$ is the *start variable*, and P is a finite set of *grammar*, or *production*, *rules* (also: *productions*).[6]

1. A production (rule) is a pair of strings (α, β), written $\alpha \rightarrow \beta$, where α must contain at least one non-terminal symbol. In the production (rule) $\alpha \rightarrow \beta$, α is called the *head* (or *antecedent*), and β the *body* (or *consequent*).

2. Let $\alpha, \beta \in [(V \cup T)^* = (V \cup T \cup \{\epsilon\})]$ be strings. We say that β is *directly derivable* from α (or α *yields* β) with respect to G, and write $\alpha \underset{G}{\Longrightarrow} \beta$, if there is a production $\gamma \rightarrow \delta$ and strings $\zeta_1, \zeta_2 \in (V \cup T)^*$ such that $\alpha = \zeta_1 \gamma \zeta_2$ and $\beta = \zeta_1 \delta \zeta_2$.

3. A *derivation* of the string β–called the *yield*–from the string α is a sequence of n direct derivations (steps)

$$\alpha \underset{G}{\Longrightarrow} \gamma_1, \gamma_1 \underset{G}{\Longrightarrow} \gamma_2, ..., \gamma_n \underset{G}{\Longrightarrow} \beta = \alpha \underset{G}{\overset{n}{\Longrightarrow}} \beta$$

or $\alpha \underset{G}{\overset{*}{\Longrightarrow}} \beta$, for *zero or more* steps. $\underset{G}{\overset{n}{\Longrightarrow}}$, or $\underset{G}{\overset{*}{\Longrightarrow}}$, is the *reflexive and transitive closure* of $\underset{G}{\Longrightarrow}$, as we have (i) $\alpha \underset{G}{\overset{*}{\Longrightarrow}} \alpha$, and (ii) if $\alpha \underset{G}{\overset{*}{\Longrightarrow}} \beta$ and $\beta \underset{G}{\overset{*}{\Longrightarrow}} \gamma$, then we have $\alpha \underset{G}{\overset{*}{\Longrightarrow}} \gamma$.

   a) A derivation $\alpha \Longrightarrow \beta$ is called a *leftmost derivation*, denoted by $\alpha \Longrightarrow_l \beta$, if at each step a production is applied to the leftmost variable in α.

---

[6]We often abbreviate "(non-)terminal symbols" as "(non-)terminals."

    b) A derivation $\alpha \Longrightarrow \beta$ is called a *rightmost derivation*, denoted by $\alpha \Longrightarrow_r \beta$, if at each step a production is applied to the rightmost variable in α.

4. A string $\alpha \in (V \cup T)^*$ is called a *sentential form* if $S \xLongrightarrow[G]{*} \alpha$. If $S \xLongrightarrow[G]{*}_l \alpha$ $\left(S \xLongrightarrow[G]{*}_r \alpha \right)$, then α is called a *left-sentential form* (a *right-sentential form*, respectively).

5. The *language* $L \subseteq T^*$ *generated by the grammar* G, denoted by $L(G)$, is defined as[7]

$$L(G) = \left\{ w \in T^* \mid S \xLongrightarrow[G]{*} w \right\}.$$

    a) The *leftmost language generated by the grammar* G, denoted by $L_l(G)$, is the language of strings of terminals with leftmost derivations from the start variable S.

    b) The *rightmost language generated by the grammar* G, denoted by $L_r(G)$, is the language of strings of terminals with rightmost derivations from the start variable S.

6. The grammars $G_1 = (V_1, T_1, S_1, P_1)$ and $G_2 = (V_2, T_2, S_2, P_2)$ are *equivalent* if and only if $L(G_1) = L(G_2)$.

A rule of production written as $\alpha \to \beta$ (often $\alpha ::= \beta$ in other texts) is said to be in BNF, or *Backus-Naur form*, or *notation*. Unless otherwise stated, we shall also use the following conventions:

- $A, B, C, ..., G$ denote variables;

- $a, b, c, ..., g$ denote terminals;

- $\alpha, \beta, \gamma, \delta, \zeta$ denote strings of variables and terminals;

- $u, v, ..., z$ denote strings of terminals;

---

[7] This explains the meaning of "non-terminal" symbols: They do not occur in the generated language.

- X, Y denote a symbol that may be either a variable or a terminal.

It should be noted that productions are, in practical terms, rules for *rewriting*, or, to be more precise, *replacement*. This will become clear in the many examples below.

3.1.3.2. Rules, symbols, and grammar cleaning

3.1.12. (Def.) Let there be given a grammar $G = (V, T, S, P)$. We say of a symbol $A \in V$ that:

1. It is *reachable*, or *accessible*, if there exists the derivation

$$S \overset{*}{\underset{G}{\Longrightarrow}} \alpha A \beta.$$

   Otherwise, it is *unreachable*, or *inaccessible*.

2. It is *well defined* if it generates a language $L \neq \emptyset$. Otherwise, it is *ill defined* (or *non-defined*).

It should be noted with respect to Definition 3.1.12.1 that any symbol occurring on the body of a production with S in its head is a reachable symbol, and any symbol occurring on the body of a production with an accessible symbol in the head is likewise a reachable symbol. Ill-definition is the case of productions of the kind $A \overset{*}{\Longrightarrow} \emptyset$ such that they do not generate a string of terminals–reason why we may also call these symbols *non-generating*.

Example 3.1.8. Let the grammar $G = (\{S, A, B\}, \{a, b\}, S, P)$ with

$$P = \left\{ \begin{array}{l} S \to AB \\ A \to Aa \\ A \to a \\ B \to Bb \end{array} \right\}$$

be given. The symbol B is ill defined, despite being reachable. On the contrary, A is both reachable and well defined.

Note in the grammar above that for the antecedent A there are two *alternative* consequents. Given this, we can write one single production rule where "|" means *or*:

$$A \to Aa \,|\, a.$$

3.1.13. (Def.) A grammar $G = (V, T, S, P)$ is said to be *clean* if it has neither unreachable nor ill-defined symbols.

The process of obtaining a clean grammar from any given grammar is called simply *grammar cleaning*. Although detecting unreachable and ill-defined symbols is crucial to the process of cleaning a grammar, in fact we also want to avoid circularity and superfluous derivations, so that productions of the kind $A \rightarrow B$, called *unitary* (or *unit productions*) and of which the *recursive* production $A \rightarrow A$ is a special case, should also be eliminated in the process. Evidently, productions of the kind $A \rightarrow \epsilon$ should also be eliminated. Thus, before even starting the process of cleaning a grammar, these two kinds of productions–known as *renaming* (or *copying*) and *empty productions* (or ϵ*-productions*), respectively–must be removed while leaving the grammar unchanged. We show how in the following examples.

Example 3.1.9. Let there be given $G = (\{S, A, B\}, \{a, b, c, d\}, S, P)$ with the production set

$$P = \left\{ \begin{array}{c} S \rightarrow aAB \,|\, Ab \\ A \rightarrow cBd \,|\, \epsilon \\ B \rightarrow cBA \,|\, a \end{array} \right\}.$$

We eliminate the production $A \rightarrow \epsilon$, but do so after adding to P productions in which A has been rewritten as ϵ (marked with $\cdot$):

$$P' = \left\{ \begin{array}{c} S \rightarrow aAB \,|\, Ab \,|\, \underline{aB} \,|\, \underline{b} \\ A \rightarrow cBd \\ B \rightarrow cBA \,|\, a \,|\, \underline{cB} \end{array} \right\}$$

Example 3.1.10. Let $G = (\{S, A, B, C\}, \{a, b, c, d\}, S, P)$ with the production set

$$P = \left\{ \begin{array}{c} S \rightarrow aAB \,|\, A \,|\, C \\ A \rightarrow cBd \,|\, Bc \,|\, b \\ B \rightarrow cBA \,|\, a \\ C \rightarrow cAd \,|\, c \end{array} \right\}$$

be given. There are two rules of renaming, to wit, $S \rightarrow A$ and $S \rightarrow C$. We remove these two rules by replacing these single right-side variable occurrences by the bodies of the productions with A and C on the left sides (marked with $\cdot$), so that we have the following production set:

$$P' = \left\{ \begin{array}{c} S \rightarrow aAB \,|\, \underline{cBd} \,|\, \underline{Bc} \,|\, \underline{b} \,|\, \underline{cAd} \,|\, \underline{c} \\ A \rightarrow cBd \,|\, Bc \,|\, b \\ B \rightarrow cBA \,|\, a \\ C \rightarrow cAd \,|\, c \end{array} \right\}$$

These two actions having been performed, we are ready to clean a grammar, for which we may apply an algorithm that essentially detects accessible and well-defined symbols and subsequently, by exclusion, identifies the ill-defined and inaccessible symbols. This is Algorithm 3.1.

Example 3.1.11. Let $G = (\{S, A, B, C, D, E, F, G\}, \{0, 1\}, S, P)$ with

$$P = \begin{cases} S \to A01 \mid CS0 \mid 1 \mid 1B \\ A \to 0A \mid C1 \mid 0 \mid 0BAE \\ B \to 1B \mid 0BC \mid 0F \\ C \to CG \mid DC \\ D \to 0C1 \mid 0 \\ E \to 00E \mid 1B \\ F \to 0F \mid 01 \\ G \to 0F \end{cases}$$

be given. Conveniently, this grammar does not have either non-generative or renaming productions, reason why we can proceed to apply the cleaning algorithm (Algorithm 3.1) right away. We first obtain $WDF = \{S, A, B, D, F\}$ and then $WDF' = \{S, A, B, D, E, F, G\}$. This leaves C outside WDF', because none of the alternative consequents in the body of the production with head C contains exclusively symbols from WDF (DC does contain $D \in WDF$, but $C \notin WDF$). After Step 1, we have the following production set in which the symbol C has been wholly removed along with the productions containing it:

$$P_{step1} = \begin{cases} S \to A01 \mid 1 \mid 1B \\ A \to 0A \mid 0 \mid 0BAE \\ B \to 1B \mid 0F \\ D \to 0 \\ E \to 00E \mid 1B \\ F \to 0F \mid 01 \\ G \to 0F \end{cases}.$$

We now (Step 2) first compute $ACCS = \{S, A, B\}$ and then $ACCS' = \{S, A, B, E, F\}$. Thus we have $V - ACCS' = \{D, G\}$. We remove from P_{step1} these two symbols and obtain the final production set

$$P_{step2} = P' = \begin{cases} S \to A01 \mid 1 \mid 1B \\ A \to 0A \mid 0 \mid 0BAE \\ B \to 1B \mid 0F \\ E \to 00E \mid 1B \\ F \to 0F \mid 01 \end{cases}.$$

Algorithm 3.1 Grammar cleaning

Input: A grammar $G = (V, T, S, P)$ possibly with inaccessible and ill- or non-defined symbols
Output: A clean grammar $G' = (V', T, S, P')$

STEP 1

1. Compute the set $WDF \subseteq V$ defined as

$$WDF = \{A|\, (A \to x) \in P, x \in T^*\}\,.$$

2. Compute the set WDF' defined as

$$WDF' = WDF \cup \{B|\, (B \to C_1 C_2 ... C_n) \in P\}$$

where every $C_i \in WDF$.

3. Compute

$$V - WDF' = \overline{WDF}.$$

These symbols are ill or non-defined and must be eliminated from the grammar along with the productions in which they occur on the left side.

STEP 2

1. Compute the set of accessible symbols $ACCS \subseteq V$ defined as

$$ACCS = \{S, A|\, (S \to \alpha A \beta) \in P\}\,.$$

2. Compute the set $ACCS'$ defined as

$$ACCS' = ACCS \cup \{B|\, (A \to \alpha B \beta) \in P, A \in ACCS\}\,.$$

3. Compute

$$V - ACCS' = \overline{ACCS}.$$

These are inaccessible symbols and must be eliminated from the grammar along with the productions in which they occur on the left side.

TERMINATE

Exercises

Exercise 3.1.1. Show that for any strings u, v over some alphabet Σ:

1. $|uv| = |u| + |v|$.

2. $|uv| = |vu|$.

3. $(uv)^R = v^R u^R$.

Exercise 3.1.2. Let $\Sigma = \{a, b, c\}$ be an alphabet and let $u = abbcbb$, $v = baaacb$, and $w = ccc$ be strings over Σ. Find:

1. all substrings of v.

2. uv.

3. wu^2.

4. ϵu.

5. $v \epsilon w$.

6. $v \square u$.

7. v^3.

8. $|v^3|$.

9. $|v|_a$, $|v|_b$, $|v|_c$.

10. $|vw|_a$, $|vw|_b$, $|wv|_c$.

Exercise 3.1.3. Let $\Sigma = \{0, 1\}$ be an alphabet. Give examples of strings generated by the following languages over Σ:

1. $L = \{0^2 1^l 0^2 | l > 0\}$.

2. $L = \{(01)^n | n > 0\}$.

3. $L = \{1^l 01^m 01^n | l > 0, m, n \geq 0\}$.

Exercise 3.1.4. Let $L_1 = \{pit, tip, pip\}$ and $L_2 = \{la, di, da\}$ be two languages over the alphabet $\Sigma = \{a, b, c, ..., y, z\}$. Find:

1. L_1^0.

2. L_2^1.

3. L_1^2.

4. L_1^R.

5. $L_1^1 L_2^R$

6. $L_2 L_1$.

7. $L_1 \,\square\, L_2$.

8. $L_1 \cup L_2$.

Exercise 3.1.5. For an arbitrary language L, or for any two languages L_1 and L_2, show that:

1. $L^+ = L^*$ if and only if $\epsilon \in L$.

2. $L^* = (L^*)^n$ for $n \geq 1$.

3. $\bigcup_{i=0}^n L^i = (\{\epsilon\} \cup L)^n$ for $n \geq 1$.

4. $(L_1 \cup L_2)^* = L_1^* (L_2 L_1^*)^*$.

5. $(L_1 \cup L_2)^* = (L_1^* L_2^*)^*$.

6. $(L_1 L_2)^R = L_2^R L_1^R$.

7. $(L_1 \cup L_2)^R = L_1^R \cup L_2^R$.

Exercise 3.1.6. Find the language generated by the grammar $G = (V, T, S, P)$

1. with $V = \{S, A\}$, $T = \{a, b, c\}$, and the production set

$$P = \left\{ \begin{array}{c} S \to aSb \\ Aab \to c \\ aS \to Aa \end{array} \right\}.$$

2. with $V = \{S, A, B\}$, $T = \{0, 1\}$, and the production set

$$P = \left\{ \begin{array}{c} S \to 0B \\ A \to 0B \\ B \to 1A \,|\, 1 \end{array} \right\}.$$

3. with $V = \{S, A, B\}$, $T = \{a, b\}$, and the production set

$$P = \left\{ \begin{array}{c} S \to aA \\ A \to aAB \mid a \\ B \to b \mid \epsilon \end{array} \right\}.$$

4. with $V = \{S, A, B, C\}$, $T = \{0, 1\}$, and the production set

$$P = \left\{ \begin{array}{c} S \to AS0 \mid BS1 \mid C \\ AC \to 0C \\ A0 \to 0A \\ A1 \to 1A \\ BC \to 1C \\ B0 \to 0B \\ B1 \to 1B \\ C \to \epsilon \end{array} \right\}.$$

5. with $V = \{S, A, B\}$, $T = \{0, 1\}$, and the production set

$$P = \left\{ \begin{array}{c} S \to 0AB \\ AB \to 0 \mid 1 \\ B \to AB \end{array} \right\}.$$

6. with $V = \{S, A, B\}$, $T = \{0, 1\}$, and the production set

$$P = \left\{ \begin{array}{c} S \to 0AB \\ A0 \to S0B \\ A1 \to SB1 \\ B \to SA \mid 01 \\ 1B \to 0 \end{array} \right\}.$$

7. with $V = \{S, A, B\}$, $T = \{a, b, c\}$, and the production set

$$P = \left\{ \begin{array}{c} S \to aAbc \mid abc \\ Ab \to bA \\ Ac \to Bbcc \\ aB \to aaA \mid aa \\ bB \to Bb \end{array} \right\}.$$

Exercise 3.1.7. Clean the given grammars:

1. $G = (\{S, A, B, C, D, E\}, \{a, b, c, d\}, S, P)$ with

$$P = \left\{ \begin{array}{c} S \rightarrow S \,|\, aA \,|\, Ba \,|\, aaa \\ A \rightarrow aa \\ B \rightarrow aa \\ C \rightarrow b \,|\, DE \\ D \rightarrow EC \,|\, c \\ E \rightarrow CD \,|\, d \end{array} \right\}.$$

2. $G = (\{S, A, B, C\}, \{a, b\}, S, P)$ with

$$P = \left\{ \begin{array}{c} S \rightarrow A \,|\, AB \,|\, aSB \,|\, C \\ A \rightarrow aAB \\ B \rightarrow \epsilon \,|\, Bb \end{array} \right\}.$$

3. $G = (\{S, A, B, C, D, E, F\}, \{0, 1\}, S, P)$ with

$$P = \left\{ \begin{array}{c} S \rightarrow 0A1 \,|\, 1DA \,|\, AE1 \\ A \rightarrow 00A \,|\, C01A \,|\, DC10 \\ B \rightarrow 1AB \,|\, 00D \\ C \rightarrow A0 \,|\, \epsilon \\ D \rightarrow 1010 \,|\, AD \\ E \rightarrow E11CB \\ F \rightarrow 11B \,|\, \epsilon \,|\, 00A \end{array} \right\}.$$

Exercise 3.1.8. As seen above, recursion is the case when we have a (recursive) production of the form $A \rightarrow \alpha A \beta$, where $\alpha, \beta \in (V \cup T)^*$. For example, for $\alpha \neq \epsilon$ and $A \notin \alpha$, $A \rightarrow \alpha A$ is a *right-recursive* production.

1. Prove that, given a clean grammar G, the language $L(G)$ is infinite if and only if G has at least one recursive production.

2. Is recursion a property simply to be eliminated in a formal grammar? (Hint: How many strings does one want a grammar G to be able to generate?)

Exercise 3.1.9. Although unit productions are required to be removed from a clean grammar, they are actually advantageous in some situations and are frequently to be found. Comment on this observation.

3.2. Regular languages

Regular languages are the simplest formal languages in the Chomsky hierarchy (see Section 3.5). Limited though they are–for instance, they are not Turing-complete–, they have multiple applications in classical computing, and hence an adequate knowledge of these languages and of the regular grammars is important.

3.2.1. Regular expressions

3.2.1. (Def.) Let Σ be an alphabet. The set of *regular expressions* over Σ is defined as follows:

1. $\emptyset$ and ϵ are regular expressions.

2. Each letter $a \in \Sigma$ is a regular expression.

3. If r is a regular expression, then so is r^*.

4. If r_1 and r_2 are regular expressions, then so are $(r_1 + r_2)$ and $(r_1 \cdot r_2)$.

5. Nothing else is a regular expression over Σ.

Example 3.2.1. Let $\Sigma = \{a, b, c, ..., y, z\}$ be an alphabet. The following are regular expressions over Σ:[8]

1. $\emptyset$

2. ϵ

3. f

4. $((c \cdot u) \cdot p) = (c \cdot u \cdot p)$

5. $(((y \cdot a) \cdot (w^*)) \cdot n) = (y \cdot a \cdot w^* \cdot n)$

6. $(p + (f + (e + (r + d)))) = (p + f + e + r + d)$

7. $(a + (b \cdot (b^*))) = (a + b \cdot b^*)$

---

[8]Note the omission of superfluous parentheses on the right side of the equalities.

3.2.2. (Def.) The language $L(r)$ over Σ defined by a regular expression r over Σ is as follows:

1. $L(\emptyset) = \emptyset$ and $L(\epsilon) = \{\epsilon\}$.

2. $L(a) = \{a\}$, where $a \in \Sigma$.

3. $L(r^*) = (L(r))^*$.

4. $L(r_1 + r_2) = L(r_1) \cup L(r_2)$.

5. $L(r_1 \cdot r_2) = L(r_1) L(r_2)$.

3.2.3. (Def.) Let L be a language over an alphabet Σ. Then, L is called a *regular language* over Σ if there is a regular expression r over Σ such that $L = L(r)$.

Example 3.2.2. The following are the regular languages corresponding to the regular expressions of Example 3.2.1:

1. $L(\emptyset) = \emptyset$

2. $L(\epsilon) = \{\epsilon\}$

3. $L(f) = \{f\}$

4. $L(c \cdot u \cdot p) = \{cup\}$

5. $L(y \cdot a \cdot w^* \cdot n) = \{yaw^*n\} = \{yan, yawn, yawwn, ...\}$

6. $L(p + f + e + r + d) = \{p, f, e, r, d\}$

7. $L(a + bb^*) = \{a, bb^*\} = \{a, b^+\} = \{a, b, bb, bbb, ...\}$

3.2.4. (Prop.) Let α, β, γ be regular expressions. The following are the properties of the operations on regular expressions:

1. Union (+):

    a) *Associativity:* $(\alpha + \beta) + \gamma = \alpha + (\beta + \gamma)$

    b) *Commutativity:* $\alpha + \beta = \beta + \alpha$

    c) *Identity element:* $\alpha + \emptyset = \alpha$

d) *Idempotency:* $\alpha + \alpha = \alpha$

e) If $\epsilon \in L(\alpha)$, then $\alpha + \epsilon = \alpha$

2. Concatenation $(\cdot)$:

a) *Associativity:* $(\alpha\beta)\gamma = \alpha(\beta\gamma)$

b) *Distributivity with respect to union:* $\alpha(\beta + \gamma) = \alpha\beta + \alpha\gamma$

c) *Identity element:* $\alpha\epsilon = \epsilon\alpha = \alpha$

d) *Annihilating element:* $\alpha\emptyset = \emptyset$

3. Kleene star $(*)$:

a) $\epsilon^* = \epsilon$

b) $\emptyset^* = \epsilon$

c) $\alpha^*\alpha^* = \alpha^*$

d) $\alpha^*\alpha = \alpha\alpha^* = \alpha^+$

e) $(\alpha^*)^* = \alpha^*$

f) $\alpha^* = \epsilon + \alpha\alpha^* = (\epsilon + \alpha)^*$

g) $\alpha^* = \epsilon + \alpha + \alpha^2 + \ldots + \alpha^n + \alpha^{n+1}\alpha^*$

h) $(\alpha^* + \beta^*)^* = (\alpha^*\beta^*)^* = (\alpha + \beta)^* = (\alpha^*\beta^*)\alpha^*$

For expressions implying more than one operation, the following prece-dence properties are to be considered:

3.2.5. **(Prop.)** Given any regular expression(s), the operations thereon take the precedence corresponding to their place on the following list:

1. Kleene star

2. Concatenation

3. Union

With respect to the above Proposition, it should be noted that the parentheses take precedence over all the operations listed in it.

Propositions 3.2.4-5 are extremely useful, one of their purposes being the determination of equivalent regular expressions.

3.2.6. **(Def.)** Two regular expressions r_1 and r_2 are said to be *equivalent* if $L(r_1) = L(r_2)$.

Example 3.2.3. Given the alphabet $\Sigma = \{0, 1\}$, the regular expressions $r_1 = ((\emptyset^* + 0)^* (\emptyset^* + 1)^*)^*$ and $r_2 = (\epsilon(1 + 0) + (0 + 1))^* \emptyset^*$ are equivalent, as

$$L(r_1) = L(r_2) = L((0 + 1)^*).$$

In effect, we have with respect to r_1

$$((\emptyset^* + 0)^* (\emptyset^* + 1)^*)^* = ((\epsilon + 0)^* (\epsilon + 1)^*)^* \text{ by Prop. 3.2.4.3.b}$$

$$= (0^*1^*)^* \text{ by Prop. 3.2.4.3.f}$$

$$= (0 + 1)^* \text{ by Prop. 3.2.4.3.h}$$

With respect to r_2, we have

$$(\epsilon(1 + 0) + (0 + 1))^* \emptyset^* = (\epsilon(1 + 0) + (0 + 1))^* \epsilon \text{ by Prop. 3.2.4.3.b}$$

$$= ((1 + 0) + (0 + 1))^* \text{ by Prop. 3.2.4.2.c}$$

$$= (0 + 1)^* \text{ by Prop. 3.2.4.1.b, d}$$

Propositions 3.2.4-5 are also important when considering one of the crucial aspects of regular expressions, to wit, their representation by means of labeled digraphs. This property is at the basis of automata theory, to be discussed in Chapter 4. We first give the central theorem and then concentrate on this graphical representation.

Theorem 3.2.1. *Let r be a regular expression. Then, a string x belongs to $L(r)$ if and only if there is a path in the digraph $\vec{\mathfrak{G}}(r)$ from vertex v_0 (the initial vertex) to vertex v_n (the final vertex) associated with x.*

Proof: (Sketch) Let us assume that for any regular expression r, a string x belongs to $L(r)$ if and only if there is a path $\pi = v_0, ..., v_n \in \vec{\mathfrak{G}}(r)$ such that $x \in L(r_1) L(r_2) ... L(r_{n-1})$ for r_i the label of the arc (v_i, v_{i+1}), $i = 1, ..., n - 1$. We give the proof of the $\Leftarrow$-direction, and leave the $\Rightarrow$-proof as an exercise.[9]

---

[9] A mathematical proof of a statement involving the logical expression "if and only if" (abbreviated *iff* and denoted by the symbol $\Leftrightarrow$) requires two proofs, one of the *if* direction (denoted by $\Rightarrow$), and another of the *only-if* direction (denoted by $\Leftarrow$). This requirement is accounted for by the logical definition of such a statement, to

($\Leftarrow$) Let the graph representation of a regular expression r be given by

$$v_0 \xrightarrow{r} v_n$$

if $v_0 \neq v_n$; if $v_0 = v_n$, we have

$$
\begin{array}{c}
r \\
\circlearrowright \\
v_0
\end{array} .
$$

Then, the digraph $\vec{\mathfrak{G}} = \left(\{v_0, v_n\}, \{r\}, \vec{f} \right)$ with $\vec{f} : \{v_0\} \xrightarrow{r} \{v_n\}$ is a labeled digraph $\vec{\mathfrak{G}}(r)$. Let us now extend $V_{\vec{\mathfrak{G}}}$ into $V'_{\vec{\mathfrak{G}}} = \{v_0, ..., v_n\}$ such that $\left| V'_{\vec{\mathfrak{G}}} \right| \geq 3$.

(i) If $r = \alpha_1 \alpha_2 ... \alpha_n$, then we must have a path in $\vec{\mathfrak{G}}(r)$ of the form

$$(\pi (\cdot)) \qquad \xrightarrow{\cdots} v_{i-1} \xrightarrow{\alpha_i} v_i \xrightarrow{\alpha_{i+1}} v_{i+1} \xrightarrow{\cdots}$$

for any two consecutive regular expressions $\alpha_i \alpha_{i+1} \in r$.

(ii) If $r = \alpha_1 + \alpha_2 + ... + \alpha_n$, then we must have a path in $\vec{\mathfrak{G}}(r)$ of the form

$$(\pi (+)) \qquad \xrightarrow{\cdots} v_k \xrightarrow{\alpha_1, \alpha_2, ..., \alpha_n} v_l \xrightarrow{\cdots} =$$

$$
= \xrightarrow{\cdots} v_k
\begin{array}{c}
\xrightarrow{\alpha_1} \\
\xrightarrow{\alpha_2} \\
\vdots \\
\xrightarrow{\alpha_n}
\end{array}
v_l \xrightarrow{\cdots}
$$

between any pair of successive vertices $(v_k, v_l) \in \{v_0, ..., v_n\}$.

(iii) If $r = \alpha_1 \alpha_2 ... \alpha_n = \alpha^*$, we must have a path in $\vec{\mathfrak{G}}(r)$ of the form

$$(\pi (^*)) \qquad \xrightarrow{\cdots} v_{i-1} \xrightarrow{\epsilon}
\begin{array}{c}
\alpha \\
\circlearrowright \\
v_i
\end{array}
\xrightarrow{\epsilon} v_{i+1} \xrightarrow{\cdots} .$$

It is evident that we can further analyze the α_i into substrings up to individual symbols $\sigma \in (\Sigma \cup \{\epsilon\})$, and we still have the three paths (i) - (iii) above. These paths agree with our initial assumption. This holds

---

wit,

$$p \Leftrightarrow q \equiv (p \Rightarrow q) \wedge (q \Rightarrow p) .$$

for r a regular expression over $\Sigma \cup \{\epsilon\}$, as it is obvious that ϵ can label an arc on any path $\pi_i \in \vec{\mathfrak{G}}(r)$. In any case, an ϵ-arc can always be deleted by Propositions 3.2.4.1.e and 3.2.4.2.c. Let us further delete arcs for $r = \emptyset$; this does not change our initial assumption, as $L(\emptyset) = \emptyset$. **QED**

Theorem 3.2.1 makes it clear that every path π_i in a labeled digraph $\vec{\mathfrak{G}}(r)$ corresponding to a regular expression r is associated with a (sub)string of r obtained by concatenating all the symbols labeling the arcs in π_i.

Example 3.2.4. Figure 3.2.1 shows the step-by-step construction of the labeled digraph $\vec{\mathfrak{G}}(r)$ for the regular expression over $\Sigma = \{a, b, c\}$ $r = (c + ba)^* a (c + ab^*)$. The final labeled digraph is depicted in 3.2.1.vi. Empty circles denote the vertices of the digraph. We mark the initial vertex with an incoming arrow, and do so for the final vertex by means of two concentric circles. Note how a path of the form $\pi(+)$ actually requires $n + 1$ edges for n the number of occurrences of the symbol $+$.

3.2.2. Regular grammars

Recall the definition of a formal grammar (Def. 3.1.11). A regular language is generated by a specific formal grammar known as *type-3* grammar.

3.2.7. (Def.) A grammar $G = (V, T, S, P)$ is *regular* (or of *type 3*) if in each rule $r \in P$, $r = \alpha \rightarrow \beta$, it is the case that $\alpha \in V$, $|\alpha| = 1$, and $\beta \in (V \cup T)^*$. A language $L \subseteq T^*$ is a *regular language* if there is a regular grammar G such that $L = L(G)$.

Regular grammars are actually a subset of linear grammars.

3.2.8. (Def.) A *linear grammar* is a grammar $G = (V, T, S, P)$ with rules of the form $\alpha \rightarrow \beta$ in which $\alpha \in V$, $\beta \in (V \cup T)^*$, and $|V(\beta)| \leq 1$. A linear grammar can be *right-* or *left-linear* if it has rules of the form $\alpha \rightarrow vA$ or $\alpha \rightarrow Av$, respectively, for $A \in V^*, v \in T^*$.

3.2.9. (Def.) A regular grammar is either a right-linear or a left-linear grammar.

Example 3.2.5. Consider the following grammars:

- The grammar $G_1 = (\{S, A\}, \{a\}, S, P_1)$ with

$$P_1 = \left\{ \begin{array}{c} S \rightarrow aS \,|\, aA \\ A \rightarrow a \,|\, \epsilon \end{array} \right\}$$

generating strings $r_1 = a^n, n \geq 1$, is a right-linear grammar.

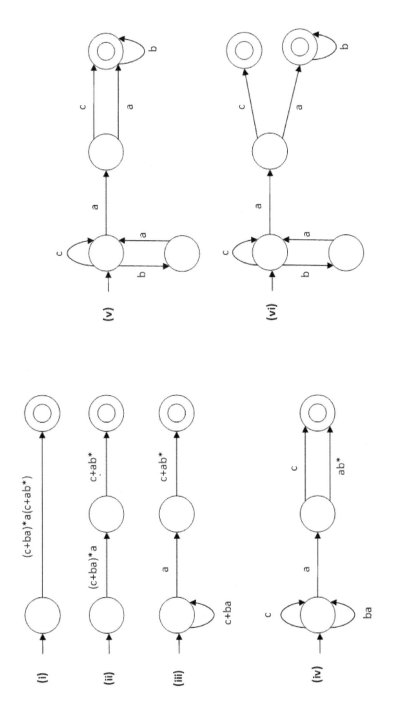

Figure 3.2.1.: A labeled digraph $\vec{\mathfrak{G}}(r)$ for a regular expression r.

- The grammar $G_2 = (\{S, A, B\}, \{a, b\}, S, P_2)$ with

$$P_2 = \left\{ \begin{array}{c} S \to Aab \\ A \to Aab \mid Bb \\ B \to b \mid \epsilon \end{array} \right\}$$

generating strings $r_2 = b^n (ab)^m$, $n = 1, 2, m \geq 1$, is a left-linear grammar.

- The grammar $G_3 = (\{S, A, B\}, \{a, b\}, S, P_3)$ with

$$P_3 = \left\{ \begin{array}{c} S \to aA \mid Bb \\ A \to abB \mid ab \\ B \to Aba \mid ba \end{array} \right\}$$

generating strings r_3 (left as an exercise) is a linear grammar.

Grammars G_1 and G_2 are regular grammars. Grammar G_3 is not a regular grammar.

3.2.10 (Prop.) A language is regular if and only if it has both a right- and a left-linear grammar that generate it.

Proof: (Sketch) ($\Rightarrow$) If L is a regular language, then $L = L(G)$ for some grammar G of type 3. Let $G = (V, T, S, P)$ be a left-linear grammar with rules of the form $A \to Bv$ for $A, B \in V, |B| \leq 1$. Then, we can construct a right-linear grammar G' from G by reverting the bodies of the productions of G, i.e. by making

$$A \to v^R B.$$

Let our terminal string be $v_k...v_1$, so that in G we have the derivation $S \xRightarrow[G]{k} v_k...v_1$ in k steps

$$S \Longrightarrow A_1 v_1 \Longrightarrow A_2 v_2 v_1 \Longrightarrow ... \Longrightarrow A_{k-1} v_{k-1}...v_1 \Longrightarrow v_k...v_1.$$

Then, in G' we have the corresponding derivation

$$S \Longrightarrow v_1^R A_1 \Longrightarrow v_1^R v_2^R A_2 \Longrightarrow ... \Longrightarrow v_1^R...v_{k-1}^R A_{k-1} \Longrightarrow v_1^R...v_k^R.$$

If we begin with a right-linear grammar G, then we can obtain a left-linear grammar G' by rewriting $A \to vB$ as

$$A \to Bv^R.$$

As above, we obtain a left-linear derivation in k steps. In either case, we have

$$v_k...v_1 = (v_1...v_k)^R$$

and

$$L\left(G'\right) = L\left(G\right)^R.$$

($\Leftarrow$) If G is a left-linear (right-linear) grammar, then G' is right-linear (left-linear, respectively). By the construction process above, we have

$$L\left(G'\right) = L\left(G\right)^R.$$

In either side of the equality, we have a regular language. **QED**

3.2.11. In order to design the algorithm to make an equivalent left-linear (right-linear) grammar $G' = (V, T, S, P')$ from a right-linear (left-linear, respectively) grammar $G = (V, T, S, P)$ (Algorithm 3.2), we need to construct a labeled digraph $\vec{\mathfrak{G}} = \left(V, E, \vec{f}\right)$ such that $V_{\vec{\mathfrak{G}}} = V_G \cup \{\epsilon\}$, $E = T_G$, and $\vec{f}$ corresponds to P in the following way:

- If there is in P a rule of the type $A \rightarrow B\sigma$ (or $A \rightarrow \sigma B$) for $\sigma \in T$, then create the incidence function $\vec{f} : A \overset{\sigma}{\rightarrow} B$ for $A, B \in \left(V_{\vec{\mathfrak{G}}} = V_G\right)$ where σ labels the arc in E with tail A and head B.

- If there is in P a rule of the type $A \rightarrow \sigma$ for $\sigma \in T$, then create the incidence function $\vec{f} : A \overset{\sigma}{\rightarrow} \epsilon$, where $A, \epsilon \in \left(V_{\vec{\mathfrak{G}}} = V_G \cup \{\epsilon\}\right)$ and σ labels the arc in E with tail A and head ϵ.

Example 3.2.6. Let there be given the left-linear grammar $G = (\{S, A, B\}, \{a, b\}, S, P)$ with

$$P = \left\{ \begin{array}{c} S \rightarrow b \mid Ab \\ A \rightarrow Ba \\ B \rightarrow b \mid Ab \end{array} \right\}.$$

Then, the corresponding labeled digraph $\vec{\mathfrak{G}}\left(G\right)$ is shown in Figure 3.2.2.

3.2.12. The input for the algorithm must be a left-/right-linear grammar $G = (V, T, S, P)$ such that in no rule r in P it is the case that S occurs in the body thereof. If it does, then we must add a new variable V_{n+1} to $V = \{S, V_1, ..., V_n\}$. This done, two further steps are required:

- a rule of the form $V_{n+1} \rightarrow \alpha$ must be added to P for each rule in P of the form $S \rightarrow \alpha$;

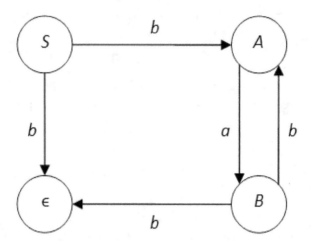

Figure 3.2.2.: A labeled digraph $\vec{\mathfrak{G}}\,(G)$ corresponding to a left-linear grammar G.

- replace all occurrences of S in the bodies of productions by V_{n+1}.

3.2.13. (Def.) The grammar $G' = (V', T, S, P')$ obtained as above is called a *S-restricted left-/right-linear grammar.*

Example 3.2.7. Let there be given the right-linear grammar $G = (\{S, A\}, \{a, b\}, S, P)$ with

$$P = \left\{ \begin{array}{c} S \to bA \\ A \to aS \,|\, a \end{array} \right\}.$$

By proceeding as in §3.2.12, we obtain the S-restricted right-linear grammar $G' = (\{S, A, B\}, \{a, b\}, S, P')$ with

$$P' = \left\{ \begin{array}{c} S \to bA \\ A \to aB \,|\, a \\ B \to bA \end{array} \right\}.$$

Example 3.2.8. Let our S-restricted left-linear grammar be the one given in Example 3.2.6. By applying Step 2 of Algorithm 3.2, we obtain the labeled digraph $\vec{\mathfrak{G}}'\,(G')$ in Figure 3.2.3. Reading the rules off $\vec{\mathfrak{G}}'\,(G')$

Algorithm 3.2 Left-/Right-linear grammar to right-/left-linear grammar

---

Input: A S-restricted left-/right-linear grammar $G = (V, T, S, P)$
Output: A S-restricted right-/left-linear grammar $G' = (V, T, S, P')$

---

1. Construct the labeled digraph $\vec{\mathfrak{G}}$ corresponding to G.

2. Change the vertex for $S \in \vec{\mathfrak{G}}$ for the vertex for $\epsilon \in \vec{\mathfrak{G}}$ (and vice-versa), and reverse the incidence function, i.e. reverse the direction of the arcs, so that you obtain the labeled digraph $\vec{\mathfrak{G}}'$.

3. Obtain P' by reading the rules off the connections in $\vec{\mathfrak{G}}'$.

(Step 3), we have

$$P' = \left\{ \begin{array}{c} S \to b \,|\, bB \\ A \to b \,|\, bB \\ B \to aA \end{array} \right\}$$

for $G' = (V, T, S, P')$ the S-restricted right-linear grammar equivalent to G.

3.2.3. Properties of regular languages

3.2.3.1. The pumping lemma for regular languages (I)

3.2.14. (Prop.) Every finite language is regular.
   Proof: Left as an exercise.

But is an arbitrary infinite language regular? This is a relevant question, as it turns out that most interesting and useful languages are infinite. The following theorem, known as the *pumping lemma for regular languages*, provides the means for a proof by contradiction: If a language L does not satisfy the specified conditions, then it is not a regular language. These conditions are necessary, but not sufficient: A language may satisfy the conditions and be non-regular. The typical method for proving the regularity of a language L is by constructing a regular expression based on this lemma. Another method is by constructing a finite-state automaton; in fact, this is the standard proof.

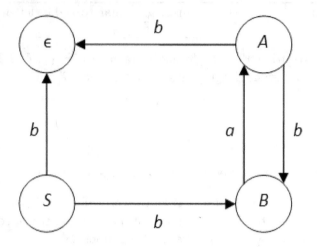

Figure 3.2.3.: The digraph $\vec{\mathfrak{G}}'\,(G')$ obtained from $\vec{\mathfrak{G}}\,(G)$.

Theorem 3.2.2. *(Pumping lemma for regular languages I) Let L be a regular language. Then, there is a constant m such that if z is any word in L and $|z| \geq m$ (the "pumping length"), we can write $z = uvw$ in such a way that*

1. $|uv| \leq m$;

2. $|v| \geq 1$;

3. *for all $i = 0, 1, 2, ...$, $z_i = uv^i w \in L$.*

Proof: (Idea) See Example 3.2.9. (See below, Section 4.1.1.3, for a proof using a finite-state automaton.) **QED**

Informally, the pumping lemma states that if a regular language L contains a (sufficiently) long string z, then it contains an infinite set of strings of the form $uv^i w$ where v is the substring that can be "pumped," i.e. repeated at will, or removed, with z remaining a string in L.

Example 3.2.9. Consider language L_1 of Example 3.1.5. This language is not regular. We can easily prove this by contradiction. (i) Let the string given be $z = a^m b^m$. Using condition 1 of the pumping lemma, v must be a and $u = \epsilon$. If $v = a$, then by "pumping" a we end up with more instances of a than instances of b, so that $m \neq m$, a contradiction.

(ii) Let now $z = a^k b^k$, $k \leq 1 < m$. We can have $v = a$ or $v = b$, but in any case we end up with more instances of one letter so that $k \neq k$, a contradiction. Let now $|a^k b^k| \leq m$ so that we can have $v = ab$; then z_i will have as following bs, i.e. $z_i = (ab)^i = ababab....$ In either case, $z_i \notin L_1$, which is a contradiction. Thus L_1 is not a regular language.

3.2.3.2. Algebra and linear equations for regular languages

Just as for regular expressions, there is a well-defined algebra for the main operations on regular languages. Application of these algebraic rules allows us to determine a regular language that is a result of any of the operations concatenation, union, and Kleene star (or iteration) on regular languages.

3.2.15. (Prop.) Let L, L_i, $i = 1, 2, 3$, be arbitrary regular languages. Let $\emptyset$ denote the empty language and $L_\epsilon = \{\epsilon\}$. Then,

1. $L_1 \cup L_2 = L_2 \cup L_1$

2. $L_1 \cup (L_2 \cup L_3) = (L_1 \cup L_2) \cup L_3$ and $L_1 (L_2 L_3) = (L_1 L_2) L_3$

3. $L_1 (L_2 \cup L_3) = L_1 L_2 \cup L_1 L_3$ and $(L_1 \cup L_2) L_3 = L_1 L_3 \cup L_2 L_3$

4. $L \cup \emptyset = \emptyset \cup L = L$ and $L\emptyset = \emptyset L = \emptyset$

5. $L L_\epsilon = L_\epsilon L = L$

6. $L \cup L = L$

7. $L^* = L_\epsilon \cup \underbrace{L \cup L^2 \cup L^3 \cup ...}_{L^+} = L_\epsilon \cup L^+$

8. $L^+ = L^* L = L L^*$

9. $(L^*)^* = L^*$

Proof: Left as an exercise.

Given a grammar G conveniently in a left-/right-linear form, it is possible to determine the language it generates by means of systems of linear equations in the following way.

3.2.16. (Def.) Let $G = (V, T, S, P)$ be a left-/right-linear regular grammar. Then, every variable $A_i \in V$ defines an unknown that is actually a language, i.e.

$$L_X = L_{A_i} = \left\{ w \in T^* | A_i \overset{n}{\Longrightarrow} w \right\}.$$

Hence, given a right-linear rule of production

$$A_i \rightarrow \alpha A_1 \,|\,... \,|\alpha A_n \,|\, \epsilon$$

where $\alpha \in T^*$, we have the corresponding equation

$$L_{A_i} = \alpha A_1 \cup ... \cup \alpha A_n \cup \epsilon.$$

Similarly, for a left-linear rule of production

$$A_i \rightarrow A_1\alpha \,|\,... \,|A_n\alpha \,|\, \epsilon$$

we have the equation

$$L_{A_i} = A_1\alpha \cup ... \cup A_n\alpha \cup \epsilon.$$

In either case, it is easy to see that for a given production set P with $|V| = n$ there is a system of n equations of the form

$$\left\{ \begin{array}{l} L_{A_1} \\ L_{A_2} \\ \vdots \\ L_{A_n} \end{array} \right. .$$

It should be evident that $L_S = L(G)$ for some grammar G. Note in particular the following identity for languages, known as *Arden's lemma* (Arden, 1961):

Theorem 3.2.3. *The equation*

$$L_X = L_A L_X \cup L_B$$

where L_B is any language and $L_A \neq \emptyset$, has the unique solution

$$L_X = (L_A)^* L_B.$$

Proof: Left as an exercise.

Example 3.2.10. Let there be given grammar G_1 of Example 3.2.5. Then, we have the system of linear equations

$$\left\{ \begin{array}{l} L_S = aL_S \cup aL_A \\ \quad L_A = a \cup \epsilon \end{array} \right. .$$

Solving for L_A in L_S we have

$$L_S = aL_S \cup a\left(a \cup \epsilon\right).$$

Applying Arden's lemma, we obtain the language

$$L_S = a^*a\left(a \cup \epsilon\right)$$

corresponding to

$$L\left(a^*a\left(a + \epsilon\right)\right) = \{a^*a\left(a + \epsilon\right)\}.$$

3.2.3.3. Closure properties of the regular languages

Recall now Definition 3.1.10. In what follows, we show the closure properties of the regular languages, whose class we denote by $\mathscr{RGL}$. Closure properties are important, because we can construct a regular language L' from a regular language L by (repeated) application of operations that preserve closure. We begin with the main operations, to wit, union, concatenation, and Kleene star (cf. Def. 3.2.2.3-5).[10]

3.2.17. (Prop.) The class $\mathscr{RGL}$ of regular languages is closed under union, concatenation, and Kleene star.

Proof: (Sketch) We give the proof for union; the proofs for the remaining operations are similar and are left as an exercise. Let L_1 and L_2 be regular languages. Then, there must be regular expressions r_1 and r_2 such that $L_1 = L\left(r_1\right)$ and $L_2 = L\left(r_2\right)$. Then, by Definition 3.2.2.4, we have

$$L\left(r_1\right) \cup L\left(r_2\right) = L\left(r_1 + r_2\right).$$

QED

Additionally, regular languages are closed under all other operations in Definition 3.1.3, as well as under further operations (e.g., homomorphisms).

3.2.18. (Prop.) The class $\mathscr{RGL}$ is closed under difference.

Proof: Let L_1, L_2 be regular languages. Then, it is obvious that $L_1 - L_2 = L_1$ (or $L_2 - L_1 = L_2$) such that L_1 (L_2) is the set of strings that

---

[10]Some closure proofs are "better" if we make finite-state automata feature in them, despite the fact that regular expressions/languages and finite-state automata are equivalent mathematical structures, as it was already touched upon (cf. Example 3.2.4; cf. also Examples 3.2.6 and 3.2.8). This will become clearer in Section 4.1, where the reader is asked to repeat some of these proofs by employing finite-state automata.

are in L_1 (in L_2) but not in L_2 (L_1, respectively) is a regular language. **QED**

3.2.19. (Prop.) The class $\mathscr{RGL}$ is closed under reversal.

Proof: (Sketch) Let $L = L(r)$ for some regular expression r. We claim that L^R is regular. In effect, we must show that $L(r)^R = (L(r))^R$. The proof is by structural induction on the basis provided by $\epsilon = \epsilon^R$, $\emptyset = \emptyset^R$, and $a = a^R$ for some symbol a. The structural induction falls on the three main operations of union, concatenation, and Kleene star.

(i) With respect to union, let $r = r_1 + r_2$. Then, we have

$$r^R = r_1^R + r_2^R.$$

Hence,

$$L\left(r_1^R + r_2^R\right) = L\left(r_1^R\right) + L\left(r_2^R\right) = (L(r_1 + r_2))^R$$

and $(L(r_1 + r_2))^R$ is a regular language.

(ii) For concatenation, let $r = r_1 r_2$. Then,

$$r^R = r_2^R r_1^R.$$

Hence,

$$L\left(r_2^R r_1^R\right) = L\left(r_2^R\right) L\left(r_1^R\right) = (L(r_1 r_2))^R$$

and $(L(r_1 r_2))^R$ is a regular language.

(iii) As for the Kleene-star operation, let $r = r_1^*$. Then,

$$r^R = \left(r_1^R\right)^*.$$

We now need to show that for any string $x = x_1 x_2 ... x_n$, $x \in L(r)$ if and only if its reversal $x_n^R x_{n-1}^R ... x_1^R = x^R \in L\left(\left(r_1^R\right)^*\right)$. **QED**

3.2.20. (Prop.) The class $\mathscr{RGL}$ is closed under complementation.

Proof: Recall from Definition 3.1.9.8 that the complement of a language L is

$$\overline{L} = \{w \in \Sigma^* | w \notin L\}.$$

This is the same as stating that

$$\overline{L} = \Sigma^* - L.$$

If Σ^* is regular, then $\overline{L}$, for any language L, is also regular. **QED**

3.2.21. (Prop.) The class $\mathscr{RGL}$ is closed under intersection.

Proof: (Hint) Apply the De Morgan's laws and invoke Proposition 3.2.20.

3.2.22. (Prop.) The class $\mathscr{RGL}$ is closed under homomorphisms.

Proof: (Sketch) We let $L = L(r)$ for some regular expression r. For $r \in \Sigma^*$, we let $h(r)$ be the expression obtained by substituting each symbol $\sigma \in \Sigma^*$ in r by $h(\sigma)$. We apply structural induction to show that

$$(\heartsuit) \qquad L(h(r')) = L(r') = h(L(r'))$$

for r' a sub-expression of r. Let $r' = \epsilon$ or $r' = \emptyset$; then, $r' = h(r')$ and we have the equality $\heartsuit$. Let now $r' = \sigma$ for some individual symbol $\sigma \in \Sigma$. Then, $h(\sigma)$ may be a string of symbols, and in any case

$$\{\sigma\} = \{h(\sigma)\}$$

and the equality $\heartsuit$ holds. This exhausts the induction basis. For the induction step, we have union, concatenation, and Kleene star. We prove the theorem with respect to union and leave the other two operations as an exercise. Let now $r' = r_1' + r_2'$. Then, by the definitions of homomorphism, according to which we have $h(r') = h\left(r_1' + r_2'\right) = h\left(r_1'\right) + h\left(r_2'\right)$, and union we have

$$L(h(r')) = L\left(h\left(r_1'\right) + h\left(r_2'\right)\right) = L\left(h\left(r_1'\right) \cup h\left(r_2'\right)\right) =$$

$$= h\left(L\left(r_1'\right) \cup L\left(r_2'\right)\right) = h(L(r'))$$

and the equality $\heartsuit$ holds. **QED**

Exercises

Exercise 3.2.1. Let $\Sigma = \{a, b\}$. Describe the language $L(r)$ with:

1. $r = ab^*a^*$.

2. $r = aa + ab + bb$.

3. $r = a^* + b^*$.

4. $r = abb^*a$.

5. $r = a^*ba^*ba^*$.

6. $r = (aa + bb + (ab + ba)(aa + bb)^*(ab + ba))^*$.

7. $r = b^*a(a + ab^*a)^*$.

8. $r = (b + ab^*a)^* ab^*$.

9. $r = (a + bbb)^*$.

Exercise 3.2.2. Construct the labeled digraph $\vec{\mathfrak{G}}(r)$ for each regular expression r in Exercise 3.2.1.

Exercise 3.2.3. For each of the regular expressions in Exercise 3.2.1, give two examples of strings $v, w \in L(r)$, $v \neq w$.

Exercise 3.2.4. Given the following languages, determine the corresponding regular expressions:

1. $L(r) = \{w \in \{0,1\}^* \,|\, w$ has at least two consecutive $0\}$.

2. $L(r) = \{w \in \{0,1\}^* \,|\, w$ has at most two consecutive $0\}$.

3. $L(r) = \{w \in \{0,1\}^* \,|\, w$ has exactly two consecutive $0\}$.

4. $L(r) = \{w \in \{0,1\}^* \,|\, w$ has no two consecutive $0\}$.

5. $L(r) = \{0^n 1^m \,|\, (n+m)$ is odd$\}$.

6. $L(r) = \{0^n 1^m \,|\, n \geq 1, m \geq 1, nm \geq 2\}$.

7. $L(r) = \{w \in \{0,1\}^* \,|\, w$ ends in $01\}$.

8. $L(r) = \{w \in \{0,1\}^* \,|\, |w|_0$ is even, $|w|_1$ is odd$\}$.

Exercise 3.2.5. Prove that, given an alphabet $\Sigma = \{a,b\}$,

1. $\{\epsilon\}$ is a regular language.

2. $(aa + aaa)^* = \epsilon + aaa^*$.

3. $(a+b)^* ab (a+b)^* + b^*a^* = (a+b)^*$.

Exercise 3.2.6. Determine whether the following regular expressions over $\Sigma = \{a,b,c\}$ are equivalent:

1. $r_1 = (b + ab)^*(a + \epsilon)$; $r_2 = (b^*abb^*)^*(a + \epsilon) + b^*(a + \epsilon)$.

2. $r_1 = (a^* (b + c)^* + b^*)^* \, ; r_2 = (a + b + c)^*.$

Exercise 3.2.7. Show that the following languages over the alphabet $\Sigma = \{a, b\}$ are not regular:

1. $L = \{a^n b^{2n} | n > 0\}.$

2. $L = \{a^n b^m | 0 < n \leq m\}.$

3. $L = \left\{ a^{n^2} | n \geq 0 \right\}.$

Exercise 3.2.8. Determine the regular expression r_3 of Example 3.2.5.

Exercise 3.2.9. The language $L = \{a (ba)^*\}$ is regular. Determine the productions of each of the right- and left-linear grammars generating L.

Exercise 3.2.10. Show by means of systems of linear equations that the following grammars are regular:

1. Grammar G_2 of Example 3.2.5.

2. Grammar G of Example 3.2.6.

3. Grammar G of Example 3.2.7.

Exercise 3.2.11. Prove the following Propositions:

1. Prop. 3.2.4.3.b

2. Prop. 3.2.4.3.d

3. Prop. 3.2.4.3.f

4. Prop. 3.2.4.3.h

Exercise 3.2.12. Prove (Complete the proof of) the theorems and propositions in this Section that were left as an exercise (with a sketchy proof, respectively).

Exercise 3.2.13. Let $\Sigma_1 = \{a, b, c, ..., z\}$, $\Sigma_2 = \{0, 1, ..., 9\}$, and $\Sigma_3 = \{-, ., \_\}$ be alphabets. Let further $\Sigma = \Sigma_1 \cup \Sigma_2 \cup \Sigma_3 \cup \{@\}$.

1. Give three regular expressions over Σ that can be employed for email address validation.

2. Construct an algorithm for email address validation based on regular expressions over Σ.

Exercise 3.2.14. For each language L over Σ, let

$$L' = \{y|xy \in L \text{ for some string } x\}.$$

1. Identify L'.

2. Show that if L is a regular language, then so is L'.

3.3. Context-free languages

Regular languages are too simple and limited for, say, a high-level programming language. In order to be able to generate complex languages of this kind we need more complex grammars. A context-free grammar (abbr.: CFG) is just such a grammar. This will be easily realized once it is shown that these grammars are capable of generating rather complex sentences of a natural language like English. However, it must be remarked that the context-free languages, just like the regular languages, are not Turing-complete. Additionally, albeit more expressive than the regular languages, decidability is worse than for these. In any case, they can be considered the central languages in classical computation; for instance, most programming languages are in this language class.

3.3.1. Context-free grammars

3.3.1.1. Context-free vs. context-sensitive grammars

3.3.1. (Def.) A grammar $G = (V, T, S, P)$ is *context-free* (or of *type 2*) if each production $r \in P$ has the form $\alpha \rightarrow \beta$, where $\alpha \in V$, $|\alpha| = 1$, and $\beta \in (V \cup T)^*$. A language $L \subseteq T^*$ is a *context-free language* (CFL) if there is a CFG G such that $L = L(G)$.

Example 3.3.1. We begin with a very simple example of a CFG. Consider the language $L = \{a^m b^m | m > 0\}$. This is language L_1 of Example 3.1.5 that was proven to be non-regular in Example 3.2.9. L is a CFL. In effect, consider the grammar $G = (V, T, S, P)$ with $V = \{S\}$,

$T = \{a, b\}$, and $P = \{r_1, r_2\}$, where $r_1 = S \rightarrow aSb$ and $r_2 = S \rightarrow ab$. By applying $m - 1$ times production r_1 and then r_2 we obtain the derivation

$$\underbrace{S \Longrightarrow aSb \Longrightarrow a^2Sb^2 \Longrightarrow \ldots \Longrightarrow a^{m-1}Sb^{m-1}}_{(m-1)r_1} \underbrace{\Longrightarrow a^mb^m}_{r_2}.$$

Note that r_2 is a final production, i.e. once it is applied, no S remains in the resulting string, and so this resulting string is terminal.

Example 3.3.2. As seen in Definition 3.3.1, CFGs are characterized by productions with a single variable in the head and strings of both variables and terminals in the body. These productions can generate–or better: parse (see below)–sentences in a natural language like English. For instance, let $G = (V, T, S, P)$ be a CFG with

$$V = \left\{ \begin{array}{c} \langle SENTENCE \rangle, \langle NOUN\_PHR \rangle, \langle VERB\_PHR \rangle, \\ \langle ARTICLE \rangle, \langle ADJECTIVE \rangle, \langle NOUN \rangle, \\ \langle VERB \rangle, \langle ADVERB \rangle, \langle DEFINITE \rangle \\ \langle INDEFINITE \rangle \end{array} \right\},$$

where the start symbol is $\langle SENTENCE \rangle$,

$$T = \{the, a, an, ants, resourceful, diligently, work, little\},$$

and

$$P = \left\{ \begin{array}{c} \langle SENTENCE \rangle \rightarrow \langle NOUN\_PHR \rangle \langle VERB\_PHR \rangle \\ \langle NOUN\_PHR \rangle \rightarrow \langle ARTICLE \rangle \langle ADJECTIVE \rangle \langle NOUN \rangle \\ \langle ARTICLE \rangle \rightarrow \langle DEFINITE \rangle | \langle INDEFINITE \rangle | \epsilon \\ \langle ADJECTIVE \rangle \rightarrow \langle ADJECTIVE \rangle \langle ADJECTIVE \rangle | \epsilon \\ \langle VERB\_PHR \rangle \rightarrow \langle VERB \rangle \langle ADVERB \rangle \\ \langle DEFINITE \rangle \rightarrow the \\ \langle INDEFINITE \rangle \rightarrow a \,|\, an \\ \langle ADJECTIVE \rangle \rightarrow resourceful \,|\, little \\ \langle NOUN \rangle \rightarrow ants \\ \langle VERB \rangle \rightarrow work \\ \langle ADVERB \rangle \rightarrow diligently \end{array} \right\}.$$

It is easy to see that this CFG generates the English sentence *Resourceful little ants work diligently*. Note the application of the production

$$\langle ARTICLE \rangle \rightarrow \epsilon.$$

Note also how the rules in P are simplified: The variables $\langle NOUN \rangle$ and

$\langle VERB \rangle$ would require subdivision into further variables, so that we would have the variables $\langle NOUN\_SINGULAR \rangle$, $\langle NOUN\_PLURAL \rangle$, and $\langle VERB\_3RD\_PERSON \rangle$.

Before we begin elaborating on CFGs and the corresponding CFLs, we should contrast these with the context-sensitive grammars (CSGs).

3.3.2. (Def.) A grammar $G = (V, T, S, P)$ is *context-sensitive* (or of *type 1*) if each production $r \in P$ has the form $\gamma A \delta \to \gamma X \delta$, where $A \in V$, $\gamma, \delta \in (V \cup T)^*$, and $X \in (V \cup T)^+$ (i.e. $X \neq \epsilon$). Put differently, every production in a CSG is of a form $\alpha \to \beta$ such that $|\beta| \geq |\alpha|$, i.e. no production is length-decreasing.[11] A language $L \subseteq T^*$ is a *context-sensitive language* (CSL) if there is a CSG G such that $L = L(G)$.

The informal explanation for the label "context-sensitive" is that the production $\gamma A \delta \to \gamma X \delta$ allows the substitution of A by X only in the context "$\gamma \cdots \delta$".

We retake the CSGs in Section 4.3.3.2. below. We now move on with our elaboration on the CFLs. Simple though they are, it may be a tricky affair to generate a language from a CFG, or to test for membership of a string w in the class $\mathcal{CFL}$. As a matter of fact, a CFG G may have simpler rules, having only one or at most two types of productions. We call these simplifications *normal forms*, of which we consider two, to wit, the Chomsky and Greibach normal forms.

3.3.1.2. Normal forms for CFGs (I): Chomsky normal form

3.3.3. (Def.) A CFG G in which every production is of the two forms $A \to BC$ and $A \to a$, where $A, B, C \in V$ and $a \in T$, is said to be in *Chomsky normal form (ChNF)*.

We provide the algorithm for the transformation of a CFG into ChNF below (Algorithm 3.3), but before we do so we anticipate some remarks. Firstly, the given grammar should be cleaned prior to applying the algorithm (cf. Section 3.1.3.2). With respect to the removal of ϵ-productions and unit productions, it will prove useful to first handle the following propositions from the viewpoint of proof.

3.3.4. (Prop.) For every CFG G there is a CFG G' such that $L(G') = L(G) - \{\epsilon\}$.

Proof: Left as an exercise. (Hint: Cf. Example 3.1.9.)

---

[11] The production $S \to \epsilon$ is allowed only in case S does not occur in the consequent of any of the remaining productions.

Algorithm 3.3 Chomsky-normal-form transformation

Input: A clean CFG $G = (V, T, S, P)$
Output: A CFG $G' = (V', T, S, P')$ in Chomsky normal form (ChNF)

INITIATE with P

STEP I: Given a rule $r_i \in P$ of the form $\alpha \to \beta_1 \mid \beta_2 \mid ... \mid \beta_n$:

1. If r_i is a production with body $|\beta_j| = 1, \beta \in T$, then **output** $P_{I.1} = P$ and go to step 2.

2. If r_i is a production with body $|\beta_j| > 1$:

   a) for $|\beta_j| = 2$, $\beta \in V$, **output** $P_{I.2.a} = P$.

   b) for each symbol a in β_j such that $a \in T$, create a new symbol $U_a \in V$. Add a rule $U_a \to a$ to G and replace a in the bodies β_j of rules r_i by U_a. **Output** $P_{I.2.b}$.

   c) for $|\beta_j| \geq k, k \geq 3, \beta \in V$, such that β_j has the form $A \to B_1 B_2 ... B_k$, introduce $k - 2$ new variables $W_1, W_2, ..., W_{k-2}$ and replace rule r_i by $k - 1$ rules r' such that

$$A \to B_1 W_1 \qquad\qquad \left(r'_1 \right)$$
$$W_1 \to B_2 W_2 \qquad\qquad \left(r'_2 \right)$$
$$\vdots \qquad\qquad\qquad \vdots$$
$$W_{k-3} \to B_{k-2} W_{k-2} \qquad \left(r'_{k-2} \right)$$
$$W_{k-2} \to B_{k-1} B_k \qquad \left(r'_{k-1} \right)$$

   and **output** $P_{I.2.c}$.

STEP II: Introduce a new start symbol S_0 and add the rule $S_0 \to S$ to $P_{I.2.c}$. **Output** P'.

TERMINATE

3.3.5. (Prop.) For every CFG G there is a CFG G' without unit productions such that $L(G') = L(G)$.

Proof: Left as an exercise. (Hint: Cf. Example 3.1.10.)

With these proofs in the hand, the following theorem will be easy to prove:

Theorem 3.3.1. *Let G be a CFG generating a language that contains at least one string other than ϵ. Then, there is a CFG G' such that G' is a clean grammar and $L(G') = L(G)$.*

Proof: Left as an exercise.

It should be easy to see how important it is to have a clean CFG G before we start the process of its transformation into ChNF. In a clean grammar G, all the productions are of the form $\alpha \to \beta$ where β is either a terminal or a string $|\beta| \geq 2$ of terminals and variables: If the former, then the rule is already in ChNF; if the latter, then we must make it so that $|\beta| = 2$ consists solely of variables, and $|\beta| \geq 3$ must be broken into a group of productions such that $|\beta| = 2, \beta \in V$.

Example 3.3.3. Let $G = (\{S, A, B, C, D\}, \{a, b\}, S, P)$ have the following production set:

$$P = \left\{ \begin{array}{c} S \to Aab \,|\, b \,|\, bB \\ A \to aA \,|\, a \,|\, aBAC \\ B \to bB \,|\, aD \\ C \to aaC \,|\, bB \\ D \to aD \,|\, ab \end{array} \right\}$$

We apply Algorithm 3.3 to this CFG. Note that this grammar just is the clean grammar of Example 3.1.11; we renamed the variables E and F as C and D, respectively, for convenience, and renamed the terminals 0 and 1 as a and b, respectively. Because this is a clean grammar, we can proceed directly to the application of Algorithm 3.3. Step I.1 leaves the production set unchanged, and thus $P_{I.1} = P$, where the subscript indicates the step of the algorithm just applied. Application of Step I.2.a also leaves P unchanged. With respect to Step I.2.b, we create the variables U_a and U_b, introduce the rules $U_a \to a$ and $U_b \to b$, and proceed to the replacements stipulated in this step of the algorithm. This done, for convenience (only) we rename the variables U_a and U_b as E and F, respectively, so that we now have the following production set $P_{I.2.b}$:

$$P_{I.2.b} = \left\{ \begin{array}{c} S \to AU_aU_b \,|\, b \,|\, U_bB \\ A \to U_aA \,|\, a \,|\, U_aBAC \\ B \to U_bB \,|\, U_aD \\ C \to U_aU_aC \,|\, U_bB \\ D \to U_aD \,|\, U_aU_b \\ U_a \to a \\ U_b \to b \end{array} \right\} = \left\{ \begin{array}{c} S \to AEF \,|\, b \,|\, FB \\ A \to EA \,|\, a \,|\, EBAC \\ B \to FB \,|\, ED \\ C \to EEC \,|\, FB \\ D \to ED \,|\, EF \\ E \to a \\ F \to b \end{array} \right\}$$

We now have the productions $S \to AEF$, $A \to EBAC$, and $C \to EEC$, which require application of Step I.2.c. In the case of the first mentioned production, we have $|\beta| = 3$, so that we need to introduce only a single new variable; we choose G and have the new rules:

$$S \to AG$$
$$G \to EF$$

As for the second mentioned rule, we have $|\beta| = 4$, so that we now need two new variables; we choose H and I, and have now the three new productions:

$$A \to EH$$
$$H \to BI$$
$$I \to AC$$

With respect to the third mentioned rule, we have $|\beta| = 3$, and introduce the new variable J, obtaining the new rules:

$$C \to EJ$$
$$J \to EC$$

We have now the following production set:

$$P_{I.2.c} = \left\{ \begin{array}{c} S \to AG \,|\, b \,|\, FB \\ A \to EA \,|\, a \,|\, EH \\ B \to FB \,|\, ED \\ C \to EJ \,|\, FB \\ D \to ED \,|\, EF \\ E \to a \\ F \to b \\ G \to EF \\ H \to BI \\ I \to AC \\ J \to EC \end{array} \right\}$$

Application of Step II gives us:

$$P' = \begin{cases} S_0 \rightarrow AG \,|\, b \,|\, FB \\ S \rightarrow AG \,|\, b \,|\, FB \\ A \rightarrow EA \,|\, a \,|\, EH \\ B \rightarrow FB \,|\, ED \\ C \rightarrow EJ \,|\, FB \\ D \rightarrow ED \,|\, EF \\ E \rightarrow a \\ F \rightarrow b \\ G \rightarrow EF \\ H \rightarrow BI \\ I \rightarrow AC \\ J \rightarrow EC \end{cases}$$

Our grammar $G' = (V', T', S_0, P')$ in ChNF has the production set immediately above, and has $V' = \{S, S_0, A, B, C, D, E, F, G, H, I, J\}$ and $T' = \{a, b\}$. Note that $T' = T$, as expectable (otherwise, we would have $L(G) \neq L(G')$).

From the above, it will be easy to prove the following result:

Theorem 3.3.2. *For every CFG G there is an equivalent CFG G' in ChNF such that $L(G') = L(G) - \{\epsilon\}$.*

Proof: Left as an exercise.

3.3.1.3. Normal forms for CFGs (II): Greibach normal form

Whereas the Chomsky normal form is a restriction on the length of the body of rules, the Greibach normal form imposes restrictions on the positions of variables and terminals in the body of productions. The steps of the transformation of a clean CFG into this form are complex, but it has important applications, namely in the construction of pushdown automata, the models of computation for the CFLs (cf. Section 4.2).

3.3.6. (Def.) A CFG G in which every production is of the form $A \rightarrow a\alpha$, where $a \in T$ and $\alpha = B_1 B_2...B_n$, $n \geq 0$, $A, \alpha \in V$, is said to be in *Greibach normal form* (abbr.: GNF).

In order to obtain the GNF of a CFG, we start with a CFG in ChNF. However, in order to apply the algorithm for the former (Algorithm 3.4), we remove the rule $S_0 \rightarrow S$ from the latter.

Algorithm 3.4 Greibach-normal-form transformation

Input: A CFG $G = (V, T, S, P = P_0)$ in ChNF
Output: A CFG $G' = (V', T' = T, A_1, P' = P_4)$ in Greibach normal form (GNF)

START with P_0

1. Relabel all the k variables of P_0 as $A_1, A_2, ..., A_k$ making $S = A_1$ and ordering the rules such that $r_1 = A_1 \to \beta, ..., r_k = A_k \to \beta$. **Output** P_1.

2. Verify that for every rule $r_i \in P_1$ of the form $A_i \to A_j \alpha$, $|\alpha| = n - 1$ if $n > 0$, it is the case that $i < j$. If not, substitute A_j in the body of r_i by the body of A_j. Repeat until $j \geq i$ or $A_j \to \sigma \in T$. **Output** P_2.

3. If for any $r \in P_2$ we have a rule of the form

$$A_i \to A_i \alpha_1 \,|\, A_i \alpha_2 \,|\, ... \,|\, A_i \alpha_k \,|\, \beta_1 \,|\, \beta_2 \,|\, ... \,|\, \beta_l$$

   for $|\alpha| = n - 1$ if $n > 0$, and $\beta = \sigma_1 \sigma_2 ... \sigma_n \in (T \cup V)^*$ and $\sigma_1 \neq A_i$, then replace r by

   a) $Z \to \alpha_j \,|\, \alpha_j Z$ for $1 \leq j \leq k$, Z is a new variable, and
   b) $A_i \to \beta_j \,|\, \beta_j Z$ for $1 \leq j \leq l$.
   c) **Output** P_3.

4. If for any $r_i \in P_3$ we have a rule of the form $A_i \to \alpha$, for $A_i, \alpha \in V$, replace the initial variables of productions in the body of r_i until r_i is of the form $A_i \to a_1 \alpha \,|\, a_2 \alpha \,|\, ... \,|\, a_m \alpha$, where $a_j \in T$. Proceed in the order $i = n, n - 1, n - 2, ..., 1$ for the A_j. **Output** P_4.

TERMINATE

Example 3.3.4. We apply Algorithm 3.4 to the CFG in ChNF obtained in Example 3.3.3. This (without the rule $S_0 \to S$) is our input CFG G. Application of Step 1 of Algorithm 3.4, in which we rename S as A_1 and then proceed in alphabetical order to rename A as A_2, B as A_3, and so on until we rename J as A_{11}, gives us the production set:

$$P_1 = \left\{ \begin{array}{c} A_1 \to A_2 A_8 \,|\, b \,|\, A_7 A_3 \\ A_2 \to A_6 A_2 \,|\, a \,|\, A_6 A_9 \\ A_3 \to A_7 A_3 \,|\, A_6 A_5 \\ A_4 \to A_6 A_{11} \,|\, A_7 A_3 \\ A_5 \to A_6 A_5 \,|\, A_6 A_7 \\ A_6 \to a \\ A_7 \to b \\ A_8 \to A_6 A_7 \\ A_9 \to A_3 A_{10} \\ A_{10} \to A_2 A_4 \\ A_{11} \to A_6 A_4 \end{array} \right\}$$

In application of Step 2, we verify that the condition $j \geq i$ stipulated is not satisfied for the rules with heads A_8 through A_{11}. We proceed with the substitutions indicated and obtain:

$$A_8 \to \underbrace{a}_{A_6} A_7$$

$$A_9 \to \underbrace{A_7}_{A_3} A_3 A_{10} \,|\, \underbrace{A_6 A_5}_{A_3} A_{10} \to \underbrace{b}_{A_7} A_3 A_{10} \,|\, \underbrace{a}_{A_6} A_5 A_{10}$$

$$A_{10} \to \underbrace{A_6}_{A_2} A_2 A_4 \,|\, \underbrace{a}_{A_2} A_4 \,|\, \underbrace{A_6 A_9}_{A_2} A_4 \to \underbrace{a}_{A_6} A_2 A_4 \,|\, a A_4 \,|\, \underbrace{a}_{A_6} A_9 A_4$$

$$A_{11} \to \underbrace{a}_{A_6} A_4$$

Complete application of Step 2 gives us the production set:

$$P_2 = \left\{ \begin{array}{c} A_1 \to A_2 A_8 \,|\, b \,|\, A_7 A_3 \\ A_2 \to A_6 A_2 \,|\, a \,|\, A_6 A_9 \\ A_3 \to A_7 A_3 \,|\, A_6 A_5 \\ A_4 \to A_6 A_{11} \,|\, A_7 A_3 \\ A_5 \to A_6 A_5 \,|\, A_6 A_7 \\ A_6 \to a \\ A_7 \to b \\ A_8 \to a A_7 \\ A_9 \to b A_3 A_{10} \,|\, a A_5 A_{10} \\ A_{10} \to a A_2 A_4 \,|\, a A_4 \,|\, a A_9 A_4 \\ A_{11} \to a A_4 \end{array} \right\}$$

P_2 has no occurrence of the case considered in Step 3 of Algorithm 3.4, a case known as *left recursion*, and we have $P_2 = P_3$. Thus we move straight on to Step 4. Luckily, productions with heads A_{11} through A_6 are already in GNF, so we need only tackle those with heads A_5 through A_1. Complete application of Step 4 gives us the production set:

$$P' = \left\{ \begin{array}{c} A_1 \to a A_2 A_8 \,|\, a A_8 \,|\, a A_9 A_8 \,|\, b \,|\, b A_3 \\ A_2 \to a A_2 \,|\, a \,|\, a A_9 \\ A_3 \to b A_3 \,|\, a A_5 \\ A_4 \to a A_{11} \,|\, b A_3 \\ A_5 \to a A_5 \,|\, a A_7 \\ A_6 \to a \\ A_7 \to b \\ A_8 \to a A_7 \\ A_9 \to b A_3 A_{10} \,|\, a A_5 A_{10} \\ A_{10} \to a A_2 A_4 \,|\, a A_4 \,|\, a A_9 A_4 \\ A_{11} \to a A_4 \end{array} \right\}$$

Our CFG in GNF is $G' = (V', T', A_1, P')$ with P' as just shown, $V' = (A_1, A_2, ..., A_{11})$, and, as expectable, $T' = T$.

Example 3.3.5. We give now an Example of a CFG in whose transformation into GNF we are confronted with left recursion. Suppose that, having started with a clean CFG $G = (\{S, A, B, C\}, \{a, b\}, S, P)$, after application of Step 2 of Algorithm 3.4 we have the production set:

$$P_2 = \left\{ \begin{array}{c} A_1 \to A_2 A_3 \,|\, A_4 A_4 \\ A_2 \to b \\ A_3 \to a \\ A_4 \to b A_3 A_4 \,|\, A_4 A_4 A_4 \,|\, b \end{array} \right\}$$

We do indeed have a case of left recursion in the rule with head A_4.

Application of Step 3.a of Algorithm 3.4 gives us the additional rule

$$Z \rightarrow A_4 A_4 \mid A_4 A_4 Z$$

and application of Step 3.b gives us the altered rule with head A_4

$$A_4 \rightarrow b A_3 A_4 \mid b \mid b A_3 A_4 Z \mid bZ.$$

Complete application of Step 3 gives us the production set:

$$P_3 = \left\{ \begin{array}{c} A_1 \rightarrow A_2 A_3 \mid A_4 A_4 \\ A_2 \rightarrow b \\ A_3 \rightarrow a \\ A_4 \rightarrow b A_3 A_4 \mid b \mid b A_3 A_4 Z \mid bZ \\ Z \rightarrow A_4 A_4 \mid A_4 A_4 Z \end{array} \right\}$$

We proceed now to applying Step 4, obtaining the production set:

$$P' = \left\{ \begin{array}{c} A_1 \rightarrow b A_3 \mid b A_3 A_4 A_4 \mid b A_4 \mid b A_3 A_4 Z A_4 \mid bZ A_4 \\ A_2 \rightarrow b \\ A_3 \rightarrow a \\ A_4 \rightarrow b A_3 A_4 \mid b \mid b A_3 A_4 Z \mid bZ \\ Z \rightarrow b A_3 A_4 A_4 \mid b A_4 \mid b A_3 A_4 Z A_4 \mid bZ A_4 \mid \\ b A_3 A_4 A_4 Z \mid b A_4 Z \mid b A_3 A_4 Z A_4 Z \mid bZ A_4 Z \end{array} \right\}$$

Note the exponential increase in the bodies of some rules. Note also that $V' = \{A_1, A_2, A_3, A_4, Z\} = V \cup \{Z\}$.

Algorithm 3.4 finds its mathematical support in two lemmas. We give these lemmas, and leave their proofs as exercises. With these proofs in the hand, it will be easy to prove the central theorem for GNF.

Lemma 3.3.3. *Let $G = (V, T, S, P)$ be a CFG and $(B \rightarrow \gamma_1 \mid \gamma_2 \mid ... \mid \gamma_m) \in P$. If there is in G a production $r \in P$ of the form $A \rightarrow \alpha B \beta$, then if we replace $A \rightarrow \alpha B \beta$ by $(A \rightarrow \alpha \gamma_1 \beta \mid \alpha \gamma_2 \beta \mid ... \mid \alpha \gamma_m \beta) \in P'$, we have $L(G) = L(G')$.*

Proof: Left as an exercise.

Lemma 3.3.4. *Let there be given a CFG $G = (V, T, S, P)$ and a rule $(A \rightarrow A_i \alpha_1 \mid A_i \alpha_2 \mid ... \mid A_i \alpha_m) \in P$. If $A_i \rightarrow \beta_1 \mid \beta_2 \mid ... \mid \beta_k$ where each β_j begins with either a terminal or a variable $A_j, j > i$, then if we replace the m productions by*

$$r_1 = A_i \rightarrow \beta_1 \mid \beta_2 \mid ... \mid \beta_l \mid \beta_1 B_i \mid \beta_2 B_i \mid ... \mid \beta_l B_i$$

and

$$r_2 = B_i \rightarrow \alpha_1 \,|\, \alpha_2 \,|\, ... \,|\, \alpha_k \,|\, \alpha_1 B_i \,|\, \alpha_2 B_i \,|\, ... \,|\, \alpha_k B_i$$

$r_1, r_2 \in P'$, *then* $L(G) = L(G')$ *for* $G' = (V', T, S, P')$, $V' = V \cup \{B_i\}$.

Proof: Left as an exercise.

Theorem 3.3.5. *For every CFG G there is an equivalent CFG G' in GNF such that* $L(G') = L(G) - \{\epsilon\}$.

Proof: Left as an exercise.

3.3.1.4. Derivation, or parse, trees

The CFG of Example 3.3.1 is a rather simple example in the sense that it is easy to determine the language generated solely by looking at the productions. However, as said, this is not the norm. One way to determine more complex languages is by constructing derivation, or parse, trees.

3.3.7. (Def.) Let $G = (V, T, S, P)$ be a CFG. We say that an ordered labeled tree is a *derivation*, or *parse*, *tree* for a string $w \in G$, denoted by $\mathcal{T}_w$ (abbreviating $\mathcal{T}_{G_w}$), if and only if:

1. The root of $\mathcal{T}_w$ is S;

2. Each and every interior vertex of $\mathcal{T}_w$ is labeled with an element from V;

3. Each and every leaf of $\mathcal{T}_w$ is labeled with an element from $T \cup \{\epsilon\}$;

4. If a vertex has a label $A \in V$ and its children are labeled from left to right with $X_1, X_2, ..., X_n$, then P must contain a production of the form $A \rightarrow X_1 X_2 ... X_n$;

5. A leaf labeled with ϵ has no siblings.

3.3.8. (Def.) A derivation tree $\mathcal{T}_w$ is called a *partial derivation tree*, denoted by $\mathcal{T}_w^i$, $i = 0, 1, ..., n$, if $S = \mathcal{T}_w^0$ is the root and every leaf is labeled with an element from $V \cup T \cup \{\epsilon\}$.

This should be distinguished from a *subtree*, in which the root can be any particular vertex of the derivation tree (cf. Def. 2.2.16.1). We denote a subtree of a string w by $\mathcal{T}_w'$.

Example 3.3.6. Let the following be the productions of a CFG $G = (V, T, S, P)$ with $V = \{S, A, B\}$ and $T = \{a, b, c\}$:

$$P = \left\{ \begin{array}{c} S \to aAB \\ A \to Bba \\ B \to bB \mid c \end{array} \right\}$$

The productions of this grammar generate the string $w = acbabc$ as a result of the derivation (we omit the subscript G in $\Longrightarrow$):

$$S \Longrightarrow aAB \Longrightarrow a\,(Bba)\,B \Longrightarrow acbaB \Longrightarrow acba\,(bB) \Longrightarrow acbabc$$

Figure 3.3.1 shows the different partial derivation trees and the final derivation tree. In this, the string is read in the leaves from left to right. Other strings of this grammar are any of $ab^n cbab^m c$ for $n, m \geq 0$, so that we have the CFL $L = \{ab^n cbab^m c | n, m \geq 0\}$.

Theorem 3.3.6. *Let $G = (V, T, S, P)$ be a CFG. Then, $S \overset{*}{\underset{G}{\Longrightarrow}} \alpha$ if and only if there is a derivation tree in G with yield α.*

Proof: Left as an exercise. (Hint: Prove that for any $A \in V$, $A \overset{*}{\underset{G}{\Longrightarrow}} \alpha$ if and only if there is a subtree with vertex A with α as the yield. Then make $A = S$.)

3.3.1.5. Ambiguity and inherent ambiguity

Given a CFG G, there may be more than one derivation (tree) for a single string, and they may be unequally appropriate. The following example illustrates this problem.

Example 3.3.7. Let $G = (\{S\}, \{a, +, *, (,)\}, S, P)$ be a CFG with the following productions in P:

$$S \to a \mid S + S \mid S * S \mid (S)$$

Figure 3.3.2 shows that the string $a + a * a$ has two leftmost derivations.

The problem exhibited in Example 3.3.7 is called ambiguity.

3.3.9. (Def.) A CFG G is said to be *ambiguous* if there is a string $w \in L\,(G)$ with two or more different leftmost derivations in G. Otherwise, G is *unambiguous*.

This is more rigorously captured in the following theorem:

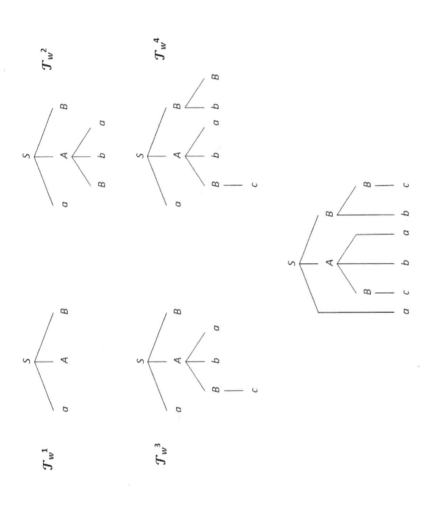

Figure 3.3.1.: Derivation tree of the string $w = acbabc \in L(G)$ with the corresponding partial derivation trees.

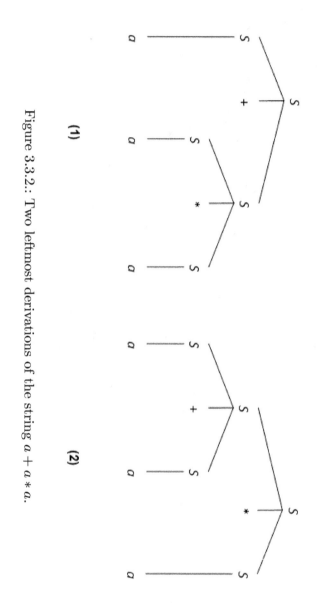

(1)   (2)

Figure 3.3.2.: Two leftmost derivations of the string $a + a * a$.

Theorem 3.3.7. *Let G be a CFG and $w \in L(G)$. Then, the following statements are equivalent:*[12]

1. *w has more than one derivation tree.*

2. *w has more than one leftmost derivation.*

3. *w has more than one rightmost derivation.*

Proof: Left as an exercise. (Hint: Given two derivation trees $\mathcal{T}_1$ (abbreviating $\mathcal{T}_{w1}$) and $\mathcal{T}_2$, specify the first step where the two corresponding derivations differ such that, given an occurrence of a variable A, there will be two nodes with different children such that $\mathcal{T}_1 \neq \mathcal{T}_2$.)

The ambiguity exhibited in Example 3.3.7 resides in the following possible *interpretations*: Derivation tree 1 interprets this string as a sum, whereas derivation tree 2 interprets the string as a product. Suppose $a = -2$; then we have $a + (a * a) = 2$ and $(a + a) * a = 8$.

This ambiguity is as highly undesirable in programming as it is in arithmetic, as programs are required to have a unique interpretation. This problem can be solved by agreeing, whenever a step has more than one variable occurrence, to use the leftmost one when *parsing* the string. As shown, a string is ambiguous if it has more than one derivation, or parse, tree, and parsing a string–i.e. constructing its parse tree–actually superimposes a structure on it. In fact, parsing is the only efficient way to recognize a string of a CFL. This entails a reformulation of grammar equivalence (cf. Def. 3.1.11.6) for the CFGs:

3.3.10. (Def.) Two grammars G_1 and G_2 are said to be *structurally equivalent* if $L(G_1) = L(G_2)$ and to each string w it is the case that G_1 and G_2 assign a similar parse tree, i.e. a parse tree with a similar structure.

We then speak of Definition 3.1.11.6 as *weak equivalence*, and of the above as *strong equivalence*.

Example 3.3.8. Let us retake the CFG of Example 3.3.7. Note that above we did not apply the production rule $S \to (S)$. By doing it now, and by agreeing to use the leftmost variable, we verify that there is only one leftmost derivation corresponding to the string $a + (a * a)$. Figure 3.3.3 shows the derivation, or parse, tree of this string. Because this

---

[12]Given a statement asserting the equivalence of propositions p, q, r, etc., it is required that one prove that $p \equiv q$, $q \equiv r$, etc.

derivation is in conformity with the intended meaning (i.e. it obeys the precedence rules of arithmetic), we say that this grammar is *structurally adequate*.

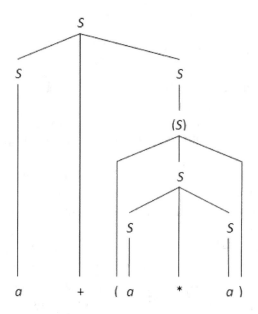

Figure 3.3.3.: Parse tree of an unambiguously derived string.

However, this convention does not always work, because there are languages that are inherently ambiguous.

3.3.11. (Def.) A CFL L is said to be *inherently ambiguous* if every CFG that generates it is ambiguous.

Example 3.3.9. The CFL $L = \{a^i b^j c^k \,|\, i = j \text{ or } j = k\}$ is inherently ambiguous. We leave the proof as an exercise.

It should be remarked, however, that inherent ambiguity is not a property that is frequent enough (actually, it is quite rare) to make us worry about it, not affecting programming languages to a significant extent. This said, one must obviously be on the lookout for this unwanted property.

3.3.2. Properties of the context-free languages

3.3.2.1. The pumping lemma for CFLs and Ogden's lemma

We often need to find out whether a language is, or is not, a CFL. Just as in the case of regular languages, there is a *pumping lemma for CFLs* that allows us to detect non-CFLs. Informally, this lemma states that in a given CFL there are always two short substrings close together that can be simultaneously "pumped" at will, i.e. can both be repeated the same number (zero or more) of times.

We begin with a lemma that shows clearly the importance of having a CFG in ChNF when working with CFLs.

Lemma 3.3.8. *Let* $S \overset{*}{\underset{G}{\Longrightarrow}} z$, *where G is in ChNF. Suppose that $\mathcal{T}_z$ is a derivation tree for z in G and that no path in $\mathcal{T}_z$ contains more than k nodes. Then $|z| \leq 2^{k-2}$.*

Proof: First, suppose that $z = a$. Then, $\mathcal{T}_z$ has only two nodes, labeled S and a respectively, and a single edge (see Fig. 3.3.4.1), i.e. $|z| = 2^{2-2} = 1$. Clearly, $|z| \leq 2^{k-2}$. Otherwise, because G is in ChNF, the root of $\mathcal{T}_z$ must have exactly two immediate successors, α and β, labeled by variables (e.g., A and B, respectively, for a production $S \to AB$). We now have two subtrees $\mathcal{T}_z' = \mathcal{T}_\alpha$ and $\mathcal{T}_z'' = \mathcal{T}_\beta$ with roots A and B, respectively (see Fig. 3.3.4.2). In each of $\mathcal{T}_\alpha, \mathcal{T}_\beta$ the longest path must contain $\leq k-1$ nodes. By induction, we may assume that each of $\mathcal{T}_\alpha, \mathcal{T}_\beta$ has $\leq 2^{k-3}$ leaves, so that we have

$$|z| \leq 2^{k-3} + 2^{k-3} = 2^{k-2}.$$

QED

We can now easily prove Theorem 3.3.9.[13]

Theorem 3.3.9. *(Pumping lemma for CFLs) Let L be any CFL. Then there is an integer n depending only on L such that, if $z \in L$ and $|z| \geq n$, then we can write $z = uvwxy$ satisfying the following three conditions:*

1. $|vx| \geq 1$;

2. $|vwx| \leq n$;

3. $uv^i wx^i y \in L$ for all $i \geq 0$.

---

[13] Firstly published in Bar-Hillel, Perles, & Shamir (1961).

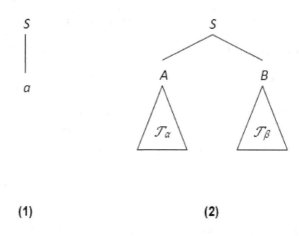

(1)   (2)

Figure 3.3.4.: Parse trees for productions (1) $S \to a$ and (2) $S \to AB$.

Proof: (Sketch) Clearly, given a grammar G in ChNF, if we start with a derivation

$$(D) \qquad S \underset{G}{\overset{*}{\Longrightarrow}} uAy \underset{G}{\overset{*}{\Longrightarrow}} uvAxy \underset{G}{\overset{*}{\Longrightarrow}} uvwxy = z$$

we can end up with a yield $uv^i wx^i y$ by the sequence

$$(D') \quad S \underset{G}{\overset{*}{\Longrightarrow}} uAy \underset{G}{\overset{*}{\Longrightarrow}} uvAxy \underset{G}{\overset{*}{\Longrightarrow}} uv^2 Ax^2 y \underset{G}{\overset{*}{\Longrightarrow}} \dots$$

$$\dots \underset{G}{\overset{*}{\Longrightarrow}} uv^i Ax^i y \underset{G}{\overset{*}{\Longrightarrow}} uv^i wx^i y.$$

That is, a sufficiently long derivation in G must contain a recursive (or self-embedded) variable A such that w can be derived from any of the occurrences of A and thus any of the strings uwy, $uvwxy$, $uv^2 wx^2 y$, ..., can be derived from S. Recall that this grammar G must generate a language $L(G) - \{\epsilon\}$ in ChNF. This means that every derivation step (i) either introduces a terminal by the application of a production of the form $A \to a$, (ii) or augments the length of the sentential form by means of a production $A \to BC$ (cf. Def. 3.3.3).

Because this grammar is in ChNF, any derivation tree must be a binary tree of the basic form shown in Figure 3.3.5, and because z is a long string, the parse tree for this string must have a long path. As a matter of fact, so long that there must be some variable that occurs more than once on this path–and near the bottom of the path, for that matter. In terms of Lemma 3.3.8, we let $n = 2^k$ for k the number of variables in G. If $z \in L(G)$ and $|z| \geq n$, then any parse tree $\mathcal{T}_z$ must have a path with length $\geq k+1$, since $|z| > 2^{k-1}$. But this path has $\geq k+2$ vertices, all labeled with variables with the exception of the last one. Hence, by Lemma 3.3.8 we have

$$|vwx| = |v [\![\mathcal{T}_\beta]\!] x| = |[\![\mathcal{T}_\alpha]\!]| \leq 2^n$$

where $[\![\mathcal{T}_\gamma]\!]$ denotes the string consisting of the labels of the leaves of the tree $\mathcal{T}_\gamma$. **QED**

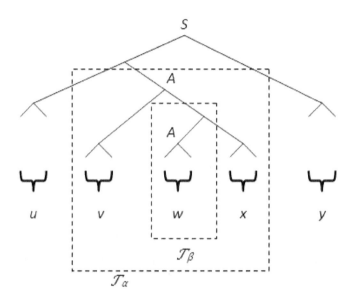

Figure 3.3.5.: Parse tree for $z = uv^i wx^i y$.

Example 3.3.10. The language $L = \{a^n b^n c^n | n > 0\}$ is not a CFL. In effect, suppose $L = L(G)$ is a CFL with G a grammar in ChNF with n variables. Now choose k so large that $|a^k b^k c^k| > 2^n$, i.e. $k > 2^n/3$. We have $a^k b^k c^k = uvwxy$. Set $z_i = uv^i wx^i y$, so that we have $z_i \in L$ for $i = 0, 1, 2, ...$ For $i = 2$, we thus have $z_2 = uv^2 wx^2 y$. But v and x must each contain only one of a, b, or c, so that one of these three letters must be left out. For $i = 3, 4, 5, ...$, z_i contains more and more copies of v and x; moreover, $vx \neq \epsilon$. Hence, it is not possible for z_i to have the same number of occurrences of a, b, and c. Thus, $z_i \notin L$, and we reached a contradiction.

However, some non-CFLs evade detection by means of the pumping lemma for CFLs. For instance, $L = \{a^i b^j c^k d^l | i = 0 \text{ or } j = k = l\}$ is not a CFL, but this lemma fails to determine this. This is so because this pumping lemma is not strong enough, namely in the sense that it does not tell us much about the location of the substrings v and x, i.e. the substrings that are pumped. The following lemma, known as *Ogden's lemma* (Ogden, 1968), allows the designation of some positions of z as "distinguished," so that some of the distinguished positions are guaranteed to appear in the pumped substrings. As a matter of fact, the pumping lemma for CFLs just is the special case of Ogden's lemma in which all the positions in z are distinguished.

Theorem 3.3.10. *(Ogden's lemma) Let L be a CFL. Then there is an integer n such that, if $z \in L$ and $|z| \geq n$, and we mark n or more positions of z as "distinguished," then we can write $z = uvwxy$ such that*

1. *the string vx has at least one distinguished position;*

2. *the string vwx has at most n distinguished positions;*

3. *$uv^i wx^i y \in L$ for all $i \geq 0$.*

Proof: Left as an exercise. (Hints: Let us call vertices of a derivation tree both of whose children have distinguished descendants *branch points*. Construct a path π in the tree beginning at the root only with branch points. It should follow that there are at least $k + 1$ branch points in π. Apply the pigeonhole principle.[14])

Example 3.3.11. Ogden's lemma allows us to determine that the language $L = \{a^i b^j c^k | i \neq j, j \neq k, i \neq k\}$ is not a CFL. We leave the explanation as an exercise.

3.3.2.2. Further properties of CFLs

We next approach the closure properties for CFLs, as well as decidability properties for this language class. We begin with the former.

Theorem 3.3.11. *Let L_1 and L_2 be CFLs. Then, $L_1 \cup L_2$, $L_1 L_2$, and $(L_i)^*$ are also CFLs.*

---

[14]The *pigeonhole principle* states that if $(n + 1)$ objects are distributed among n sets, then at least one of the sets must contain at least two objects.

Proof: We prove that $L_1 \cup L_2$ is also a CFL and leave the other two remaining cases as an exercise. Suppose that the CFGs $G_1 = (V_1, T, S_1, P_1)$ and $G_2 = (V_2, T, S_2, P_2)$ generate the CFLs L_1 and L_2, respectively. Assume further $V_1 \cap V_2 = \emptyset$. Design a new CFG $G = (V, T, S, P)$ with $V = V_1 \cup V_2 \cup \{S\}$ and $P = P_1 \cup P_2 \cup \{S \to S_1 \mid S_2\}$, $S \notin (V_1 \cup V_2)$. We can derive a string $x \in L(G)$ by starting with either $S \to S_1$ or $S \to S_2$ and continuing the derivation in either G_1 or G_2, so that $L(G) = L(G_1) \cup L(G_2)$. In effect, suppose that $S \overset{*}{\underset{G}{\Longrightarrow}} x$. Then, the first step in the derivation must be either $S \Longrightarrow S_1$ or $S \Longrightarrow S_2$. Because $V_1 \cap V_2 = \emptyset$, in the first case we remain in G_1 and $x \in L_1$; similarly for $x \in L_2$. Thus, $L_1 \cup L_2 = L(G)$. **QED**

Theorem 3.3.11 has more than its intrinsic mathematical interest; it comes in handy in practical terms. In effect, to construct a CFG may be a non-trivial task. Because a CFL can be the union of simpler CFLs, one can break a CFG into simpler parts and then construct CFGs for these parts. Similarly, practical applications can be found for concatenation and iteration.

Further closure properties of CFLs are as follows. For the reasons stated in the Preface, we present these as (multi-item) propositions rather than as theorems.

3.3.12 (Prop.) The class $\mathscr{CFL}$ is closed under (i) substitution and (ii) homomorphism.

Proof: (i) Let $L \subseteq T^*$ be a CFL and let θ be a substitution such that $\theta(a) = L_a$ is a CFL for every $a \in T$, i.e. θ is the function $\theta : T \longrightarrow L$. We assume that L (abbreviating $L(G)$) is generated by the CFG $G = (V, T, S, P)$. Let further L_a (abbreviating $L(G_a)$) be generated by the CFG $G_a = (V_a, T_a, S_a, P_a)$ and let

$$V_a \cap V = \emptyset = V_a \cap V_b$$

for $a \neq b \in T$. Then, L_a is generated by the CFG $G_\theta = (V_\theta, T_\theta, S, P_\theta)$ where

$$V_\theta = V \cup \left(\bigcup_{a \in T} V_a \right),$$

$$T_\theta = \bigcup_{a \in T} T_a$$

and

$$P_\theta = P' \cup \left(\bigcup_{a \in T} P_a \right)$$

for $P' \subseteq P$ the production set with each $a \in T$ replaced by S_a in their bodies. Then,

$$\theta\,(L) = L\,(G_\theta) = \bigcup_{a \in T} \theta\,(a)$$

is a CFL.

(ii) Given an alphabet Σ, a substitution θ is a homomorphism if for every $a \in \Sigma$ we have $|L_a| = 1$ for $L_a = \theta\,(a)$. **QED**

3.3.13. (Prop.) The class $\mathscr{CFL}$ is not closed under (i) intersection, (ii) complementation, and (iii) difference.

Proof: (i) It can be shown that the languages $L_1 = \{a^n b^n c^m | n, m > 0\}$ and $L_2 = \{a^n b^m c^m | n, m > 0\}$ are CFLs (cf. Exercise 3.3.16), but

$$L_1 \cap L_2 = \{a^n b^n c^n | n > 0\}$$

which has been shown not to be a CFL (cf. Example 3.3.10).

(ii) We proved with respect to Theorem 3.3.11 that for any two CFLs L_1 and L_2, $L_1 \cup L_2$ is also a CFL. Let us now take the complements of these languages and apply De Morgan law. Then we have

$$\overline{\overline{L_1} \cup \overline{L_2}} = L_1 \cap L_2.$$

But we know from (i) above that the CFLs are not closed under intersection. Hence, neither are they closed under complementation.

(iii) For every alphabet Σ, Σ^* is a CFL. Suppose that for every CFL $L \subseteq \Sigma^*$, $\Sigma^* - L$ is also a CFL. But by the De Morgan law we have

$$\Sigma^* - ((\Sigma^* - L_1) \cup (\Sigma^* - L_2)) = L_1 \cap L_2$$

which was shown not to be closed for $\mathscr{CFL}$. **QED**

3.3.14. (Prop.) Let L_1 and L_2 be a CFL and a regular language, respectively. Then, (i) $L_1 \cap L_2$ and (ii) $L_1 - L_2$ are CFLs.

Proof: Left as an exercise.

Many questions are relevant with respect to CFLs. However, not all relevant questions have a "Yes/No" answer; those that do not fail to have an algorithm. In effect:

3.3.15. (Prop.) For arbitrary CFGs G_1 and G_2, the questions whether (i) $L\,(G_1) = L\,(G_2)$ (for weak equivalence), (ii) $L\,(G_1) \cap L\,(G_2) = \emptyset$, (iii) $L\,(G_1) \subseteq L\,(G_2)$, and (iv) $L\,(G_i) = \Sigma^*$ are undecidable.

Proof: Left as a research exercise.

We present now theorems for the decidable questions (complete proofs are left as exercises).

Theorem 3.3.12. *Given a CFG G, there are algorithms to determine whether (i) $L(G) = \emptyset$, (ii) $L(G)$ is finite, and (iii) $L(G)$ is infinite.*

Proof: (Idea) (i) Given a CFG $G = (V, T, S, P)$, if we have $S \overset{*}{\underset{G}{\Rightarrow}} w$ for at least one string $w \in T^* - \{\epsilon\}$, then $L(G) \neq \emptyset$. Otherwise, $L(G) = \emptyset$.

(ii) (Sketch) Apply Algorithm 3.3 to G. For every production in the obtained G' of the form $A \to BC$ or $A \to CB$, draw a digraph $\vec{\mathfrak{G}}$ with vertices A, B (or A, C). $L(G') = L(G) - \{\epsilon\}$ is finite if and only if there are no cycles in this digraph.

(iii) (Sketch) Let G be a grammar in ChNF with exactly n variables. Check whether there is a string $w \in L(G)$ such that

$$2^n < |w| \leq 2^{n+1}.$$

$L(G)$ is infinite if and only if there is such a string. (Hint: Invoke the pumping lemma for CFLs.) **QED**

Theorem 3.3.13. *Let G be a CFG and w be a string. Then there is an algorithm to determine whether $w \in L(G)$.*

Proof: (Idea) The CYK Algorithm (cf. Section 5.5) is one such algorithm. **QED**

Exercises

Exercise 3.3.1. Determine the CFLs given the indicated productions:

1. $S \to SaS \mid b \mid \epsilon$

2. $S \to aS \mid bS \mid \epsilon$

3. $S \to aA \mid bA; \quad A \to aS \mid bS$

4. $S \to aS \mid aSbS \mid \epsilon$

5. $S \to ab \mid bS \mid a \mid b$

6. $S \to SS \mid a \mid b$

Exercise 3.3.2. Transform the grammars of Exercise 3.1.7.1-3 into:

1. Chomsky normal form.

2. Greibach normal form.

Exercise 3.3.3. Obtain the derivation trees of the following strings given the indicated productions of CFGs:

1. $w = abaabaa$ given the production set

$$P = \left\{ \begin{array}{c} S \to aAS \mid a \\ A \to bS \end{array} \right\} .$$

2. $w = a^5$ given the production set

$$P = \{S \to SS \mid a\} .$$

3. $w = a^3 b^5$, given the production set

$$P = \left\{ \begin{array}{c} S \to aS \mid aA \\ A \to bA \mid b \end{array} \right\} .$$

Exercise 3.3.4. Construct the parse tree for the English sentence *Resourceful little ants work diligently* generated by the CFG of Example 3.3.2.

Exercise 3.3.5. Let $G = (V, T, S, P)$ with $V = \{A, B\}$ and $T = \{a, b\}$ be a CFG. The productions of G are as follows:

$$P = \left\{ \begin{array}{c} S \to aB \mid bA \\ A \to aS \mid bAA \mid a \\ B \to bS \mid aBB \mid b \end{array} \right\} .$$

Obtain the string $aaabbabbba$ by (i) a leftmost derivation and (ii) a rightmost derivation.

Exercise 3.3.6. Show that the CFGs G with the following productions are ambiguous:

1.

$$P = \left\{ \begin{array}{c} S \to a \mid aAb \mid abSb \\ A \to aAAb \mid bS \end{array} \right\} .$$

2.

$$P = \{S \to SS \mid a \mid b\} .$$

3.

$$P = \left\{ \begin{array}{l} S \rightarrow A \,|\, B \\ A \rightarrow a\,Ab \,|\, ab \\ B \rightarrow abB \,|\, \epsilon \end{array} \right\} .$$

Exercise 3.3.7. With respect to the grammars in Exercise 3.3.6.1-3, find an equivalent unambiguous grammar for each of them.

Exercise 3.3.8. In Examples 3.3.7-8, we saw how CFGs with arithmetical operations can generate ambiguous strings and discussed generally the topic of disambiguation. In a programming context, however, we need to be more precise. Let our CFG $G = (V, T, \langle EXP \rangle, P)$ where $T = \{id, ct, (,), +, *\}$, "$id$" denotes an identifier and "ct" does so for a constant, and $V = \{\langle EXP \rangle, \langle OP \rangle\}$, "EXP" denoting an expression and "OP" an operation.

1. Give the production set P of G such that G is an ambiguous grammar when generating the string $id + ct * id$.

2. Change G so that the operation of multiplication, denoted by $*$, always has priority over addition. Verify with a parse tree for the string $id + ct * id$.

3. Augment T with the symbols for subtraction $(-)$ and division $(/)$ and change G further such that the conventional precedence of the arithmetical operations is always respected in G.

Exercise 3.3.9. Given the following ambiguous CFGs, (i) identify the source of ambiguity in each grammar, and (ii) find a way to disambiguate it.

1. $G = (\{S\}, \{a, b, c\}, S, P)$ with the production set

$$P = \{ \; S \rightarrow aS \,|\, Sb \,|\, c \; \} .$$

2. $G = (\{S, A\}, \{0, 1\}, S, P)$ with the production set

$$P = \left\{ \begin{array}{l} S \rightarrow A0A \\ A \rightarrow 0A \,|\, 1A \,|\, \epsilon \end{array} \right\} .$$

3. $G = (\{S\}, \{0, 1\}, S, P)$ with the production set

$$P = \{ \; S \rightarrow 00S1 \,|\, 0S1 \,|\, \epsilon \; \} .$$

4. $G = (\{S, A\}, \{a, b\}, S, P)$ with the production set

$$P = \left\{ \begin{array}{l} S \to aS \mid Sb \mid A \\ A \to aA \mid bA \mid \epsilon \end{array} \right\}.$$

5. $G = (\{S, A, B\}, \{a, b, c, d\}, S, P)$ with the production set

$$P = \left\{ \begin{array}{l} S \to A \mid B \\ A \to aAb \mid \epsilon \\ B \to cBd \mid \epsilon \end{array} \right\}.$$

Exercise 3.3.10. Explain why the following languages are inherently ambiguous:

1. $L = \{a^i b^j c^k \mid i = j \text{ or } j = k\}$ (cf. Example 3.3.9).

2. $L = \{a^n b^m c^m d^n \mid n, m > 0\} \cup \{a^n b^n c^m d^m \mid n, m > 0\}$.

Exercise 3.3.11. Determine whether the following languages are CFLs:

1. $L = \{a^{n^2} \mid n \geq 1\}$.

2. $L = \{w \in \{a, b, c\}^* \mid |w|_a = |w|_b = |w|_c\}$.

3. $L = \{a^i b^j c^i d^j \mid i, j \geq 1\}$.

4. $L = \{w^2 \mid w \in \{0, 1\}^*\}$.

Exercise 3.3.12. Show why the pumping lemma for CFLs fails in the case of the language $L = \{a^i b^j c^k d^l \mid i = 0 \text{ or } j = k = l\}$.

Exercise 3.3.13. Show why Ogden's lemma allows us to determine that the language of Example 3.3.11, $L = \{a^i b^j c^k \mid i \neq j, j \neq k, i \neq k\}$, is not a CFL.

Exercise 3.3.14. Give an intuitive account of Ogden's lemma.

Exercise 3.3.15. With respect to Theorem 3.3.9:

1. Give an intuitive account of each of the conditions 1 through to 3.

2. Does it hold for (i) $L = \emptyset$ and/or (ii) $L = \{\epsilon\}$?

3. Comment on the importance of parse trees for the proof of this theorem.

Exercise 3.3.16. With respect to the proof of Proposition 3.3.13.i:

1. Show that L_1 and L_2 are indeed CFLs. (For instance, construct the sets of productions for their associated CFGs.)

2. Reflect on why this is a constructive proof, i.e. a proof that actually produces, or constructs, specific desired objects or structures.

Exercise 3.3.17. Prove (Complete the proof of) the theorems and propositions above that were left as an exercise (with a sketchy proof, respectively).

Exercise 3.3.18. In which way is it (more) adequate to speak of a CFL L as a *tree language* rather than as a *string language*?

Exercise 3.3.19. Reflect on the trade-off between ambiguity and complexity/size in a CFG.

Exercise 3.3.20. As stated above (cf. Prop. 3.3.15.i), weak equivalence of CFLs is not decidable. What about strong equivalence? Justify your answer.

Exercise 3.3.21. With respect to the (sketchy) proofs of Theorems 3.3.12-13:

1. Prove the rationale behind the algorithms.

2. Write the algorithms.

Exercise 3.3.22. Let $L = \{w \in T^* || w|_a = |w|_b\}$, $L_a = \{c^n d^n | n \geq 1\}$, and $L_b = \{ww^R | w \in (c + e)^*\}$. Let the production sets

$$P = \{S \rightarrow aSbS \,|\, bSaS \,|\, \epsilon\}$$

$$P_a = \{S_a \rightarrow cS_a d \,|\, cd\}$$

$$P_b = \{S_b \rightarrow cS_b c \,|\, eS_b e \,|\, \epsilon\}$$

be given for G, G_a, and G_b, respectively. Find the production set of $\theta(L)$ for θ the substitution $\theta(a) = L_a$ and $\theta(b) = L_b$.

Exercise 3.3.23. Rewrite Definition 3.3.7 as an algorithm (call it "Parse-tree Algorithm").

Exercise 3.3.24. Show that the class $\mathscr{CFL}$ is closed under *inverse homomorphisms*, i.e. if L is a CFL, then $h^{-1}(L)$, for h a homomorphism, is also a CFL.

3.4. Recursively enumerable languages

In this Section, we discuss briefly the basic features of the recursively enumerable languages as far as formal grammars are concerned, and we elaborate further on them below, namely in Chapter 5. The languages that we approach next are fundamental for classical computation in more than one way. This notwithstanding, the reader will realize that our discussion of these languages is by far shorter than for the regular languages and, in particular, the CFLs. In effect, their "unrestricted" nature contributes to a lack of precise knowledge with respect to them. Moreover, the fact that they are not–very or at all–relevant for programming languages limits their interest from the viewpoint of applied research. Were this book on formal languages/grammars and machines alone, we would dispense with more than a brief paragraph on these languages; it is the fact that we are here also concerned with the theory of classical computing that accounts for a more extended discussion of these languages, namely insofar as they are associated to the Turing machine, the *non-plus-ultra* construct of computability and complexity theory.

3.4.1. (Def.) A grammar $G = (V, T, S, P)$ is an *unrestricted grammar* (UG; also: *type-0 grammar*) if it has productions of the form $\alpha \to \beta$ for strings α, β such that $\alpha \in (V \cup T)^{+}$, $\beta \in (V \cup T)^{*}$, with $|V(\alpha)| \geq 1$. A language $L \subseteq T^*$ is a *recursively enumerable language* (REL) if and only if there is a UG G such that $L = L(G)$.

Contrarily to CFGs, UGs allow for productions in which a variable may *depend on the context*. For instance, the production $Bc \to bc$ allows the substitution of the variable B by the terminal b only if B is immediately followed by c on the antecedent. In particular, given a UG G, the assumption $S \underset{G}{\overset{*}{\Longrightarrow}} vAx \underset{G}{\overset{*}{\Longrightarrow}} z$ no longer implies that $z = vwx$ for some string w. Nevertheless, just as in the case of regular languages and CFLs, a UG production is terminal when its body has no variables.

Example 3.4.1. Recall from Example 3.3.10 that the language $L = \{a^n b^n c^n | n > 0\}$ is not a CFL. But this language is a REL. We show how a UG can generate it. We begin by creating a variable L denoting "left end of a string." We now require productions that (i) allow us to obtain strings of the form $L(ABC)^n$, and (ii) allow for an alphabetical (re)arrangement of the variables A, B, and C. These productions are as follows:

$$(i) \qquad S \rightarrow SABC \mid LABC$$

$$(ii) \qquad BA \rightarrow AB; CB \rightarrow BC; CA \rightarrow AC$$

Now, of course, we need productions that (iii) allow us to replace variables that are already in alphabetic order by terminals:

$$(iii) \qquad LA \rightarrow a; aA \rightarrow aa; aB \rightarrow ab; bB \rightarrow bb; bC \rightarrow bc; cC \rightarrow cc$$

Because the heads of productions in a UG typically have more than one symbol we cannot construct parse trees for strings of RELs. However, we can still construct some sort of derivation graph; more precisely, a labeled derivation digraph.

3.4.2. (Def.) Given a UG $G = (V, T, S, P)$, let there be given a name f_i for each $r_i \in P$ such that $f_i \notin (V \cup T)$. Then, f_i is called the *name of rule* r_i. We then have the set

$$V_P = \{f_1, f_2, ..., f_n\}$$

such that $V_P \cap (V \cup T) = \emptyset$.

The name f_1 should be assigned to the/a production with the start symbol S in the head. If there is a rule of the form $S \rightarrow \beta_1 \mid \beta_2 \mid ... \mid \beta_n$ make $f_1, f_2, ..., f_n$ the first names in V_P for the productions $S \rightarrow \beta_1, S \rightarrow \beta_2, ..., S \rightarrow \beta_n$, respectively. Further occurrences of S in the body of productions can be distinguished (for example, by indexing S).

3.4.3. (Def.) A *derivation graph* for a string $w = w_1 w_2 ... w_k$ generated by a UG G with productions of the form $r_i = \alpha_i \rightarrow \beta_i = f_i$ is a labeled digraph $\vec{\mathfrak{G}}(w)$ with nodes labeled by $(V \cup T \cup V_P)$ such that for some $f_i \in V_P$ we can have a path π of the form

$$X$$
$$\downarrow$$
$$f_i$$
$$\downarrow$$
$$Y$$

where $X \subseteq \alpha_i$ and $Y \subseteq \beta_i$, $|X| = 1$ and $|Y| = 0, 1$, $X \in (V \cup T)^+$ and

$Y \in (V \cup T)^*$, and there is a (sub)graph $\vec{\mathfrak{G}}'(w_j) \subseteq \vec{\mathfrak{G}}(w)$ of the form

$$
\begin{array}{ccc}
X_1 & \cdots & X_n \\
\searrow \;\; \downarrow \;\; \swarrow & & \\
f_i & & \\
\swarrow \;\; \downarrow \;\; \searrow & & \\
Y_1 & \cdots & Y_m
\end{array}
$$

for $\alpha_i = X_1 X_2 ... X_n$ and $\beta_i = Y_1 Y_2 ... Y_m$.

Example 3.4.2. Let there be given the UG $G = (\{S, A, B\}, \{a, b\}, S, P)$ with the following production set:

$$
P = \left\{
\begin{array}{l}
S \to SAa \mid SaAB \mid B \\
AB \to aB \\
Aa \to aA \\
aA \to AB \\
B \to b \mid \epsilon
\end{array}
\right\}
$$

It is now required that we have productions with a single body, so that we have the following production set with assigned names:

$$
P = \left\{
\begin{array}{ll}
(f_{1.1}) & S \to SAa \\
(f_{1.2}) & S \to SaAB \\
(f_{1.3}) & S \to B \\
(f_2) & AB \to aB \\
(f_3) & Aa \to aA \\
(f_4) & aA \to AB \\
(f_5) & B \to b \\
(f_6) & B \to \epsilon
\end{array}
\right\}
$$

We have the corresponding set of names of rules $V_P = \{f_1, f_2, f_3, ..., f_6\}$ where there are three f_1-rules distinguished by further indexing. The derivation graph of the string bab generated by G in the derivation

$$
S \underset{f_{1.1}}{\Longrightarrow} SAa \underset{f_{1.3}}{\Longrightarrow} BAa \underset{f_5}{\Longrightarrow} bAa \underset{f_3}{\Longrightarrow} baA \underset{f_4}{\Longrightarrow} bAB \underset{f_2}{\Longrightarrow} baB \underset{f_5}{\Longrightarrow} bab
$$

is shown in Figure 3.4.1.

Recall from the discussion of CFLs that a few questions with respect to these languages are undecidable. In fact, the problem of undecidability is even more acute for the RELs: The questions of equivalence, inclusion,

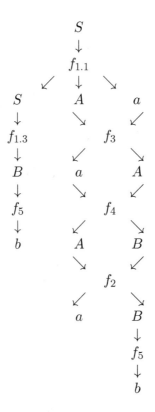

Figure 3.4.1.: A derivation graph of the string *bab* generated by a UG.

membership, finiteness, and emptiness are all *undecidable*. Furthermore, the class of RELs is not closed under complementation. Nevertheless, we have the following result:

Theorem 3.4.1. *Let L_1 and L_2 be RELs. Then, $L_1 \cup L_2$ and $L_1 \cap L_2$ are also RELs.*

Proof: The proof requires the notion of a Turing machine, so it is left as an exercise in Section 4.3.

Exercises

Exercise 3.4.1. Despite being called unrestricted, UGs do not allow any production of the form $\epsilon \to \alpha$, for $\alpha \in (V \cup T)^*$. Explain why.

Exercise 3.4.2. Show that for each UG $G = (V, T, S, P)$ there is a UG $G' = (V', T', S, P')$ all of whose productions are either of the form

$$\alpha \to \beta$$

with $\alpha, \beta \in (V_1 \cup T_1)^+$ and $|\alpha| \leq |\beta|$, or of the form

$$A \to \epsilon$$

for $A \in V'$.

Exercise 3.4.3. Find a UG generating the following RELs:

1. $L = \{a^{2^n} | n \in \mathbb{N}\}$.

2. $L = \{xxx | x \in \{a, b\}^*\}$.

3. $L = \{a^n b^n a^n b^n | n \geq 0\}$.

Exercise 3.4.4. Find the REL generated by the following productions of the UG $G = (\{S, A, B, C\}, \{a, b, c\}, S, P)$:

$$P = \begin{cases} S \to ABCS \mid ABC \\ AB \to BA \\ BC \to CB \\ CA \to AC \\ AC \to CA \\ BA \to AB \\ CB \to BC \\ A \to a \\ B \to b \\ C \to c \end{cases}$$

Exercise 3.4.5. Find the REL generated by the following productions of the UG $G = (\{S, S_1, A\}, \{a, b\}, S, P)$:

$$P = \left\{ \begin{array}{c} S \rightarrow S_1 A \\ S_1 \rightarrow aS_1 b \\ aS_1 b \rightarrow aa \\ bA \rightarrow bbbA \\ A \rightarrow \epsilon \end{array} \right\}$$

Exercise 3.4.6. Find the REL generated by the following productions of the UG $G = (\{S, L, R, 2\}, \{a\}, S, P)$:

$$P = \left\{ \begin{array}{c} S \rightarrow LaR \\ L \rightarrow L2 \,|\, \epsilon \\ 2a \rightarrow aa2 \\ 2R \rightarrow R \\ R \rightarrow \epsilon \end{array} \right\}$$

Exercise 3.4.7. From each grammar of Exercises 3.4.3-6, choose some terminal string $w \neq \epsilon$ and draw its corresponding derivation graph.

Exercise 3.4.8. Find all the strings generated by the grammar of Example 3.4.2. Draw the corresponding derivation graphs.

Exercise 3.4.9. Rewrite Definitions 3.4.2-3 as an algorithm (call it "Derivation-graph Algorithm").

Exercise 3.4.10. Show that the language $L = \{a^n b^n c^n | n > 0\}$ is a CSL. (Hint: Change the consequent $LABC$ in production (i); cf. Example 3.4.1.)

3.5. The Chomsky hierarchy (I)

Recall the general definition of a formal grammar (Def. 3.1.11). Note that the definition of a UG (Def. 3.4.1) is the closest one to this general definition of a formal grammar. Actually, they are one and the same definition, often assembled under the label "phrase-structure grammar."[15] In effect, this type-0 grammar provides the "framework" into which the other studied grammars must fit. N. Chomsky, the designer of this 0-3 typology, established the following strict-containment hierarchy known as the *Chomsky hierarchy* (Chomsky, 1956; 1959), in which we abbreviate "regular language" as "RGL" and indicate between brackets the type of grammar that generates each language class:

---

[15]Which, of course, is often confusing, reason why we avoid this label.

$$\mathscr{RGL}\,(3) \subset \mathscr{CFL}\,(2) \subset \mathscr{CSL}\,(1) \subset \mathscr{REL}\,(0)$$

The following theorem states this in a different formulation.

Theorem 3.5.1. *There are regular languages that are not CFLs, and there are CFLs that are not CSLs, and CSLs that are not RELs.*

Proof: This is a strict containment relation, which means that there is at least one language generated by a grammar of type j that is not generated by a grammar of type i, where $j < i$, i covers j, and $i, j = 0, 1, 2, 3$. In effect:

- The language $L = \{a^n b^n | n > 0\}$ is not regular (cf. Example 3.2.9), but it is a CFL (cf. Example 3.3.1).

- The language $L = \{a^n b^n c^n | n > 0\}$ is not a CFL (cf. Example 3.3.10), but it is a CSL (cf. Exercise 3.4.10).

- Because RELs are generated by UGs, there are CSLs that are not RELs, as the former are generated by grammars with restrictions, namely by CSGs.

QED

We now analyze this hierarchy from the viewpoint of its implications. Firstly, this is obviously a hierarchy from the most restricted to the less restricted–or most general–grammars, and it is thus a hierarchy with practical implications: If, given a language L, there is an algorithm that decides that L is a regular language, then we need search no more, because this language class is included in all the other classes of formal languages. In other words, the more restricted a grammar is, the simpler a program can be written to decide on the type of language. We summarize the main features of this hierarchy in Table 3.1.1 and then provide an algorithm (Algorithm 3.5) for deciding on the language class.[16] (We leave the algorithm for deciding on the type of grammar as an exercise.)

The importance of this hierarchy will become clearer in the next Chapter, as it is the case that each language class is associated to a mathematical object–*an abstract machine*–that is in fact a model of computation implementing a specific (decision) program. This has, again, practical importance: The more restricted a language is, the simpler it is to devise a (decision) program for it. Indeed, programming a Turing machine, the

---

[16]For this particular algorithm, a pseudo-code that simulates a frequent structure in programming languages is quite appropriate.

Type	Name of G	$\alpha \rightarrow \beta$
0	Unrestricted (UG)	$\alpha \in (V \cup T)^+, \lvert V(\alpha) \rvert \geq 1$ $\beta \in (V \cup T)^*$
1	Context-sensitive (CSG)	$\alpha, \beta \in (V \cup T)^+, \lvert \beta \rvert \geq \lvert \alpha \rvert$ $\alpha = \gamma A \delta$ $\beta = \gamma X \delta$ $\gamma, \delta \in (V \cup T)^*$ $X \in (V \cup T)^+$
2	Context-free (CFG)	$\alpha \in V, \lvert \alpha \rvert = 1$ $\beta \in (V \cup T)^*$
3	Regular	$\alpha \in V, \lvert \alpha \rvert = 1$ $\beta = Av$ or vA $A \in V^*, v \in T^*$

Table 3.5.1.: The Chomsky hierarchy.

Algorithm 3.5 Language class by grammar type

Input: A grammar $G = (V, T, S, P)$
Output: Language class $\mathscr{C}$ such that $G \in \mathscr{C}$

```
{
if G is regular then
    return "regular"
} else {
    if G is context-free then
        return "context-free"
    } else {
        if G is context-sensitive then
            return "context-sensitive"
        } else {
            if G is unrestricted then
                return "recursively enumerable"
}
```

---

abstract machine associated to RELs, can be a daunting task for even very elementary functions (see Example 4.3.3); the reader will soon realize that, compared to it, programming a finite-state automaton for a regular language is hardly as complex a task.

But the importance of this hierarchy lies also precisely in what is left out from it. That is to say that there are (infinitely many) languages that are not RELs. This and further consequences of this hierarchy from the computational perspective are discussed below in Chapter 5.

Exercises

Exercise 3.5.1. Design an algorithm for, given a language L, determining the type of grammar G that generates $L = L(G)$ according to the Chomsky hierarchy.

Exercise 3.5.2. Identify the type (0-3) of the grammars in Exercise 3.1.6.

Exercise 3.5.3. Comment on the trade-off between expressiveness and simplicity in the Chomsky hierarchy.

4. Models of computation

With a formal language under consideration, we often need to know what kind of a language it is–or is not. The most efficient way to solve this problem is by describing the language by means of a mathematical abstraction of a machine. This machine, in turn, has associated to it a computer model. The simplest such machines are merely recognizers or acceptors in the sense that, given an input string w, their computation is limited to a "Yes/No" answer or behavior.[1] More complex models can actually produce some output, and the most complex machines–the Turing machines–can both decide languages and compute functions. Memory is associated to this growing complexity in the following way: From basically no memory for the simplest language recognizers, memory increases until it reaches virtually infinity in the Turing machine.

In this Chapter, we provide an extensive introduction to the theory of models of computation, also (more) often known as *automata theory*. Readers seeking a more comprehensive treatment of automata theory can benefit from Sakarovitch (2009). We associate the different models to the corresponding grammars and languages according to the Chomsky hierarchy, and do so in a very general way, without regard to the many practical applications. Khoussainov & Nerode (2001) and Anderson (2006) discuss automata theory from the viewpoint of general applications. For specific applications, see, e.g., Reghizzi, Breveglieri, & Morzenti (2019) and Cooper & Torcson (2012) for the field of compilation, and Gopalakrishnan (2006) for logic-based computation engineering.

One of the objectives of this Chapter is the construction of machines

---

[1] String *acceptance* and *recognition* are basically synonyms, as is evident from items 1 and 3 of Definition 4.1.5 below, and we shall use both terms, as well as their respective antonyms *rejection* and *non-recognition*, indifferently. However, we prefer to say that a machine *recognizes* (rather than *accepts*) a given language L when there is the emphasis that it both accepts strings $w \in L$ and rejects those strings $w \notin L$ (cf. Def. 4.1.1.1; see also Example 4.1.2). But this is a distinction too subtle to be strictly followed, so that we shall see an arbitrary $L(M)$ as the language L accepted, or recognized, by machine M, and M itself shall be indifferently called an *acceptor* or a *recognizer*. We generalize this usage to all the computation models for all the language classes. We remark that in the case of Turing machines (Section 4.3) there are also language *deciders*.

such as finite automata and Turing machines. For this end, the software JFLAP, freely available at www.jflap.org, might prove very useful.

4.1. Finite-state machines

Finite-state machines are the simplest machines, or models of computation, associated with a class of formal languages, namely the simplest (non-trivial) formal languages, i.e. the regular languages. Although they are often indifferently called *finite automata* (*automaton* in the singular), fine-graining is sometimes necessary. For our ends, the following distinctions suffice:

4.1.1. (Def.) A *finite-state machine* is a finite recognizer or a finite transducer. Let L be an arbitrary regular language. Then, given an input string $w \in L$:

1. A *finite-state recognizer* either accepts or rejects w.

2. A *finite-state transducer* outputs a string $w' \in L$.

In the context of formal languages, the main difference between recognizers and transducers is that whereas the former have a direct relation to regular expressions, i.e. they recognize or accept regular expressions, the latter establish a relation between strings: They "translate" a regular string w into another regular string w'. Our interest in output strings–rather than on single output symbols–allows us to see both Mealy and Moore machines as finite-state transducers. This notwithstanding, and because there are variations in the literature,[2] one can simply speak of *finite automata with output* when referring to Mealy and Moore machines.

It is important to remark that all these machines owe their coinage to the fact that, at any given time, they can be in exactly one of a finite number of possible states. This holds for pushdown automata, as well as for Turing machines generally, but current usage is such that these are not usually spoken of as finite-state machines. We prefer the label "finite automata" for referring to finite-state recognizers or acceptors, not only because it is common practice, but also to suggest the continuity with pushdown automata and with linear-bounded automata, to be studied

---

[2]Moore machines are often considered *classifiers*, as they give us an output associated to a current state.

in later Sections. We study finite automata in Section 4.1.1 and finite transducers in Section 4.1.2.[3]

As elsewhere in this book, the Chomsky hierarchy guides our elaboration on these machines. But finite-state machines have many and diverse applications. For instance, readers interested in these machines in the field of switching theory may benefit from Kohavi & Jha (2010). Further applications can be found in the literature cited above in the introductory remarks to this Chapter.

4.1.1. Finite automata

As we shall see below, a finite automaton (abbr.: FA)[4] may be either deterministic or non-deterministic; we distinguish them by the abbreviations "DFA" and "NDFA," respectively. We shall use the abbreviation "FA" whenever a specification is not essential, which is generally the case until we reach Section 4.1.1.4.

Kleene's theorem (see below) states that the class of languages recognized by FAs is exactly the class $\mathscr{RGL}$. In this Section, we go all the way from the definition of a FA to an algorithm to detect non-regular languages; in between, we see how to obtain a regular expression from the state diagram of a FA and how to minimize a FA, among other topics.

4.1.1.1. Basic aspects of finite automata

4.1.2. (Def.) A *finite-state recognizer*, or *finite automaton*, is a 5-tuple

$$M = (Q, \Sigma, q_0, A, \delta)$$

where $Q = \{q_0, q_1, ..., q_n\}$ is a finite set of *states*, Σ is a finite *input alphabet*, $q_0 \in Q$ is the *initial state*, $A \subseteq Q$ is the set of *accepting states*, and $\delta : (Q \times \Sigma) \longrightarrow Q$ is the *transition function*.

4.1.3. (Def.) The *computer model* for a FA (see Fig. 4.1.1) consists of (i) an input tape, (ii) a read-only head, (iii) a control box programmed by the transition function δ: Whenever a read-only head examines a letter $\sigma \in \Sigma$ on a cell of the input tape in state $q \in Q$, the computer switches into state $\delta(q, \sigma)$ and moves on to read the letter on the next cell (so this is single-direction tape motion).

---

[3]We henceforth more often than not abbreviate "finite-state automaton" as "finite automaton" and "finite-state transducer" as "finite transducer."

[4]We consider "FA" as an acronym, and indicate its plural as "FAs."

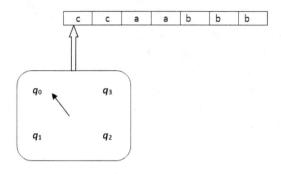

Figure 4.1.1.: Computer model of a FA.

4.1.4. (Def.) A *configuration* for a FA M is a pair $C = (q, w)$ such that $q \in Q$ and $w \in \Sigma^*$ denoting that M is at state q with the read-only head positioned at a letter of the string w.[5]

1. A *computation* for a FA M is a sequence $C_0, C_1, ..., C_n$ of configurations, $C_0 = (q_0, w_0)$ and $C_n = (q_n, w_n)$, such that $C_{i-1} \vdash_M C_i$, read "configuration C_{i-1} *yields* configuration C_i *in one step*," for $i = 1, ..., n$.

2. A configuration (q, w) *yields* a configuration (q', w'), denoted by $(q, w) \vdash_M^* (q', w')$, where $\vdash_M^*$ denotes the reflexive and transitive closure of the step relation $\vdash_M$, if there is a computation of (q', w') from (q, w) in zero or more consecutive steps.[6]

4.1.5. (Def.) Let there be given a string $w \in \Sigma^*$ and a FA $M = (Q, \Sigma, q_0, A, \delta)$. Then:

1. w is *accepted* by M if, starting at state q_0 with the first letter, its transition sequence terminates in a state $q_f \in A$ such that

$$q_0, w \vdash_M^* q_f, \epsilon.$$

Otherwise, w is *rejected*.

2. The *language accepted* by M, denoted by $L(M)$, is the set of all strings accepted by M. Formally,

$$L(M) = \{w \in \Sigma^* | w \text{ is accepted by } M\}.$$

---

[5]Some texts use the expression "instantaneous description" instead of "configuration."
[6]Cf. Def. 3.1.11.3 for the notions of reflexive and transitive closure. See also Def. 2.1.15.

3. w is *recognized* by M if the final state $q_f \in Q$ is some accepting state $q_i \in A$, $0 \leq i \leq k$.

Another way to define a FA $M = (Q, \Sigma, q_0, A, \delta)$ is by means of its state diagram $D = \vec{\mathfrak{D}}(M)$.

4.1.6. (Def.) The *state diagram* $D = \vec{\mathfrak{D}}(M)$ of a FA M is a labeled digraph with the following characteristics:

1. The vertices of $\vec{\mathfrak{D}}(M)$ are the states $q_i \in Q$, $i = 0, 1, ..., n$.

2. For each state $q_i \in Q$ and each letter $\sigma \in \Sigma$ there is an arc from vertex q_i to vertex $\delta(q_i, \sigma)$ labeled with the letter σ. If $\delta(q_i, \sigma) = q_j$, $j = 0, 1, ..., n$, then if M is in state q_i and the current input letter is σ, M will move to state q_j, $i \gtreqless j$.

3. The starting state q_0 is indicated by an entering arrow and an accepting state $q_j \in A$ is represented as two concentric circles.

Example 4.1.1. Figure 4.1.2 shows the FAs accepting the regular expressions of Examples 3.2.1-2. Note that the first FA accepts the language $L(M) = \{\epsilon\}$; in fact, a FA whose initial state coincides with an accepting state (i.e. $q_0 \in A$) accepts the empty string. Differently, a FA accepting the language $L(M) = \emptyset$ has solely the initial state q_0 (and perhaps a final state q_f, but there is no arc connecting both states).

Example 4.1.2. Let $M = (\{q_0, q_1, q_2\}, \{0, 1\}, q_0, \{q_0, q_1\}, \delta)$ be a FA with the transition function as specified in the following transitions:

$q_i \in Q$	Input $\sigma \in \{0, 1\}$	$\delta(q_i, \sigma) = q_j \in Q$
q_0	0	q_0
q_0	1	q_1
q_1	0	q_0
q_1	1	q_2
q_2	0	q_2
q_2	1	q_2

This gives the following *transition table*, where we indicate the initial state with $\rightarrow$ and an accepting state with $*$:

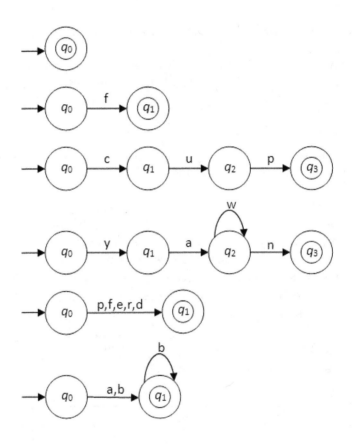

Figure 4.1.2.: State diagrams of FAs.

	$\delta\,(q,0)$	$\delta\,(q,1)$
$\rightarrow *q_0$	q_0	q_1
$*q_1$	q_0	q_2
q_2	q_2	q_2

This FA accepts all the strings that can be obtained from the regular expression $(0+10)^*\,(1+\epsilon)$ (cf. Example 4.1.6 below); for instance, the strings 0^51, 101010, and 0^{20}, including ϵ, are all accepted. The state diagram of this FA is shown in Figure 4.1.3. Note that if there are two successive 1 (e.g., 0^511), then the FA enters state q_2, which it cannot leave; thus q_2 is a non-accepting state–known as a *trapping state*, because the single arc leaving it is a loop.

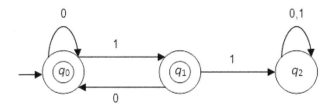

Figure 4.1.3.: A FA with two accepting states and one rejecting state.

Example 4.1.2 shows exactly what it is that FAs *recognizing a language* $L\,(M)$ do: They distinguish those strings w belonging to $L\,(M)$ from those that do not by accepting the former and rejecting all other strings. In other words, they provide a "Yes/No" (accept/reject) output. If a FA accepts no strings whatsoever, it still recognizes one language, to wit, the language $L\,(\emptyset) = \emptyset$.

Example 4.1.3. Figure 4.1.4 shows the state diagram for the FA accepting the language

$$L\,((c+ba)^*\,a\,(c+ab^*)) = \{c, ba\}^*\,\{ac, aab^*\}$$

(cf. Example 3.2.4). Note that this is the labeled digraph of Figure 3.2.1.vi, now with the states indicated in the vertices and given the following transition table:

	$\delta\,(q,a)$	$\delta\,(q,b)$	$\delta\,(q,c)$
$\rightarrow q_0$	q_2	q_1	q_0
q_1	q_0	–	–
q_2	q_4	–	q_3
$*q_3$	–	–	–
$*q_4$	–	q_4	–

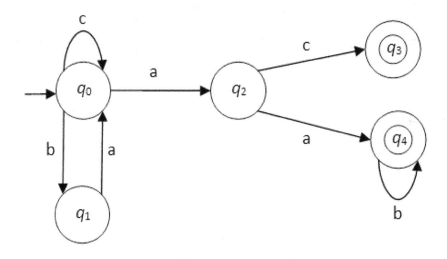

Figure 4.1.4.: A FA for the regular language $L = \{c, ba\}^* \{ac, aab^*\}$.

Example 4.1.4. In Figures 3.2.2-3, replace the vertices for ϵ with final states and make the vertices for S the initial states; then, $\vec{\mathfrak{G}}\,(G)$ and $\vec{\mathfrak{G}}'\,(G')$ are state diagrams for the corresponding FAs M and M'.

Besides the transition function, we often also require the extended transition function of a FA. This is particularly so for the definition of language acceptance by a FA.

4.1.7. (**Def.**) Let $M = (Q, \Sigma, q_0, A, \delta)$ be a FA. The transition function for a string of input symbols, denoted by $\hat{\delta}$, is called the *extended transition function*. Clearly,

$$\hat{\delta} : (Q \times \Sigma^*) \longrightarrow Q$$

which is defined as,

1. for every $q \in Q$ and ϵ,
$$\hat{\delta}(q, \epsilon) = q$$

2. for every $q \in Q$, every $y \in \Sigma^*$, and every $\sigma \in \Sigma$,
$$\hat{\delta}(q, y\sigma) = \delta\left(\hat{\delta}(q, y), \sigma\right).$$

In point 2 of the definition above, our interest falls obviously on $x = y\sigma$ for some $x \in \Sigma^*$, as we want to evaluate $\hat{\delta}(q, x)$. We can do this, because we know what state the FA is in after having started in q and having finished reading the letters in y; then, we apply the last transition, corresponding to σ. Similarly, we can evaluate the concatenation of two strings $x, y \in \Sigma^*$ by the equality

$$\hat{\delta}(q, xy) = \hat{\delta}\left(\hat{\delta}(q, x), y\right).$$

4.1.8. (Def.) We say that a FA $M = (Q, \Sigma, q_0, A, \delta)$ *accepts* a string $x \in \Sigma^*$ if $\hat{\delta}(q, x) \in A$; otherwise, M is said to *reject* x.

It should be obvious that we have $\hat{\delta}(q_0, w) = q_f$ for a string $w \in \Sigma^*$ if and only if we have a computation

$$q_0, w \vdash_M^* q_f, \epsilon$$

for some $q_f \in A$.

Example 4.1.5. Let it be given the input string *ccaabbb* and the FA M of Example 4.1.3. Then, the following is the accepting computation of this string by M, where we indicate the letter being read by underlining it and for convenience do not write a comma between the current state and the first letter of the string:

$$q_0\underline{c}caabbb \vdash q_0c\underline{c}aabbb \vdash q_0cc\underline{a}abbb \vdash q_2cca\underline{a}bbb$$

$$\vdash q_4ccaa\underline{b}bb \vdash q_4ccaab\underline{b}b \vdash q_4ccaabb\underline{b} \vdash q_4ccaabbb\underline{\epsilon}$$

Note that *ccaabbb*$\underline{\epsilon}$ denotes that the read-only head has actually fallen off the input tape. We thus have

$$q_0\underline{c}caabbb \vdash_M^7 q_4ccaabbb\underline{\epsilon}$$

and, correspondingly,

$$\hat{\delta}(q_0, ccaabbb) = q_4.$$

We can now equivalently reformulate the definition of language acceptance by a FA M (cf. Def. 4.1.5.2) by appealing to the extended transition function:

4.1.9. (Def.) The *language accepted* by a FA $M = (Q, \Sigma, q_0, A, \delta)$, denoted by $L(M)$, is the set of all strings accepted by M. Formally,

$$L(M) = \left\{ w \in \Sigma^* | \hat{\delta}(q_0, w) \in A \right\}.$$

This, in turn, allows for seeing two FAs as equivalent whenever they accept exactly the same language:

4.1.10. (Def.) FAs M_1 and M_2 are said to be *equivalent* if $L(M_1) = L(M_2)$.

4.1.1.2. Characteristic equations

Given a FA M, it is not always easy to identify the regular expressions accepted by M by merely looking at the state diagram of M. The characteristic equations of M provide a reliable method to obtain such expressions. We show how.

4.1.11. (Def.) Given a FA $M = (Q, \Sigma, q_0, A, \delta)$, to each state $q_i \in Q$ we associate the corresponding equation X_i with the form

$$(\eth) \qquad X_i = \sum_{j=1}^{n} \sigma_{ij} X_j + \alpha$$

for $\sigma_{ij} X_j$ the i-th symbol σ_j such that there is in M the transition $\delta(q_i, \sigma) = q_j$ and

$$\alpha = \begin{cases} \epsilon & \text{if } q_i \in A \\ \emptyset & \text{otherwise} \end{cases}.$$

Equation X_i is the *characteristic equation* of state $q_i \in Q$.

4.1.12. (Def.) Given a FA $M = (|Q| = n, \Sigma, q_0, A, \delta)$, we can obtain the regular expression accepted by M by solving the *system of characteristic equations*

$$L(M) = L(r) = \begin{cases} X_0 \\ X_1 \\ \vdots \\ X_n \end{cases}$$

where each X_i, $0 \le i \le n$, has the form $\eth$.

The properties of the operations with regular expressions in Proposition 3.2.4 are now to be applied also to help us to solve systems of characteristic equations for a given FA. It actually is the case that it might not be necessary to solve the whole system, as we are interested only in finding X_0. When solving the system, Arden's lemma must be taken into consideration, just as in the case of the linear equations for regular languages in Section 3.2 above. For convenience, we reformulate it with regular expressions in mind.

Theorem 4.1.1. *If $X = \alpha X + \beta$ for some regular expressions $\alpha \neq \epsilon, \beta$ and a variable X, then $X = \alpha^* \beta$.*

Proof: Left as an exercise.

Example 4.1.6. Let there be given the FA in Figure 4.1.3. The corresponding system of characteristic equations is:

$$
\begin{cases}
X_0 = & (0X_0 + \epsilon) + (1X_1 + \epsilon) \\
X_1 = & (0X_0 + \epsilon) + (1X_2 + \emptyset) \\
X_2 = & 0X_2 + 1X_2 + \emptyset
\end{cases}
$$

We begin by solving for X_2, for which we require only Arden's lemma and the property of the annihilating element for concatenation:

$$X_2 = (0 + 1) X_2 + \emptyset = (0 + 1)^* \emptyset = \emptyset$$

We next solve for X_1:

$$X_1 = (0X_0 + \epsilon) + (1X_2 + \emptyset) = (0X_0 + \epsilon) + 1X_2 = 0X_0 + \epsilon + 1(\emptyset) = 0X_0 + \epsilon$$

The solution of X_0 is now straightforward:

$$X_0 = (0X_0 + \epsilon) + (1X_1 + \epsilon) =$$

$$= (0X_0 + \epsilon) + [1(0X_0 + \epsilon) + \epsilon] =$$

$$= (0X_0 + \epsilon) + [10X_0 + 1(\epsilon) + \epsilon] =$$

$$= (0 + 10) X_0 + (1 + \epsilon) + \epsilon =$$

$$= (0 + 10)^* (1 + \epsilon)$$

So, this FA recognizes the regular expression $(0 + 10)^* (1 + \epsilon)$ and it thus accepts the language $L((0 + 10)^* (1 + \epsilon)) = \{0, 10\}^* \{1, \epsilon\}$. See Example 4.1.2 for some strings in this language. In this particular FA, the alternative acceptance of the empty string is explained by the fact that the initial state is also an accepting state.

4.1.1.3. The pumping lemma for regular languages (II)

As language recognizers, FAs are useful for proving non-regular languages, as well as for distinguishing finite from infinite languages. Recall the pumping lemma for regular languages (Theorem 3.2.2); the proof of this lemma is constructed precisely by appealing to FAs. In effect, we can complete Theorem 3.2.2 in the following way:

Theorem 4.1.2. *(Pumping lemma for regular languages II) Let $L = L(M)$, where M is a FA with m states. Let $z \in L$, $|z| \leq m$. Then we can write $z = uvw$ such that z satisfies the three conditions of Theorem 3.2.2.*

Proof: If a language L is regular, then there is a FA M with a definite number of states that accepts L. Let us suppose that M has m states. Consider a string with m or more letters $a_1a_2...a_n$, $n \geq m$ and let $\delta(q_0, a_1a_2...a_i) = q_i$ for $i = 1, 2, ..., n$. This includes the initial state q_0, but since there are only m states, it is not possible for the $m + 1$ states $q_0, q_1, ..., q_m$ to be distinct. By appealing to the pigeonhole principle, we conclude that M must be in at least one state more than once, i.e. there must be two integers j and k, $0 \leq j < k \leq m$ such that $q_j = q_k$. In other words, there must be a loop. We have $|a_{j+1}...a_k| \geq 1$, because $j < k$, and because $k \leq m$ we also have $|a_{j+1}...a_k| \leq m$. If $a_1a_2...a_n$ is in $L(M)$, then $a_1a_2...a_ja_{k+1}a_{k+2}...a_n$ is also in $L(M)$, as there is a path from q_0 to q_n that goes directly through q_j without doing the loop $a_{j+1}...a_k$. But we could do this loop as many times as we want to, so that $a_1a_2...a_j(a_{j+1}...a_k)^i a_{k+1}a_{k+2}...a_n$ is also in $L(M)$ for $i = 0, 1, ...$ Simplifying by the equalities $u = a_1a_2...a_j$, $v = a_{j+1}...a_k$, and $w = a_{k+1}a_{k+2}...a_n$, and by applying the extended transition function, we have

$$\hat{\delta}(q_0, u) = q_j$$

$$\hat{\delta}(q_j, v) = q_j$$

$$\hat{\delta}(q_j, w) = q_n \in A$$

so that we have in fact

$$\hat{\delta}(q_0, uvw) = \hat{\delta}(q_0, uv^iw) = q_n \in A$$

and $z = uv^iw \in L(M)$ for $i \geq 0$. Figure 4.1.5 illustrates the FA M that accepts the regular expression $z = uv^{(i)}w$. **QED**

The acceptance or rejection of a language L by a FA is a *decision problem* (cf. Chapter 5). Two further decision problems that can be

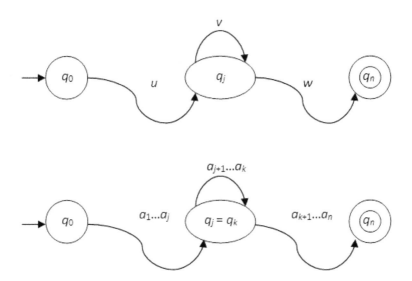

Figure 4.1.5.: A finite automaton M for the pumping lemma.

answered by a FA are whether L is non-empty and whether L is in-finite. The following two theorems (the proofs are left as exercises; hint: the pumping lemma features in the proofs) actually provide al-gorithms–albeit inefficient ones–to answer these questions.

Theorem 4.1.3. *Let M be a FA with m states. If $L(M) \neq \emptyset$, there is a string $z \in L(M)$ such that $|z| < m$.*

Theorem 4.1.4. *Let M be a FA with m states. Then $L(M)$ is infinite if and only if $L(M)$ contains a string z such that $m \leq |z| < 2m$.*

4.1.1.4. Deterministic and non-deterministic FAs

From now on, we must often specify whether a FA is deterministic or non-deterministic. *All* the examples given above are deterministic FAs. A deterministic FA (abbr.: DFA) is easily defined by contrast with the following definition:

   4.1.13. (Def.) A *non-deterministic FA* (abbr.: NDFA) is a 5-tuple

$$M = (Q, \Sigma, q_0, A, \delta)$$

where δ is the transition function $(Q \times \Sigma) \longrightarrow 2^Q$, or $(Q \times (\Sigma \cup \{\epsilon\})) \longrightarrow 2^Q$ if it includes ϵ-*transitions*, i.e. transitions $\delta(q, \epsilon) = p$.[7]

---

[7] Alternatively, one can, instead of δ, consider a *transition relation* Δ, i.e. a finite subset of $Q \times \Sigma^* \times 2^Q$.

The computer model for a NDFA is like that of a DFA, but whenever it reads a string w on the input file while on state q, it switches into *any* state of $\hat{\delta}(q, w)$ and moves on to read the next letter. The main features of a NDFA is that it allows zero, one, or more transitions from a state on a single input letter, as well as a transition on no input at all. These account for the non-determinism of these automata.

Example 4.1.7. Figure 4.1.6 shows a NDFA that accepts the language $L = \{001\}^* \{0, 010\}^*$ by allowing an ϵ-transition. Additionally, it allows the alternative transitions $\delta(q_3, 0) = q_3$ and $\delta(q_3, 0) = q_4$ on the input symbol 0 when in state q_3, so that we have $\delta(q_3, 0) = \{q_3, q_4\}$.

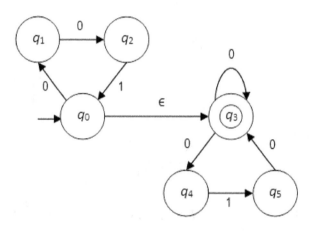

Figure 4.1.6.: A NDFA for the language $L = \{001\}^* \{0, 010\}^*$.

Importantly, ϵ-transitions can be removed from a NDFA M that accepts the language $L(M)$ without for than entailing the rejection of $L(M)$. That is, for every NDFA M with ϵ-transitions there is an equivalent NDFA M' without ϵ-transitions.

Theorem 4.1.5. *If the language L is accepted by a NDFA with ϵ-transitions M, then it is accepted by a NDFA without ϵ-transitions M'.*

Proof: (Sketch) Let $M = (Q, \Sigma, q_0, A, \delta)$ and $M' = (Q, \Sigma, q_0, A', \delta')$ where for every $q \in Q$ and every $\sigma \in \Sigma$ we have $\delta'(q, \epsilon) = \emptyset$ and $\delta'(q, \sigma) = \hat{\delta}(q, \sigma)$. Let now a string $x \in \Sigma^*$ be accepted by M if

$\left(\hat{\delta}\left(q_0, x\right) \cap A \right) \neq \emptyset.$ Furthermore, define

$$A' = \begin{cases} A \cup \{q_0\} & \text{if } \epsilon \in L \\ A & \text{otherwise} \end{cases}.$$

This definition, according to which $A \subseteq A'$, assures us that M' accepts ϵ in case $\epsilon \in L$ but $q_0 \notin A$, and the definition above of $\hat{\delta}$ (cf. Def. 4.1.14) means that, for every $q \in Q$ and every $x \in \Sigma^*$, $\hat{\delta}\left(q, x\right)$ is the set of states reachable by M by using the letters $\sigma \in x$ *and* ϵ-transitions. In turn, our definition above of δ' is intended to assure us that $\hat{\delta}'\left(q, x\right) = \hat{\delta}\left(q, x\right)$(why?). So, first of all we have to prove by induction on x that this indeed holds for every q and every x for which $|x| \geq 1$. Begin with the obvious step for $x = a \in \Sigma$. Next, let σ be an arbitrary element of Σ and let $\hat{\delta}'\left(q, y\right) = \hat{\delta}\left(q, y\right)$ for every q and some y for which $|y| \geq 1$. From

$$\hat{\delta}'\left(q, y\sigma\right) = \bigcup \left\{ \delta'\left(p, \sigma\right) | p \in \hat{\delta}'\left(q, y\right) \right\}$$

obtain (how?)

$$\hat{\delta}'\left(q, y\sigma\right) = \bigcup \left\{ \hat{\delta}\left(p, \sigma\right) | p \in \hat{\delta}\left(q, y\right) \right\}$$

which is a special case of the transition

$$\hat{\delta}\left(q, yz\right) = \bigcup \left\{ \hat{\delta}\left(p, z\right) | p \in \hat{\delta}\left(q, y\right) \right\}.$$

Now all that is left to do is to verify that $L = L\left(M\right) = L\left(M'\right)$, which is done by checking for ϵ and $|x| \geq 1$ with respect to $L\left(M\right)$ and $L\left(M'\right)$. (Hint: Check when $A = A'$ and $A \subseteq A'$.) **QED**

Another way to prove Theorem 4.1.5 (left as an exercise) would be by applying the notion of ϵ-closure.

4.1.14. **(Def.)** Given a NDFA, a state q is said to be in the ϵ-*closure* of $P \subseteq Q$, denoted by $\epsilon\left(P\right)$, if it is an element of P or it can be reached from an element thereof by means of applying $n \geq 1$ ϵ-transitions. The extended transition function $\hat{\delta} : \left(Q \times \Sigma^*\right) \longrightarrow 2^Q$ is defined in the following way:

1. For every $q \in Q$,

$$\hat{\delta}\left(q, \epsilon\right) = \epsilon\left(\{q\}\right).$$

2. For every $q \in Q$, every $y \in \Sigma^*$, and every $\sigma \in \Sigma$,

$$\hat{\delta}(q, y\sigma) = \epsilon\left(\bigcup\left\{\delta(p, \sigma) \,|\, p \in \hat{\delta}(q, y)\right\}\right).$$

Example 4.1.8. We apply the notion of ϵ-closure directly in an example. First of all, it is convenient to make, for $P \subseteq Q$:

$$\epsilon(P) = \bigcup_{q \in P} \epsilon(\{q\})$$

Define the extended transition function as in Definition 4.1.14 and extend both δ and $\hat{\delta}$ to sets of states R as, for $w \in \Sigma^*$ and $\sigma \in \Sigma$:

$$\delta(R, \sigma) = \bigcup_{q \in R} \delta(q, \sigma)$$

$$\hat{\delta}(R, w) = \bigcup_{q \in R} \hat{\delta}(q, w)$$

Let $M = (\{q_0, q_1, q_2\}, \{a, b, c\}, q_0, \{q_2\}, \delta)$ be a NDFA with the following transition table for $\delta(q, \sigma)$ and $\hat{\delta}(q, \sigma)$:

q	$\delta(q, a)$	$\delta(q, b)$	$\delta(q, c)$	$\delta(q, \epsilon)$	$\hat{\delta}(q, a)$	$\hat{\delta}(q, b)$	$\hat{\delta}(q, c)$
q_0	$\{q_0\}$	$\emptyset$	$\emptyset$	$\{q_1\}$	$\{q_0, q_1, q_2\}$	$\{q_1, q_2\}$	$\{q_2\}$
q_1	$\emptyset$	$\{q_1\}$	$\emptyset$	$\{q_2\}$	$\emptyset$	$\{q_1, q_2\}$	$\{q_2\}$
q_2	$\emptyset$	$\emptyset$	$\{q_2\}$	$\emptyset$	$\emptyset$	$\emptyset$	$\{q_2\}$

We show how we obtained $\hat{\delta}(q, \sigma)$. First, we computed:

$$\hat{\delta}(q_0, \epsilon) = \epsilon(\{q_0\}) = \{q_0, q_1, q_2\}$$

With this result, we next computed:

$$
\begin{aligned}
\hat{\delta}(q_0, a) &= \epsilon\left(\delta\left(\hat{\delta}(q_0, \epsilon)\right), a\right) \\
&= \epsilon(\delta(\{q_0, q_1, q_2\}, a)) \\
&= \epsilon(\delta(q_0, a) \cup \delta(q_1, a) \cup \delta(q_2, a)) \\
&= \epsilon(\{q_0\} \cup \emptyset \cup \emptyset) \\
&= \epsilon(\{q_0\}) = \{q_0, q_1, q_2\}
\end{aligned}
$$

and

$$
\begin{aligned}
\hat{\delta}\left(q_0, b\right) &= \epsilon\left(\delta\left(\hat{\delta}\left(q_0, \epsilon\right)\right), b\right) \\
&= \epsilon\left(\delta\left(\{q_0, q_1, q_2\}, b\right)\right) \\
&= \epsilon\left(\delta\left(q_0, b\right) \cup \delta\left(q_1, b\right) \cup \delta\left(q_2, b\right)\right) \\
&= \epsilon\left(\emptyset \cup \{q_1\} \cup \emptyset\right) \\
&= \epsilon\left(\{q_1\}\right) = \{q_1, q_2\}
\end{aligned}
$$

and so on for all the remaining states and letters. Note that $\hat{\delta}(q, \sigma)$ is not necessarily equal to $\delta(q, \sigma)$, because the latter includes only the states reachable from q by arcs labeled σ, whereas the former includes all states reachable from q by arcs labeled σ (*including arcs labeled ϵ*). From the complete transition tables above it is an easy matter to build the state diagrams of these equivalent NDFAs with and without ϵ-transitions (Fig.s 4.1.7.1 and 4.1.7.2, respectively).

Recall what was said above (remark to Def. 4.1.13) about the main features of a NDFA. A DFA is a special case of a NDFA in which for each state there is a single transition on each letter. But at the practical level they are very different: Whereas we can transform the transition table or the state diagram of a DFA into a computer program, we cannot do this (as readily) for a NDFA. Also, a FA implementing a scanner in a compiler must be a DFA. Thus, we need to be able to construct a DFA out of a NDFA. The following theorem provides the mathematical foundation for this *simulation*.

Theorem 4.1.6. *Any language that can be accepted by a NDFA M can be accepted by a DFA M'. Thus, for every NDFA M we can construct an equivalent DFA M'.*

Proof: (Sketch) A DFA $M' = \left(Q', \Sigma, q_0', A', \delta'\right)$ simulates a NDFA $M = (Q, \Sigma, q_0, A, \delta)$ by means of a correspondence between the states of the DFA and *sets of states* of the NDFA, i.e. by making $Q' = 2^Q$. More specifically, for every subset $R \in Q'$ and $\sigma \in \Sigma$, setting

$$
\delta'\left([R], \sigma\right) = \bigcup\{\delta(p, \sigma) \,|\, p \in R\}
$$

gives us

$$
\delta'\left([q_1, q_2, ..., q_i], \sigma\right) = [p_1, p_2, ..., p_j]
$$

where $[q_1, q_2, ..., q_i]$ is a single state, from

$$
\delta(R, \sigma) = \delta\left(\{q_1, q_2, ..., q_i\}, \sigma\right) = \{p_1, p_2, ..., p_j\}.
$$

Set now

$$
q_0' = [q_0]
$$

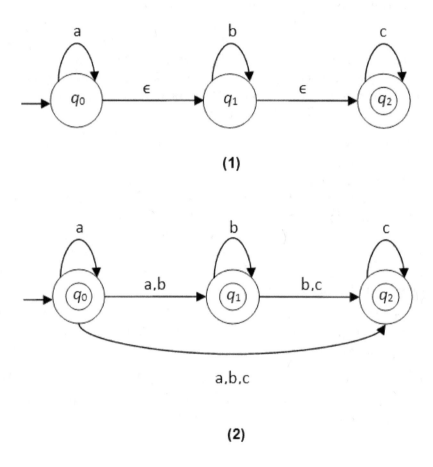

Figure 4.1.7.: Equivalent NDFAs with and without ϵ-transitions.

Algorithm 4.1 Subset construction

Input: NDFA $M = (Q, \Sigma, q_0, A, \delta)$

Output: DFA $M' = \left(Q', \Sigma, q_0', A', \delta'\right)$ such that $L(M) = L(M')$

---

1. Set $Q' = 2^Q$

2. For each $\sigma \in \Sigma$ and each subset $R \in 2^Q$ obtain $\delta'([R], \sigma) =$
   $\bigcup \{\delta(p, \sigma) \,|\, p \in R\}$ such that $\delta' \left(\underbrace{[q_1, q_2, ..., q_i]}_{\text{1 state}}, \sigma \right) = [p_1, p_2, ..., p_j]$

3. Set $q_0' = [q_0]$

4. Make $A' = \{S \in Q' \,|\, [S] \supseteq q_i \in A\}$

---

and for every $x \in \Sigma^*$

$$\hat{\delta'}\left(q_0', x\right) = \hat{\delta}(q_0, x)$$

so that we have

$$\hat{\delta'}\left(q_0', x\right) = [q_1, q_2, ..., q_i]$$

if and only if

$$\hat{\delta}(q_0, x) = \{q_1, q_2, ..., q_i\}.$$

Make the basis $|x| = 0$, and the proof follows by induction on the length m of the inputs. The proof is complete when we show that a string x is accepted by M' exactly if $\hat{\delta'}\left(q_0', x\right) \in A'$. **QED**

Example 4.1.9. The proof of this theorem provides the means to convert a NDFA into a DFA known as *subset construction* (see Algorithm 4.1).[8] Let $M = (|Q| = 5, \{a, b\}, q_0, \{q_2, q_4\}, \delta)$ be a NDFA (cf. Fig. 4.1.8.1) whose transition function δ is given by the following table:

---

[8]This method can also be applied to convert a NDFA with, into one without, ϵ-transitions.

	$\delta\left(q,a\right)$	$\delta\left(q,b\right)$
$\rightarrow q_0$	$\{q_0,q_1\}$	$\{q_0,q_3\}$
q_1	$\{q_2\}$	$\emptyset$
$*q_2$	$\emptyset$	$\emptyset$
q_3	$\emptyset$	$\{q_4\}$
$*q_4$	$\emptyset$	$\emptyset$

We obtain the DFA $M' = \left(Q', \{a,b\}, q_0', A', \delta'\right)$ in which $Q' = 2^Q = \{\emptyset, \{q_1\}, ..., \{q_0, q_1, ..., q_4\}\}$, $q_0' = [q_0]$, $A' = \{[q_0, q_1, q_2], [q_0, q_3, q_4]\}$, and $\delta'\left([R], \sigma\right)$ for every subset $R \in Q'$ is obtained as, for instance,

$$\begin{aligned}
\delta'\left([q_0, q_1], a\right) &= \delta\left(q_0, a\right) \cup \delta\left(q_1, a\right) \\
&= \{q_0, q_1\} \cup \{q_2\} \\
&= \{q_0, q_1, q_2\} \\
&= [q_0, q_1, q_2]
\end{aligned}$$

The states that interest us are those which can be reached from the initial state, with those that do not satisfy this requirement being omitted. We obtain this result by computing the transition table for δ for all the subsets R of Q:

	$\delta\left(R,a\right)$	$\delta\left(R,b\right)$
$\rightarrow \{q_0\}$	$\{q_0,q_1\}$	$\{q_0,q_3\}$
$\{q_1\}$	$\{q_2\}$	$\emptyset$
$\vdots$	$\vdots$	$\vdots$
$\{q_0,q_1\}$	$\{q_0,q_1,q_2\}$	$\{q_0,q_3\}$
$\vdots$	$\vdots$	$\vdots$
$\emptyset$	$\emptyset$	$\emptyset$

The table for δ' is as follows:

	$\delta'\left([R],a\right)$	$\delta'\left([R],b\right)$
$\rightarrow [q_0]$	$[q_0,q_1]$	$[q_0,q_3]$
$[q_0,q_1]$	$[q_0,q_1,q_2]$	$[q_0,q_3]$
$[q_0,q_3]$	$[q_0,q_1]$	$[q_0,q_3,q_4]$
$* [q_0,q_1,q_2]$	$[q_0,q_1,q_2]$	$[q_0,q_3]$
$* [q_0,q_3,q_4]$	$[q_0,q_1]$	$[q_0,q_3,q_4]$

Figure 4.1.8.2 shows the state diagram of M'. For graphical convenience, we abbreviate q_i as i. Verify that $L\left(M\right) = L\left(M'\right)$, both automata accepting strings ending in a^2 or b^2. Note that, as expectable, there are more transitions in M' than in M.

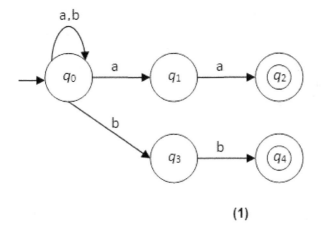

(1)

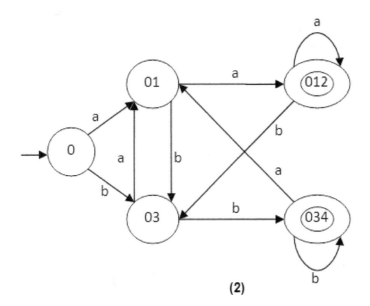

(2)

Figure 4.1.8.: Equivalent NDFA (1) and DFA (2).

4.1.1.5. The Myhill-Nerode theorem and FA minimization

It is often the case that at first construal we end up with a discouragingly complex FA; this not only influences our cognitive readiness but it also impacts on practical terms–for instance, in the context of compilation. Nevertheless, FAs can be minimized in the sense that for every FA M there is a minimal FA M' that is equivalent to it. This, in turn, depends on the notion of an equivalence relation and equivalence classes (cf. Def.s 2.1.11.6 and 2.1.12), namely applied to strings of a regular language L and to states of a FA M.

4.1.15. (Def.) We say that two strings x and y are *indistinguishable* with respect to a language L over Σ^* if

$$\{z \in \Sigma^* | xz \in L\} = \{z \in \Sigma^* | yz \in L\}.$$

Otherwise, x and y are said to be *distinguishable* strings.

1. We say that strings x and y are *equivalent with respect to* L, and write $x \approx_L y$, if and only if x and y are indistinguishable.

Example 4.1.10. Let $L = \{w \in \Sigma^* | w = xz, |w| = 2n\}$ for $\Sigma = \{0, 1\}$. Let z be an odd-length string if $|x|$ is odd and let z be an even-length string if $|x|$ is even. Then, some equivalent strings are $0 \approx_L 1$, $10 \approx_L 00$, $1 \approx_L 101$, $01 \approx_L 0000$, and there are two equivalence classes of the relation $\approx_L$.

This is an important definition, as it so happens that for a regular language L there are finitely many equivalence classes of the relation $\approx_L$. In particular, we can associate the relation $\approx_L$ to a FA M in the following way:

4.1.16. (Def.) Let M be a FA such that, for a regular language L, we have $L = L(M)$. Then, two strings x and y are *equivalent with respect to* M, denoted by $x \approx_M y$, if and only if they cause M to end in the same state. More specifically, we have $x \approx_M y$ if and only if $\hat{\delta}(q_0, x) = q_i$ and $\hat{\delta}(q_0, y) = q_j$ implies that $q_i = q_j$.

4.1.17. (Prop.) The equivalence relation $\approx_M$ is a refinement over $\approx_L$.

Proof: (Sketch) Let us suppose that $x \approx_M y$ for two strings $x, y \in L$. Then, we have $\hat{\delta}(q_0, x) = q_i = \hat{\delta}(q_0, y)$. This means that for any $z \in \Sigma^*$, it is also the case that $\hat{\delta}(q_0, xz) = q_i = \hat{\delta}(q_0, yz)$, and thus either $xz, yz \in L$ or $xz, yz \notin L$. Hence, x and y are indistinguishable, and so $x \approx_L y$. **QED**

Informally, Proposition 4.1.17 tells us that the number of equivalence classes of the relation $\approx_L$ is at most the number of states of a FA M.

4.1.18. (Def.) Let there be given a FA M. We say that two states $p, q \in Q_M$ are *equivalent* with respect to M, and we write $p \approx_M q$ if, for all input strings w, $\hat{\delta}(q, w)$ is an accepting state if and only if $\hat{\delta}(p, w)$ is an accepting state. Otherwise, i.e. if there is at least one string w such that one of $\hat{\delta}(q, w)$ and $\hat{\delta}(p, w)$ is accepting and the other is non-accepting, the states q and p are said to be *distinguishable*.

Theorem 4.1.7. *(Myhill-Nerode theorem)[9] Let $L \subseteq \Sigma^*$ be a regular language. Then, there is a minimal FA that has a number of states equal to the number of equivalence classes of the relation $\approx_M$.*

Proof: (Idea) Informally put, in order to construct the minimal FA M' out of the FA M we have to "merge together" states of M until no further "merging" is required, the rationale behind this being that each class of equivalent states of M can be considered a single state of M'. In other words, given $\delta(q, \sigma) = p$ for states q and p, if p constitutes the equivalence class $[p]_{\approx_\sigma}$ with respect to a symbol σ, then $[\delta(q, \sigma)]_{\approx_\sigma}$ can lead to any other state in $[p]_{\approx_\sigma}$, as we have, for finite $i \geq 1$ and arbitrary q,

$$[p]_{\approx_\sigma} = \left\{ p_i \mid [\delta(q, \sigma)]_{\approx_\sigma} = p_i \right\}$$

and

$$[\delta(q, \sigma)]_{\approx_\sigma} = \left\{ q_j \mid \delta(q_j, \sigma) \in [p]_{\approx_\sigma} \right\}$$

for each $\sigma \in w$, $w \in \Sigma^*$. We have here to do with a specification of the equivalence relation $\approx_L$, as we have for a string $x = \sigma_1 \sigma_2 ... \sigma_n$

$$\hat{\delta}(q_0, xz) = \left(\bigcup_{i=1}^{n} \delta(q, \sigma_i) \right) \cdot \hat{\delta}(q, z).$$

The aim is to obtain, after n iterations, the partition of Q into

$$Q' = Q/\approx_n = \{ [p_1]_\approx, ..., [p_k]_\approx \}$$

where $\approx$ abbreviates now the equivalence relation $\approx_M$. This defines, in turn, a transition function δ' such that

$$\delta'[\delta(q, \sigma)]_\approx = [p_j]_\approx$$

for arbitrary (many) q and from which the unique minimal equivalent FA M' can be constructed. **QED**

---

[9]This is a version of the theorem originally formulated in Nerode (1958).

This "merging" can be done in more than one way, each way corresponding to a different algorithm (cf. Exercise 4.1.11) with different computational costs (cf. Exercise 5.4.4). We apply here a *partition-refinement algorithm* (Algorithm 4.2), before application of which one needs to check if the DFA at hand is connected (otherwise, remove the inaccessible states).

4.1.19. (Def.) Given a FA $M = (Q, \Sigma, q_0, A, \delta)$, a state $q_i \in Q$ is said to be *accessible* if there is some string $w \in \Sigma^*$ such that

$$\hat{\delta}(q_0, w) = q_i.$$

Otherwise, we say that q_i is *inaccessible*.

1. A FA $M = (Q, \Sigma, q_0, A, \delta)$ is said to be *connected* if all its states are accessible.

It should be noted that every state $q_i \in Q_M$ is accessible from itself and/or by means of ϵ.

Algorithm 4.2 is based on Definitions 2.1.10 and 2.1.12. In practical terms, the algorithm succeeds if $|Q'| \leq |Q|$, as the DFA at hand may already be minimal, and the minimal equivalent FA is unique.[10]

We show this procedure in Example 4.1.11.

Example 4.1.11. Let there be given the FA of Figure 4.1.9.1. We begin by computing $E_0 = A$ and $E_1 = Q - A$, which constitute the coarsest partition of equivalence classes (i.e. the quotient set) of Q:

$$Q/\approx_0 = \{E_0 = \{q_2, q_3, q_4\}, E_1 = \{q_0, q_1, q_5\}\}$$

With respect to each of these two sets, we determine the transitions from each symbol of the alphabet, which gives us:

$$E_0, 0 = \begin{cases} \delta(q_2, 0) = q_4 \in E_0 \\ \delta(q_3, 0) = q_4 \in E_0 \\ \delta(q_4, 0) = q_4 \in E_0 \end{cases}$$

$$E_0, 1 = \begin{cases} \delta(q_2, 1) = q_5 \in E_1 \\ \delta(q_3, 1) = q_5 \in E_1 \\ \delta(q_4, 1) = q_5 \in E_1 \end{cases}$$

---

[10]In any case, it might be required to show that k is indeed finite, in order to prove the Myhill-Nerode theorem. This depends on the theorem being formulated in such a way that the finite index of Definition 2.1.10 features in it.

Algorithm 4.2 DFA minimization

Input: A connected DFA $M = (Q, \Sigma, q_0, A, \delta)$
Output: A minimal DFA $M' = (Q', \Sigma, E_j, A', \delta')$ equivalent to M where $Q' = Q/\approx_n = \{E_0, E_1, ..., E_m\}$, $q_0 \in E_j$ for some j, and $A' = \{E_i | q_{f_k} \in E_i\}$ for $q_{f_k} \in A$, $k \geq 1$

Initiate to $Q/\approx_0 = \{E_0 = A, E_1 = Q - A\}$ such that $E_0 = [q_f]_\approx$
Terminate when $Q/\approx_n = Q/\approx_{n-1}$

For every symbol $\sigma \in \Sigma$, every $E_i \subseteq Q/\approx_{k-1}$, and every state $q_1, ..., q_n \in E_i$ with $n > 1$:

while $Q/\approx_k \neq Q/\approx_{k-1}$, **do**
    if $\delta(q_1, \sigma), ..., \delta(p_n, \sigma) \notin E_j$ for some unique j, **then** divide E_i into E_k, E_l
        and repeat for $|E| > 1$
            else add E_i to $Q/\approx_k$
            end else
        end if
end while

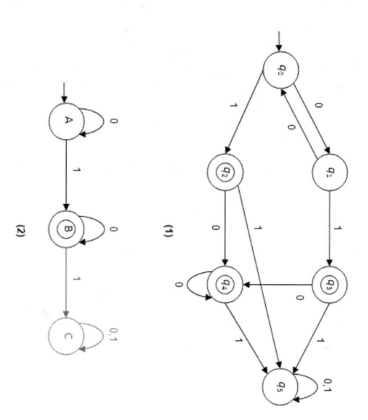

Figure 4.1.9.: A FA (1) and its minimal equivalent FA (2).

We verify that all the transition functions of $(E_0, 0)$ result in states $q_i \in E_1$ and all the transition functions of $(E_0, 1)$ give us states $q_i \in E_2$, and we leave E_0 as is. We now turn to E_1 and apply the same procedure:

$$E_1, 0 = \begin{cases} \delta\left(q_0, 0\right) = q_1 \in E_1 \\ \delta\left(q_1, 0\right) = q_0 \in E_1 \\ \delta\left(q_5, 0\right) = q_5 \in E_1 \end{cases}$$

$$E_1, 1 = \begin{cases} \delta\left(q_0, 1\right) = q_2 \in E_0 \\ \delta\left(q_1, 1\right) = q_3 \in E_0 \\ \delta\left(q_5, 1\right) = q_5 \in E_1 \end{cases}$$

With respect to $(E_1, 1)$, we verify that $\delta\left(q_0, 1\right), \delta\left(q_1, 1\right) \in E_0$ but $\delta\left(q_5, 1\right) \in E_1$; we refer to this property as *partition instability*. We thus have to divide E_1 into the partitions $E_1 = \{q_0, q_1\}$ and $E_2 = \{q_5\}$, thus obtaining

$$Q/\approx_1 = \{E_0 = \{q_2, q_3, q_4\}, E_1 = \{q_0, q_1\}, E_2 = \{q_5\}\}.$$

Another iteration of the procedure above gives us $Q/\approx_2 = Q/\approx_1$ and the process of refining the partition of equivalence classes of Q is completed. We have three states, to wit, E_0, E_1, and E_2, it being the case that $q_0 \in E_1$, and E_1 is the initial state, and the final state is clearly E_0. For convenience, we relabel E_1 as A, E_0 as B, and E_2 as C. The transition table of this FA is as follows:

	$\delta\left(E_i, 0\right)$	$\delta\left(E_i, 1\right)$
$\rightarrow A$	A	B
$*B$	B	C
C	C	C

Figure 4.1.9.2 shows the minimal equivalent FA M'. M' accepts the regular expression $r' = 0^*10^*$, which is equivalent to the regular expression $r = (00)^*(1 + 01 + (10 + 010)0^*)$ accepted by M. Clearly, state C could be removed from M', as the regular expression $0^*10^*1(0+1)^*$ (i.e. r' with suffix $1\left(0 + 1\right)^*$) is rejected (cf. Example 4.1.2 above).

4.1.1.6. Kleene's theorem and the properties of $\mathscr{RGL}$

So far, we have simply accepted that the class $\mathscr{RGL}$ is precisely the class of languages accepted by FAs. It is now time to prove this, in order to be able to prove further properties of this class. The main theorem is known as Kleene's theorem, as it was first formulated in Kleene (1956):

Theorem 4.1.8. *(Kleene's theorem) A language L over an alphabet Σ is regular if and only if $L = L(M)$ for some FA M.*

Proof: (Sketch) Recall the definitions of regular expression and regular language (Def.s 3.2.1 and 3.2.2, respectively). The proof of this theorem is by induction on $r = \emptyset, \epsilon, a \in \Sigma$, which constitutes the basis for the induction step (i.e. there are no operators involved). For the induction step, i.e., for $L(M_1) \cup L(M_2)$, $L(M_1)L(M_2)$, and $L(M_1)^*$, let $M_1 = (Q_1, \Sigma, q_1, \{f_1\}, \delta_1)$ and $M_2 = (Q_2, \Sigma, q_2, \{f_2\}, \delta_2)$ where f_i abbreviates q_{f_i}, for q_f denoting final state. Let q_0 be a new initial state and f_0 a new final state. In the first case, we have to construct a NDFA

$$M = (Q_1 \cup Q_2 \cup \{q_0, f_0\}, \Sigma, q_0, \{f_0\}, \delta)$$

where $Q_1 \cap Q_2 = \emptyset$. In the second case, we have to construct a NDFA

$$M = (Q_1 \cup Q_2, \Sigma, q_1, \{f_2\}, \delta).$$

For the third case, we have to construct a NDFA

$$M = (Q_1 \cup \{q_0, f_0\}, \Sigma, q_0, \{f_0\}, \delta).$$

The correctness of the proof falls on the right definitions of the several $\delta(\cdot, \cdot)$ involved; Figure 4.1.10 provides clues thereto. Then apply Theorems 4.1.6-7. **QED**

Kleene's theorem provides the theoretical foundation for the construction of a FA for any regular language, namely by converting the regular expression(s) that constitute it into a NDFA.[11] This construction is given in Algorithm 4.3, which can also be called *Thompson conversion*, as it shows how to convert a regular expression into a FA.

Example 4.1.12. The FA in Figure 4.1.11 accepts the language $L = L_1 \cup L_2$ where $L_1 = \{0^2(0,1)^n \mid n \geq 0\} = \{00\}\{0,1\}^*$ and $L_2 = \{1^2(01)^n \mid n \geq 0\} = \{11\}\{01\}^*$. The ϵ-transitions introduced in the Thompson construction (Fig. 4.1.11.1) can be eliminated (cf. Theorem 4.1.5), giving the final FA in Fig. 4.1.11.2. For the sake of simplicity, the construction is shown exclusively for the union of L_1 and L_2, all other details (e.g., Thompson construction of the Kleene star) having been omitted.

---

[11] The only case in which the conversion is directly into a DFA is when $r = a \in \Sigma$, all the other cases entailing ϵ-transitions and as such a NDFA as output. However, the ϵ-transitions can be removed from the NDFA once the construction has been carried out and, if the resultant automaton is not a DFA, the conversion into one can be made. (Cf. Section 4.1.1.5 above.)

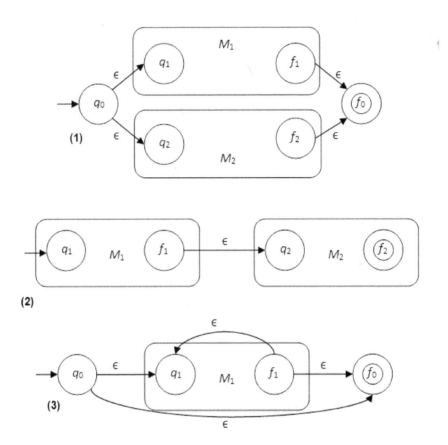

Figure 4.1.10.: Schematic diagrams for FAs accepting (1) $L_1 \cup L_2$, (2) $L_1 L_2$, and (3) $(L_1)^*$.

Algorithm 4.3 Thompson construction

Input: Languages $L(r), L(s)$ for r, s regular expressions
Output: A state digraph $\vec{\mathfrak{D}}(M(\alpha))$, where $\alpha = \{r\}$, $\alpha = \{r\} \cup \{s\}$, $\alpha = \{rs\}$, or $\alpha = \{r\}^*$

STEPS

- For $L = L(r) = \{\epsilon\}$ with $M(\epsilon) = (\{q_0, q_f\}, \Sigma, q_0, \{q_f\}, \delta)$, construct $\vec{\mathfrak{D}}(M(\epsilon))$ with a single transition $\delta(q_0, \epsilon) = q_f$ such that there is a single arc, namely from q_0 to q_f, and it is labeled "ϵ".

- For $L = L(r) = \{a\}$ with $M(a) = (\{q_0, q_f\}, \Sigma, q_0, \{q_f\}, \delta)$, construct $\vec{\mathfrak{D}}(M(a))$ with a single transition $\delta(q_0, a) = q_f$ such that there is a single arc, namely from q_0 to q_f, and it is labeled "a".

- For $L = L(r) \cup L(s) = \{r\} \cup \{s\}$ with $M(r) = M_1 = (Q_1, \Sigma, q_1, \{f_1\}, \delta_1)$ and $M(s) = M_2 = (Q_2, \Sigma, q_2, \{f_2\}, \delta_2)$, construct $\vec{\mathfrak{D}}(M(r) \cup M(s))$ for $M(r) \cup M(s) = M_1 \cup M_2$ as in Fig. 4.1.10.1.

- For $L = L(r) L(s) = \{r\}\{s\} = \{rs\}$ with $M(r) = M_1 = (Q_1, \Sigma, q_1, \{f_1\}, \delta_1)$ and $M(s) = M_2 = (Q_2, \Sigma, q_2, \{f_2\}, \delta_2)$, construct $\vec{\mathfrak{D}}(M(r) M(s))$ for $M(r) M(s) = M_1 M_2$ as in Fig. 4.1.10.2.

- For $L = L(r^*) = \{r\}^*$ with $M(r) = (Q, \Sigma, q_0, \{f_0\}, \delta)$, construct $\vec{\mathfrak{D}}(M(r^*))$ for $M(r^*)$ as in Fig. 4.1.10.3.

TERMINATE when there are no remaining regular expressions to convert.

In Section 3.2, we already saw that the class $\mathscr{RGL}$ is closed under the main operations on languages. In the mentioned Section, the proofs where completed without FAs; we leave now the proofs of those properties by invoking FAs as exercises. The following theorem respects the operations of union, intersection, and difference; one can then invoke this theorem for the closure of $\mathscr{RGL}$ under these operations. The same procedure can be used for the other operations under which the class $\mathscr{RGL}$ is closed.

Theorem 4.1.9. *Let $M_1 = (Q_1, \Sigma, q_{0,1}, A_1, \delta_1)$, $M_2 = (Q_2, \Sigma, q_{0,2}, A_2, \delta_2)$ be FAs accepting the languages L_1 and L_2, respectively. Let further $M = (Q, \Sigma, q_0, A, \delta)$ be a FA where $Q = Q_1 \times Q_2$, $q_0 = (q_{0,1}, q_{0,2})$, $A = A_1 \times A_2$, and where the transition function is defined, for every p, q, σ such that $q \in Q_1$, $p \in Q_2$, and $\sigma \in \Sigma$, by*

$$\delta\left(\left[q, p\right], \sigma\right) = \left[\delta_1\left(q, \sigma\right), \delta_2\left(p, \sigma\right)\right].$$

Then, we have the following cases: (i) if $A = \{(q, p) | q \in A_1 \text{ or } p \in A_2\}$, M accepts the language $L_1 \cup L_2$; (ii) if $A = \{(q, p) | q \in A_1 \text{ and } p \in A_2\}$, M accepts the language $L_1 \cap L_2$; and (iii) if $A = \{q, p | q \in A_1 \text{ and } p \notin A_2\}$, M accepts the language $L_1 - L_2$.

Proof: (Sketch) For all the operations $\cup, \cap, -$ we consider the extended transition

$$\hat{\delta}\left(q_0, w\right) = \left(\hat{\delta}_1\left(q_{0,1}, w\right), \hat{\delta}_2\left(q_{0,2}, w\right)\right)$$

and apply structural induction on w. We give the sketch of the proof for intersection and leave the other operations as an exercise. By considering the equation above, it should be obvious that we have $w \in L_1 \cap L_2$ if and only if:

- $w \in L_1 = L(M_1)$ and $w \in L_2 = L(M_2)$,

- $\hat{\delta}_1\left(q_{0,1}, w\right) \in A_1$ and $\hat{\delta}_2\left(q_{0,2}, w\right) \in A_2$,

- $\left[\hat{\delta}_1\left(q_{0,1}, w\right), \hat{\delta}_2\left(q_{0,2}, w\right)\right] \in A_1 \times A_2$,

- $\left(\hat{\delta}\left[q_{0,1}, q_{0,2}\right], w\right) \in A_1 \times A_2$,

- $w \in L(M)$.

Hence, $L(M) = L(M_1) \cap L(M_2)$. **QED**

From Theorem 4.1.9 we can extract an algorithm for the construction of a *(cross-)product automaton*. The relevance of this FA lies in

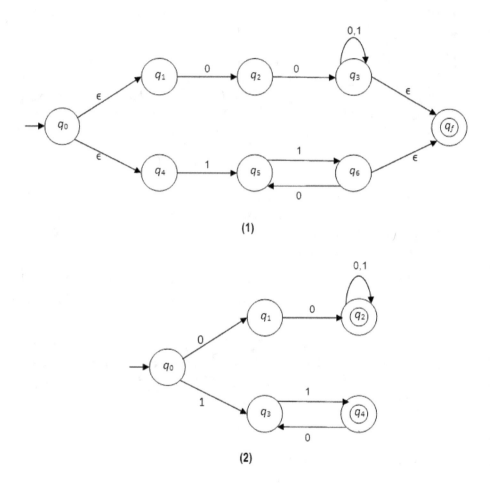

Figure 4.1.11.: A FA accepting $L = L_1 \cup L_2$ by applying the Thompson construction.

that it allows for running two FAs *in parallel*. For instance, given $L_1 = \{0,1\}^* \{00\} \{0,1\}^*$ and $L_2 = \{0,1\}^* \{01\}$, we can run M_1 and M_2 in parallel by means of a product FA $M_\times$ to check, for instance, if $0101 \in (L_1 \cup L_2)$ (cf. Exercise 4.1.17). Algorithm 4.4 outputs a product automaton for the union of two languages. For the intersection or difference of two languages, different sets of final states should be chosen (see Exercise 4.1.16).[12]

4.1.2. Finite transducers

We approach now the essential aspects of finite transducers, and we do so from a simplified perspective. For instance, we consider only those machines that compute over a symbol at a time printing also a single symbol for each input symbol. Finite transducers processing more than one symbol at a time are actually more frequent and useful, but we do not need such sophistication for our purposes. The closure properties of regular languages with FAs hold also with finite transducers, and so we also skip any discussion of this topic. The fields of application of these machines are vast, ranging from switching theory to natural language processing, and we leave it to the interested reader to search in the corresponding literature for further contents on finite transducers.

4.1.2.1. Moore and Mealy machines

It is rather obvious that a machine needs to produce some sort of output, in order to be useful for computation in practical terms. A finite(-state) transducer is just such a machine.

4.1.20. (Def.) A *finite-state transducer* (abbr.: FT) is a 6-tuple

$$M = (Q, \Sigma_I, \Sigma_O, q_0, \delta, \tau)$$

where Q, q_0 are as for a FA, Σ_I is the *input alphabet*, Σ_O is the *output alphabet*, $\delta : (Q \times \Sigma_I) \longrightarrow Q$ is the transition function, and τ is the *output function*. The specification of the output function defines two kinds of FT:

1. A FT whose output function depends on both the current state and the current input letter(s), i.e. $\tau : (Q \times \Sigma_I) \longrightarrow \Sigma_O$, is called a *Mealy machine*.

---

[12]Algorithm 4.4 preserves determinism.

Algorithm 4.4 Product-automaton construction for $L(M_\times) = L_1 \cup L_2$

Input: Two FAs $M_1 = (Q_1, \Sigma, q_{0,1}, A_1, \delta_1)$, $M_2 = (Q_2, \Sigma, q_{0,2}, A_2, \delta_2)$ accepting the languages L_1 and L_2, respectively.
Output: The product FA accepting $L_1 \cup L_2 = L(M_\times)$ for

$$M_\times = (Q_\times, \Sigma, q_{0,\times}, A_\times, \delta_\times)$$

where $Q_\times = (Q_1 \times Q_2)$, $q_{0,\times} = [q_{0,1}, q_{0,2}]$, $A_\times = (A_1 \times Q_2) \cup (A_2 \times Q_1)$, and $\delta_\times = \delta_1 \times \delta_2$.

Start with M_1 and M_2.

Step I:

1. For $q_{0,1} \in Q_1$ and $q_{0,2} \in Q_2$, do:

$$q_{0,\times} = [q_{0,1}, q_{0,2}]$$

2. For each $q_{i,1} \in Q_1$, each $q_{j,2} \in Q_2$, and each $\sigma \in \Sigma$, do:

$$\delta_\times([q_{i,1}, q_{j,2}], \sigma) = [\delta_1(q_{i,1}, \sigma), \delta_2(q_{j,2}, \sigma)]$$

3. If $q_{i,1} \in A_1$ or $q_{j,2} \in A_2$, do:

$$[q_{i,1}, q_{j,2}] \in A_\times$$

    where $A_\times = (A_1 \times Q_2) \cup (A_2 \times Q_1)$.

Step II:

1. Delete unreachable states.

2. Merge final states, if possible.

Terminate

---

2. A FT whose output function depends only on the current state, i.e. $\tau : Q \longrightarrow \Sigma_O$, is called a *Moore machine*.

In other words, the outputs of a Mealy machine are associated to its transitions, whereas those of a Moore machine are so solely to its states. Note that there are no final states for a FT, and non-determinism is not a feature we consider with respect to these machines.

4.1.21. (Def.) The computer model for a FT diverges from that of a FA in that (i) there is a read-and-write head, and (ii) there are two tapes, an input tape and an output tape.

Example 4.1.13. Figure 4.1.12.1 shows the Moore machine with the following transition and output functions over the alphabets $\Sigma_I = \Sigma_O = \{0, 1\}$:

	$\delta(q, 0)$	$\delta(q, 1)$	$\tau(q, 0) = \tau(q, 1)$
$\rightarrow q_0$	q_1	q_2	0
q_1	q_1	q_3	1
q_2	q_0	q_2	0
q_3	q_2	q_3	1

Figure 4.1.12.2 shows the Mealy machine with alphabet $\Sigma_I = \Sigma_O = \{0, 1\}$ and with the following transition and output table:

	$\delta(q, 0)$	$\delta(q, 1)$	$\tau(q, 0)$	$\tau(q, 1)$
$\rightarrow q_0$	q_1	q_2	1	0
q_1	q_1	q_3	1	1
q_2	q_0	q_2	0	0
q_3	q_2	q_3	0	1

In this Example, the input alphabet and the output alphabet are the same, but this need not be so. Note the distinct ways to indicate the output in the two machines: In a Mealy machine, the output is indicated on the edges in the form *input/output*, whereas in a Moore machine it is indicated as *state/output* on the vertices of the state diagram.

4.1.22. (Def.) A *configuration* for a FT is a triple $C = (q, w, z)$ where $q \in Q$ is the current state, $w \in \Sigma_I^*$ is the input string, and $z \in \Sigma_O^*$ is the output string.

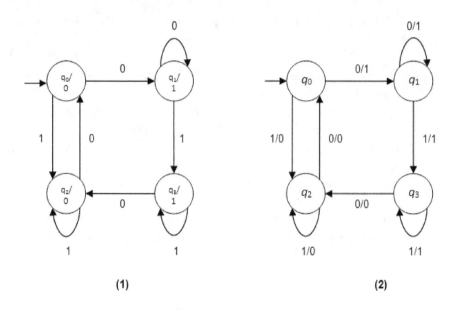

Figure 4.1.12.: Moore (1) and Mealy (2) machines.

1. The *initial configuration* of a Mealy machine on input w is $C_0 = (q_0, au, -)$ for $au = w$ denoting that a is the first symbol of w being read and $-$ indicating that no output has been produced yet. A *final configuration* for a Mealy machine on input w is $C_f = (q_i, -, z)$ where q_i is some state and z is the output string.[13]

2. The initial configuration of a Moore machine is $C_0 = (q_0, -, -)$, which indicates that when entering state q_0 a Moore machine has yet neither input nor output. The final configuration of a Moore machine is $C_f = (q_i, -, cz)$ where $c \in \Sigma_O \cup \{\epsilon\}$.

3. A *computation in one step* of a Mealy machine M is given by

$$(q, \sigma u, v) \vdash_M (p, u, v\varsigma)$$

where, for $\sigma \in \Sigma_I$ the symbol being read, $\delta(q, \sigma) = p$ and $\tau(p, \sigma) = \varsigma$ for $\varsigma \in \Sigma_O$ the output symbol. The same holds for a Moore machine once the adjustment for the initial state is made.

4. A *computation* for a FT M is a finite sequence of configurations

---

[13] Note that by "final configuration" it is just meant that the input and output strings have been entirely processed; contrarily to the case of a FA, this has no meaning of acceptance.

$C_0, C_1, ..., C_n$ such that $C_{i-1} \vdash_M C_i$, $1 \leq i \leq n$.

5. A configuration C yields a configuration C' if there is a computation of C' from C in n moves, denoted by $C \vdash_M^n C'$, or in zero or more moves, denoted by $C \vdash_M^* C'$.

Example 4.1.14. For instance, consider the Mealy machine *Me* in Figure 4.1.12.2; given an initial input string 0011, this machine performs the computation

$$q_0, 0011, - \vdash_{Me} q_1, 011, 1 \vdash_{Me} q_1 11, 11 \vdash_{Me} q_3 1, 111 \vdash_{Me} q_3, -, 1111.$$

Given the same input, the Moore machine *Mo* in Figure 4.1.12.1 beginning in state q_0 performs the computation

$$q_0, -, - \vdash_{Mo} q_0, 0011, 0 \vdash_{Mo} q_1 011, 01 \vdash_{Mo} q_1 11, 011$$

$$\vdash_{Mo} q_3 1, 0111 \vdash_{Mo} q_3, -, 01111.$$

Because, given an input string $|w| = n$, at the end of a computation both a Moore and a Mealy machine will have printed an output string $|z| \geq n$ (or $|z| \leq n$ if $\epsilon \in \Sigma_O$), we need the notion of an extended output function.

4.1.23. **(Def.)** Given a FT $M = (Q, \Sigma_I, \Sigma_O, q_0, \delta, \tau)$, the *extended output function*, denoted by $\hat{\tau}$, is defined as

$$\hat{\tau} : (Q \times \Sigma_I^*) \longrightarrow \Sigma_O^*$$

so that we have

$$\hat{\tau}(q_0, w) = z$$

for an input string w and an output string z. Given an input string $w \in \Sigma_I^*$ and some symbol $a \in \Sigma_I$, the extended output function can be further specified as follows:

1. For a Mealy machine, we have

$$\hat{\tau}(q, a) = \tau(q, a)$$

$$\hat{\tau}(q, ua) = \hat{\tau}(q, u) \tau\left(\hat{\delta}(q, u), a\right).$$

2. For a Moore machine, we have

$$\hat{\tau}(q, a) = \tau(\delta(q, a))$$

171

$$\hat{\tau}(q, ua) = \hat{\tau}(q, u)\, \tau\left(\hat{\delta}(q, ua)\right).$$

4.1.24. (Def.) Given an input $w = w_1 w_2 ... w_n$ and an output alphabet $\Sigma_O - \{\epsilon\}$, a Mealy machine Me performs a computation[14]

$$(q_0, w_1) \vdash_{Me} (\delta(q_0, w_1), w_2) \vdash_{Me} ... \vdash_{Me} \left(\hat{\delta}(q_0, w_1 w_2 ... w_{n-1}), w_n\right)$$

so that we have

$$(q_0, w_1) \vdash_{Me}^{n-1} \left(\hat{\delta}(q_0, w_1 w_2 ... w_{n-1}), w_n\right)$$

and correspondingly outputs the string

$$\underbrace{\underbrace{\tau(q_0, w_1)}_{\ell=1} \underbrace{\tau(\delta(q_0, w_1), w_2)}_{\ell=1+1} ... \tau\left(\hat{\delta}(q_0, w_1 w_2 ... w_{n-1}), w_n\right)}_{\ell=n-1}$$

and hence $\left|\hat{\tau}(q_0, w_1 w_2 ... w_{n-1})\, \tau\left(\hat{\delta}(q_0, w_1 w_2 ... w_{n-1}), w_n\right) = z\right| = n,$ whereas a Moore machine Mo performs the computation

$$q_0 \vdash_{Mo} \delta(q_0, w_1) \vdash_{Mo} \hat{\delta}(q_0, w_1 w_2) \vdash_{Mo} ... \vdash_{Mo} \hat{\delta}(q_0, w_1 w_2 ... w_n)$$

so that we have

$$q_0 \vdash_{Mo}^{n} \hat{\delta}(q_0, w_1 w_2 ... w_n)$$

and correspondingly outputs the string

$$\underbrace{\underbrace{\tau(q_0)}_{\ell=1} \underbrace{\tau(\delta(q_0, w_1))}_{\ell=1+1} \underbrace{\tau\left(\hat{\delta}(q_0, w_1 w_2)\right)}_{\ell=2+1} ... \tau\left(\hat{\delta}(q_0, w_1 w_2 ... w_n)\right)}_{\ell=n} \quad \underbrace{}_{\ell=1}$$

and hence $\left|\hat{\tau}(q_0, w_1 w_2 ... w_{n-1})\, \tau\left(\hat{\delta}(q_0, w_1 w_2 ... w_n)\right) = cz\right| = n + 1.$

The different output lengths for the same input are explained by the fact that when a Mealy machine first enters state q_0, it outputs nothing at all, doing so solely upon the first transition function. On the contrary, when first entering state q_0, a Moore machine immediately outputs the symbol associated to it.

Example 4.1.15. On input 000110110, the Moore machine in Figure

---

[14]We simplify and give only the transition configurations. Note that this impacts on the number of configurations with respect to Def. 4.1.23.

4.1.12.1 outputs the string 0111110000. On the same input, the machine of Figure 4.1.12.2 outputs the string 111110000.

4.1.2.2. Equivalence of finite transducers

Despite the different lengths of the output, the definitions above suggest the equivalence of the Mealy and Moore machine classes. In effect, a Mealy machine Me and a Moore machine Mo are equivalent if and only if both compute the same function on the same (or equivalent) input, i.e.

$$f_{Me}(x) = f_{Mo}(x) \text{ iff } Me \approx Mo.$$

It is a straightforward matter to convert a Moore machine into an equivalent Mealy machine, as according to the following intuition: Because the symbol $\sigma \in \Sigma_O$ to be printed by a Moore machine depends only on the current state, we simply assign this very σ to the *transition* of the Mealy machine that leads to this state. With respect to the difference in length of the printed strings, we just ignore the first symbol of the string printed by the Moore machine as meaningless.[15]

Example 4.1.16. In Figure 4.1.12, the Moore machine (Fig. 4.1.12.1) was converted into the equivalent Mealy machine (Fig. 4.1.12.2) by applying the intuition above. If we ignore the first symbol of the output string of the Moore machine, we verify that the outputs of both machines are the same.

The following theorem formalizes the intuition above.

Theorem 4.1.10. *Let $M = (Q, \Sigma_I, \Sigma_O, q_0, \delta, \tau)$ be a Moore machine. Then, there is an equivalent Mealy machine M' with the same number of states.*

Proof: (Idea) Define $M' = \left(Q, \Sigma_I, \Sigma_O, q_0', \delta', \tau'\right)$ such that τ' depends on the output from the state reached after the transition is made, i.e. $\tau'(q, \sigma) = \tau(\delta(q, \sigma))$ for a symbol σ and then extend this to a string w, as in Definitions 4.1.23-4. **QED**

The conversion of a Mealy machine into an equivalent Moore machine is not so straightforward, as the next theorem suggests:

Theorem 4.1.11. *Let $M = (Q, \Sigma_I, \Sigma_O, q_0, \delta, \tau)$ be a Mealy machine. Then, there is an equivalent Moore machine $M' = \left(Q', \Sigma_I, \Sigma_O, q_0', \delta', \tau'\right)$ with at most $|Q||\Sigma_O| + 1$ states.*

---

[15] Alternatively, no symbol is printed when the Moore machine first enters state q_0. In this case, we have $\Sigma_O \cup \{\epsilon\}$.

Proof: (Sketch) Let $[\cdot]$ denote a single state of M'. For all $a \in \Sigma_I$, and all $b \in \Sigma_O$, we let:

- $Q' = Q \times \Sigma_O$

$$\delta'\left([q_j, b], a\right) = \begin{bmatrix} \underbrace{\delta(q_i, a)}_{=}, \underbrace{\tau(q_i, a)}_{=} \\ q_j \qquad b \end{bmatrix} = q_{jb}$$

- $\tau'\left([q_j, b]\right) = b$

In other words, for each state $q_i \in Q$ we create $|\Sigma_O|$ states of M' labeled $q_{i\varsigma}$ such that $\tau'\left([q_i, \varsigma]\right) = \varsigma$ for all $i = 1, 2, ..., n$ and all symbols $\varsigma \in \Sigma_O$. This gives us $Q' = |Q| \, |\Sigma_O|$. Furthermore, let

$$q_0' = \begin{cases} [q_0, c] & \text{if } q_0' \in C_0 \\ \delta'\left([q_j, b], a\right) & \text{otherwise} \end{cases}$$

for arbitrary $c \in \Sigma_O$ and C_0 the initial configuration of M'. We have now $Q' = |Q| \, |\Sigma_O| + 1$ at most. Given an input $x = a_1 a_2 ... a_n$, it is verified that the strings printed by M and M' are identical. (We leave the details of the computations by both machines as an exercise.) **QED**

Example 4.1.17. Suppose there is given a Mealy machine $M = (Q, \Sigma_I, \Sigma_O, q_0, \delta, \tau)$ with $|Q| = 3$, $\Sigma_I = \{0, 1\}$ and $\Sigma_O = \{a, b\}$. Then,

$$Q' = \left(Q \times \Sigma_O = \left\{ \begin{matrix} q_{0a} & q_{0b} \\ q_{1a} & q_{1b} \\ q_{2a} & q_{2b} \end{matrix} \right\} \right) + q_{0c}$$

are the possible states of an equivalent Moore machine M'. Clearly, we have, say, state q_{0a} if and only if there is a state q_0 at which an a is printed. Hence, we need not exhaust $|Q| \, |\Sigma_O|$. Suppose M is the Mealy machine in Figure 4.1.13.1. Then we have

$$q_0 \times \{a, b\} = \begin{cases} [\delta(q_0, 0), \tau(q_0, 0)] = q_{1a} \\ [\delta(q_0, 1), \tau(q_0, 1)] = q_{2a} \end{cases}$$

$$q_1 \times \{a, b\} = \begin{cases} [\delta(q_1, 0), \tau(q_1, 0)] = q_{1b} \\ [\delta(q_1, 1), \tau(q_1, 1)] = q_{2a} \end{cases}$$

$$q_2 \times \{a, b\} = \begin{cases} [\delta\,(q_2, 0)\,, \tau\,(q_2, 0)] = q_{1a} \\ [\delta\,(q_2, 1)\,, \tau\,(q_2, 1)] = q_{2b} \end{cases}$$

Because there is no transition to q_0, we simply assign, say, a to q_0 and thus have the initial state q_{0a} for M'. We have thus

$$|Q'| = |Q|\,|\Sigma_O| + 1 = \left| \begin{cases} q_{1a} & q_{1b} \\ q_{2a} & q_{2b} \end{cases} \right| + q_{0a} = 5.$$

The transition and output table of M' is the following:

	$\delta'\,(q_{i\varsigma}, 0)$	$\delta'\,(q_{i\varsigma}, 1)$	$\tau'\,(q_{i\varsigma}, 0)$	$\tau'\,(q_{i\varsigma}, 1)$
$\rightarrow q_{0a}$	q_{1a}	q_{2a}	a	a
q_{1a}	q_{1b}	q_{2a}	b	a
q_{1b}	q_{1b}	q_{2a}	b	a
q_{2a}	q_{1a}	q_{2b}	a	b
q_{2b}	q_{1a}	q_{2b}	a	b

Figure 4.1.13.2 shows the state diagram of this Moore machine.[16]
It can be easily verified that on the input string 001110 the Mealy machine outputs the string *ababba* and its equivalent Moore machine outputs the string *aababba*.

4.1.2.3. Minimizing finite transducers

Just as in the case of FAs, the minimization of FTs is often of practical importance. In order to minimize a FT we must begin with a connected FT.

4.1.25. (Def.) Given a FT $M = (Q, \Sigma_I, \Sigma_O, q_0, \delta, \tau)$, a state $q_i \in Q$ is said to be *accessible* if there is some string $w \in \Sigma_I^*$ such that

$$\hat{\delta}\,(q_0, w) = q_i.$$

Otherwise, we say that q_i is *inaccessible*.

1. A FT $M = (Q, \Sigma_I, \Sigma_O, q_0, \delta, \tau)$ is said to be *connected* if all its states are accessible.

We also need the notion of equivalent states, but because now we have no accepting states, we need a different definition. In particular,

---

[16]For graphical convenience, we write i/ς instead of $q_{i\varsigma}/\varsigma$ in the vertices of the state diagram for M'.

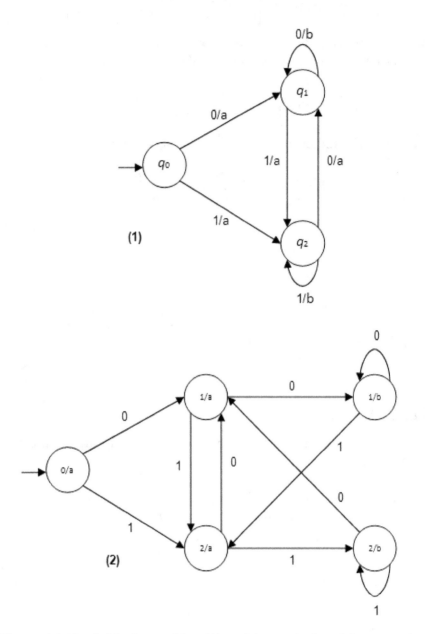

Figure 4.1.13.: A Mealy machine (1) and its equivalent Moore machine (2).

we need a definition of state equivalence that depends on the output function.[17] We give this definition for a Mealy machine; below we show how to adapt it to a Moore machine.

4.1.26. (Def.) Let $M = (Q, \Sigma_I, \Sigma_O, q_0, \delta, \tau)$ be a Mealy machine. Two states $q_i, q_j \in Q$ are said to be *equivalent*, written $q_i \approx_{Me} q_j$ if and only if, given an input string w,

$$(\approx_{Me}) \qquad \hat{\tau}(q_i, w) = \hat{\tau}(q_j, w).$$

Otherwise, they are said to be *distinguishable*. More specifically, states $q_i, q_j \in Q$ are said to be

1. *k-equivalent* if and only if $\approx_{Me}$ holds for all $|w| \le k$. Otherwise, i.e. if there is some $|w| \le k$ such that $\hat{\tau}(q_i, w) \ne \hat{\tau}(q_j, w)$, they are *k-distinguishable*.

2. *1-equivalent* if and only if there is some $\sigma \in \Sigma_I$, say a, such that $\tau(q_i, a) = \tau(q_j, a)$. Otherwise, i.e. if $\tau(q_i, a) \ne \tau(q_j, a)$, then they are *1-distinguishable*.

3. $(k-1)$-*distinguishable* if and only if there is some $|w| \le k-1$ such that

$$\delta(q_i, a) = q_k$$

and

$$\delta(q_j, a) = q_l$$

such that

$$\hat{\tau}(q_i, aw) = \tau(q_i, a)\hat{\tau}(q_k, w)$$

and

$$\hat{\tau}(q_j, aw) = \tau(q_j, a)\hat{\tau}(q_l, w)$$

but

$$\hat{\tau}(q_k, w) \ne \hat{\tau}(q_l, w).$$

Theorem 4.1.12. *Let M be a Mealy machine in which all states are distinguishable. Then, M is minimal and unique up to relabeling of the states.*

Proof: Left as an exercise. (Hint: Invoke the pigeonhole principle.)

In order to create an algorithm for the minimization of a Mealy machine (cf. Algorithm 4.6) we must retake the notion of a partition (cf.

---

[17]Compare with Definition 4.1.18.

Def. 2.1.10) and first formulate an adequate algorithm for this. This we do in Algorithm 4.5.[18]

Example 4.1.18. Let there be given the Mealy machine of Figure 4.1.14.1. Complete application of Steps 1-2 of Algorithm 4.5 gives us:

$$\mathscr{P}_Q^1 = \{E_0 = \{q_0, q_1, q_2\}, E_1 = \{q_3, q_4\}\}.$$

In Step 3 we obtain

$$E_0, a = \begin{cases} \delta(q_0, a) = q_1 \in E_0 \\ \delta(q_1, a) = q_1 \in E_0 \\ \delta(q_2, a) = q_1 \in E_0 \end{cases}$$

$$E_0, b = \begin{cases} \delta(q_0, b) = q_2 \in E_0 \\ \delta(q_1, b) = q_3 \in E_1 \\ \delta(q_2, b) = q_4 \in E_1 \end{cases}$$

$$E_1, a = \begin{cases} \delta(q_3, a) = q_4 \in E_1 \\ \delta(q_4, a) = q_4 \in E_1 \end{cases}$$

$$E_1, a = \begin{cases} \delta(q_3, b) = q_3 \in E_1 \\ \delta(q_4, b) = q_4 \in E_1 \end{cases}$$

Only with respect to (E_0, b) do we verify that the transitions lead to states in different equivalence classes, and we split E_0 into $E_0 = \{q_0\}$ and $E_2 = \{q_1, q_2\}$, thus obtaining the partition refinement

$$\mathscr{P}_Q^2 = \{E_0 = \{q_0\}, E_1 = \{q_3, q_4\}, E_2 = \{q_1, q_2\}\}.$$

Repetition of this Step 3 gives the final partition

$$\mathscr{P}_Q^2 = \mathscr{P}_Q^3 = Q/\approx_{Me} = \{E_0 = \{q_0\}, E_1 = \{q_3, q_4\}, E_2 = \{q_1, q_2\}\}.$$

For convenience, we relabel the states accordingly, obtaining

$$Q' = \{q_0, q_{12}, q_{34}\}.$$

Figure 4.1.14.2 shows the minimal Mealy machine M' equivalent to M obtained by applying Algorithm 4.6. For graphical convenience, q_{ij} is

---

[18]Compare Algorithms 4.5-6 with Algorithm 4.2.

Algorithm 4.5 Partition refinement for the states of a Mealy machine

---

Input: A set $Q = \{q_0, q_1, ..., q_m\}$ of states of a connected Mealy machine $M = (Q, \Sigma_I, \Sigma_O, q_0, \delta, \tau)$
Output: A set $Q' = \mathscr{P}_Q = Q/ \approx_{Me} = \{E_0, E_1, ..., E_k\}$ of equivalence classes

---

1. Divide Q into a first (coarse) partition $\mathscr{P}_{Q_0} = \{E_0, E_1\}$ such that

$$E_0 = \{q | q \text{ is 1-equivalent to } q_0\}$$

   and
$$E_1 = \{p | p \text{ is 1-distinguishable from } q_0\} .$$

   Repeat for $q_1, q_2, ..., q_m$ obtaining the partitions $\mathscr{P}_{Q_1}, \mathscr{P}_{Q_2}, ..., \mathscr{P}_{Q_m}$.

2. Make

$$\mathscr{P}_Q^1 = \left(\bigcup_{i=0}^{m} \mathscr{P}_{Q_i} \right) - E_i$$

   for E_i any duplicate equivalence classes.

3. For every pair q_i, q_j in the same equivalence class, determine whether there are transitions $\delta(q_i, a) = q_k$ and $\delta(q_j, a) = q_l$ such that q_k and q_l are in different equivalence classes. If so, create new equivalence classes E_r, E_s such that, say, $q_i \in E_r$ and $q_j \in E_s$.

4. Repeat Step 3 until $\mathscr{P}_Q^n = \mathscr{P}_Q^{n-1}$.

Algorithm 4.6 Mealy-machine minimization

Input: Connected Mealy machine $M = (Q, \Sigma_I, \Sigma_O, q_0, \delta, \tau)$
Output: Minimal Mealy machine $M' = (Q', \Sigma_I, \Sigma_O, E_j, \delta', \tau')$ with $Q' = \mathscr{P}_Q^m = Q/\approx_{Me} = \{E_0, E_1, ..., E_n\}$

---

1. Apply Algorithm 4.5 to Q to obtain $Q' = \mathscr{P}_Q^m = Q/\approx_{Me} = \{E_0, E_1, ..., E_n\}$

2. Choose some $q_i \in E_l$ and some $q_j \in E_m$, $l \lesseqgtr m$, and make

$$\delta'(E_l, a) = E_m$$

$$\tau'(E_l, a) = b$$

for all $a \in \Sigma_I$ and all $b \in \Sigma_O$.

3. Make E_j such that $q_0 \in E_j$ the initial state of M'.

---

abbreviated as ij in the vertex labels.

4.1.27. Algorithm 4.6 can be adapted to a Moore machine $M = (Q, \Sigma_I, \Sigma_O, q_0, \delta, \tau)$, in order to obtain the minimal equivalent Moore machine $M' = (Q', \Sigma_I, \Sigma_O, Ej, \delta', \tau')$. We obtain Q' by applying Algorithm 4.5 with minimal changes,[19] and then, when applying Algorithm 4.6, in Step 2 of this Algorithm we make

$$\delta'(E_l, a) = E_m$$

$$\tau'(E_m) = b$$

However, the assignment (in Step 3) of $\tau(q_0)$ to the equivalence state associated with q_0 can lead to non-uniqueness of the equivalent minimal Moore machine M'.

4.1.2.4. Conversion of finite transducers into acceptors

Every Moore machine with output alphabet $\Sigma_O = \{0, 1\}$ can be considered as a FA by taking outputs "1" as accepting states. A FA, in turn, can be seen as a Moore machine by considering that it enters an accepting state when it prints "1", and enters some other state when printing "0." Thus, a transition table for a Moore machine can be turned into a transition table for a FA by assigning $*$, our marker for an accepting state, to a state that outputs "1". See Example 4.1.19.

Example 4.1.19. The table below is the transition table for a FA equivalent to the Moore machine in Example 4.1.14. Figure 4.1.15. shows this FA.

	$\delta(q, 0)$	$\delta(q, 1)$
$\rightarrow q_0$	q_1	q_2
$*q_1$	q_1	q_3
q_2	q_0	q_2
$*q_3$	q_2	q_3

Exercises

Exercise 4.1.1. Let $\Sigma = \{0, 1\}$. Construct a FA M accepting precisely those strings over Σ / the language:

---

[19] We need now the notion of 0-*distinguishable states* as those states q_i, q_j such that $\tau(q_i) \neq \tau(q_j)$.

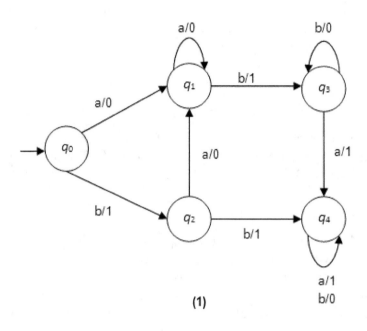

(1)

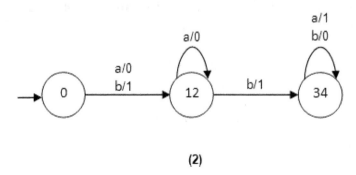

(2)

Figure 4.1.14.: A Mealy machine (1) and its minimal equivalent (2).

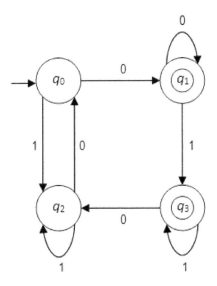

Figure 4.1.15.: A Moore machine converted into a FA.

1. with an even number of 0.

2. that end in a single 1.

3. that end in an odd number $n > 1$ of 1.

4. with the prefix 10.

5. $L = \{0, 1\}^* \{000, 111\} \{0, 1\}^*$.

6. $L = \{0, 1\}^* \{00\}$.

7. $L = \{010\}^* \{11, 0110\}^*$.

8. $L = \{00, 001\}^* \{1\}$.

9. $L = \{1, 01\}^* \{0\}$.

10. $L = \{010, 101\} \{101, 010\}^*$.

11. $L(01^* + \epsilon)$.

12. $L((1 + 01^*0)^* 01^*)$.

Exercise 4.1.2. Describe a FA recognizing all (partial) anagrams of the string *amber*.

Exercise 4.1.3. Describe a FA with the Roman alphabet for input alphabet Σ that recognizes strings with the 5 vowels occurring in the usual order, i.e. *aeiou* (e.g., the English word *facetious*). Describe its behavior when given the string *milk* as input.

Exercise 4.1.4. Show that the following languages are not regular:

1. $L = \{a^n b^m \in \Sigma^* | n \neq m\}$.

2. $L = \{ww^R | w \in \Sigma^*\}$.

3. $L = \{w \in \Sigma^* | |w|_a < |w|_b\}$.

Exercise 4.1.5. Find the regular expressions accepted by the indicated FAs by means of their characteristic equations:

1. Figure 4.1.8.1.

2. Figure 4.1.9.1.

3. Figure 4.1.11.2.

4. Figure 4.1.15.

5. Figure 4.1.16.1.

6. Figure 4.1.16.2.

7. Figure 4.1.16.3.

Exercise 4.1.6. Design the two algorithms based on Theorems 4.1.3 and 4.1.4.

Exercise 4.1.7. Construct a NDFA M accepting the language $L = \{0, 11\}^* \{10^*, \epsilon\}$ that is actually a combination of two NDFAs M_1 and M_2.

Exercise 4.1.8. Convert the NDFA with ϵ-transitions of Example 4.1.7 into a NDFA without ϵ-transitions.

Exercise 4.1.9. Construct the DFAs equivalent to the following NDFAs:

1. The NDFA without ϵ-transitions of Figure 4.1.7.2.

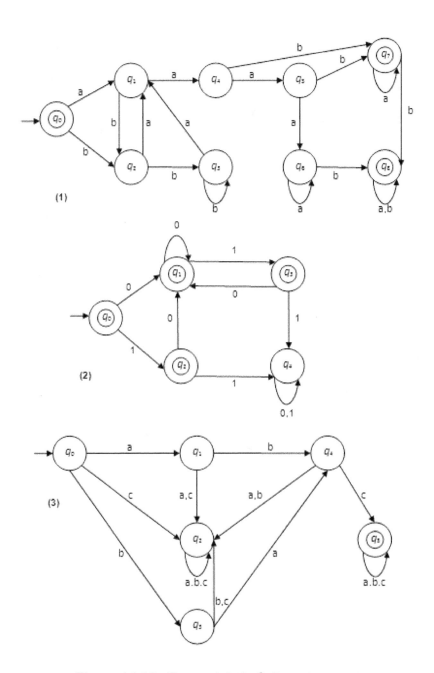

Figure 4.1.16.: Deterministic finite automata.

2. The NDFA with transition table:

	$\delta(q, a)$	$\delta(q, b)$
$\to q_0$	$\{q_0, q_1\}$	$\{q_2\}$
q_1	$\{q_3\}$	$\{q_1\}$
q_2	$\{q_2\}$	$\{q_4\}$
$*q_3$	$\emptyset$	$\{q_3\}$
$*q_4$	$\emptyset$	$\{q_4\}$

3. The NDFA with transition table:

	$\delta(q, 0)$	$\delta(q, 1)$
$\to q_0$	$\{q_0\}$	$\{q_1\}$
q_1	$\{q_0, q_2\}$	$\emptyset$
$*q_2$	$\emptyset$	$\{q_0, q_1\}$

4. The NDFA with transition table:

	$\delta(q, 0)$	$\delta(q, 1)$
$\to q_0$	$\{q_0\}$	$\{q_0, q_1\}$
q_1	$\{q_2\}$	$\{q_2\}$
$*q_2$	$\emptyset$	$\emptyset$

5. The NDFA with transition table:

	$\delta(q, a)$	$\delta(q, b)$
$\to q_0$	$\{q_0, q_1, q_3\}$	$\{q_0, q_2, q_3\}$
q_1	$\{q_3\}$	$\emptyset$
q_2	$\emptyset$	$\{q_3\}$
$*q_3$	$\{q_3\}$	$\{q_3\}$

Exercise 4.1.10. Construct the NDFA M' without ϵ-transitions equivalent to the NDFA $M = (\{q_0, q_1, q_2, q_3, q_4\}, \{0, 1\}, q_0, \{q_0\}, \delta)$ with the following transition table:

q	$\delta(q, 0)$	$\delta(q, 1)$	$\delta(q, \epsilon)$	$\hat{\delta}(q, 0)$	$\hat{\delta}(q, 1)$
q_0	$\emptyset$	$\emptyset$	$\{q_1\}$	$\{q_1, q_2\}$	$\emptyset$
q_1	$\{q_1, q_2\}$	$\emptyset$	$\emptyset$	$\{q_1, q_2\}$	$\emptyset$
q_2	$\emptyset$	$\{q_3\}$	$\emptyset$	$\emptyset$	$\{q_0, q_1, q_3\}$
q_3	$\emptyset$	$\{q_4\}$	$\{q_0\}$	$\{q_1, q_2\}$	$\{q_4\}$
q_4	$\{q_3\}$	$\emptyset$	$\emptyset$	$\{q_0, q_1, q_3\}$	$\emptyset$

Exercise 4.1.11. Research into the following algorithms for minimization of DFAs and formulate them in some sort of pseudo-code:

1. Moore's algorithm.

2. Hopcroft's algorithm.

3. Brzozowski's algorithm.

Exercise 4.1.12. With respect to the partition-refinement algorithm (Algorithm 4.2), is this the same as Moore's algorithm?

Exercise 4.1.13. Can the FA in Figure 4.1.8.2 be minimized?

Exercise 4.1.14. Minimize the automata given in the state diagram of the indicated Figures:

1. Figure 4.1.11.2.

2. Figure 4.1.15.

3. Figure 4.1.16.1.

4. Figure 4.1.16.2.

5. Figure 4.1.16.3.

Exercise 4.1.15. As seen above, a FA does not accept the language $L_1 = \{a^m b^m \in \Sigma^* | m \geq 0\}$. However, it does accept the language $L_2 = \{a^m b^n \in \Sigma^* | m, n \geq 1\}$. Explain this contrast by appealing to the computation abilities of FAs.

Exercise 4.1.16. With respect to the closure properties of regular languages (cf. Section 3.2.3.3), give proofs of closure by invoking product FAs:

1. Closure under intersection. (Hint: Given two FAs M_1 and M_2 with languages $L(M_1)$ and $L(M_2)$, the accepting states of M_1 and M_2 are a single state of the product FA $M_3 = M_\times$.)

2. Closure under difference. (Hint: Construct the product FA $M_3 = M_\times$ of M_1 and M_2 in such a way that M_3 has only the accepting states of M_1 or M_2, but not of both.)

Exercise 4.1.17. Given $L_1 = \{0, 1\}^* \{00\} \{0, 1\}^*$ and $L_2 = \{0, 1\}^* \{01\}$, construct the product FA for:

1. $L_1 \cup L_2$. (Apply Algorithm 4.4.)

2. $L_1 \cap L_2$.

3. $L_2 - L_1$.

Exercise 4.1.18. Given two DFAs $M_1 = (Q_1, \Sigma, q_{0,1}, A_1, \delta_1)$ and $M_2 = (Q_2, \Sigma, q_{0,2}, A_2, \delta_2)$, the *direct sum* of M_1 and M_2 is the DFA $M_1 + M_2 = (Q_1 \cup Q_2, \Sigma, q_0, A_1 \cup A_2, \delta) = M_+$ where $q_0 = q_{0,1}$ or $q_0 = q_{0,2}$ and the transition function is defined as:

$$\delta(q, a) = \begin{cases} \delta_1(q, a) & \text{if } q \in Q_1 \\ \delta_2(q, a) & \text{if } q \in Q_2 \end{cases}$$

Find the direct sum of the two DFAs in Figure 4.1.17. (Hint: Construct the transition table for $M_1 + M_2$.)

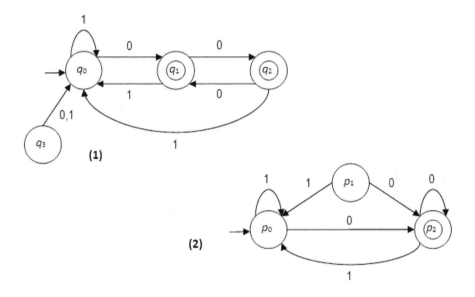

Figure 4.1.17.: Two DFAs.

Exercise 4.1.19. It can be shown that two DFAs M_1 and M_2 are equivalent if, given the equivalence classes of $M_+ = M_1 + M_2$, $q_{0,1}$ and $q_{0,2}$ are in the same equivalence class.

1. Account formally for this result.

2. Verify if the two DFAs of Figure 4.1.17 are equivalent by using this result. (Hint: Apply Algorithm 4.2.)

Exercise 4.1.20. A *two-way FA* (abbrev.: 2FA) is a FA whose read-only head can move to both the left and the right.

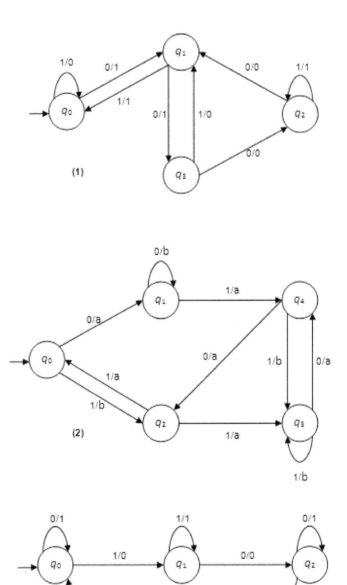

Figure 4.1.18.: Mealy machines.

1. Give a formal definition of a 2FA.

2. Describe the main aspects of its behavior when accepting a string.

3. What is the computing power of a 2FA as compared to a FA?

4. Find applications for a 2FA.

5. Do the 2FAs augment the class $\mathscr{RGL}$?

Exercise 4.1.21. With respect to the Mealy machines in Figure 4.1.18:

1. Give three different examples of strings output by them.

2. Convert them into equivalent Moore machines.

3. Find their minimal equivalent Mealy machines.

Exercise 4.1.22. The notion of direct sum of FAs (Exercise 4.1.18) generalizes directly to FTs. By applying it (cf. Exercise 4.1.19), determine whether the following FTs are equivalent:

1. M_1 (Fig. 4.1.12.2) and M_2 (Fig. 4.1.18.3).

2. M_1 (Fig. 4.1.13.1) and M_2 (Fig. 4.1.18.2).

3. M_1 (Fig. 4.1.18.1) and M_2 (Fig. 4.1.18.3).

Exercise 4.1.23. A barcode (see Fig. 4.1.19) represents data by varying the width and spacings of a series of parallel bars. A binary barcode has only two widths for the bars and the spacings between them, say, *narrow* and *wide*. A barcode reader is a machine that, given a barcode as an input, "translates" it into an output string of symbols. Elaborate on a FT as a barcode reader. In particular, elaborate on:

1. How is the "translation" carried out?

2. How does a FT validate a barcode?

Exercise 4.1.24. Design a Moore machine that works as a traffic light.

Exercise 4.1.25. Account for the problem of non-uniqueness mentioned in §4.1.27.

Figure 4.1.19.: A barcode.

Exercise 4.1.26. Prove (Complete the proof of) the theorems and propositions of Sections 4.1.1-2 that were left as an exercise (with a sketchy proof, respectively). (Hint for Proposition 4.1.17: Invoke Def. 2.1.10.)

Exercise 4.1.27. Prove Theorem 4.1.5 by invoking the notion of ϵ-closure.

4.2. Pushdown automata

Pushdown automata (PDAs) are associated to CFLs in the same way that finite-state machines are associated to regular languages: A language $L(G)$ can be generated by a CFG G if and only if it can be accepted by a PDA M such that $L(G) = L(M)$.[20] But unlike finite-state machines, non-determinism cannot always be eliminated in PDAs; if non-determinism can be eliminated in a PDA, then we have a *parser* for a certain CFL. Parsers thus accept only a subset of the CFLs, precisely that subset in which the syntax of most programming languages is included.

4.2.1. Basic aspects of PDAs

Recall the definition of a formal grammar $G = (V, T, S, P)$ (Def. 3.1.11). A PDA is essentially a (possibly non-deterministic) finite-state machine with an auxiliary stack that provides an unlimited amount of memory for P. The operation of a stack is basically on a last-in-first-out rule: Adding a symbol to the memory is interpreted as *pushing* it onto a stack so that it becomes the top symbol; this explains the coinage of these machines.

As said, its memory may be unlimited, but the PDA has access only to the symbol at the top of the stack, i.e. the most recently added symbol. Let X be the symbol currently on top of the stack; then, $\alpha = YX$, where α is a string over the stack alphabet, denotes that a new symbol

---

[20]We consider the abbreviation "PDA" as an acronym and write its plural form as PDAs.

Y is added to the stack and is now the top symbol. But the PDA can simply leave the stack unchanged, an action denoted by $\alpha = X$, or *pop X off* the stack (i.e. remove X), denoted by $\alpha = \epsilon$. Visualizing a tray dispenser at a cafeteria may help gaining an intuitive idea of a PDA; the formal description of a computer model of a PDA (see below) lends rigor to this idea.

4.2.1. (Def.) A pushdown automaton is a 7-tuple

$$M = (Q, \Sigma, \Gamma, q_0, A, Z_0, \delta)$$

where Q is a finite set of states, $q_0 \in Q$ is the initial state, Σ is a finite set of symbols called the *input alphabet,* Γ is a finite set of symbols called the *stack alphabet,* A is the set of accepting states, $Z_0 \in \Gamma$ is the *start stack symbol,* and $\delta : (Q \times (\Sigma \cup \{\epsilon\}) \times \Gamma) \longrightarrow (Q \times \Gamma^*)$ is the transition function.[21]

4.2.2. (Def.) The computer model for a PDA (see Fig. 4.2.1) consists of (i) an input tape, (ii) a read-only head, (iii) a stack, and (iv) a control box programmed by the transition function δ. The read-only head reads an input tape moving in a single direction (from the left to the right). When this head reads a substring u while in state q with substring α at the top of the stack, the machine selects a corresponding entry from δ and performs the indicated transition.

4.2.3. (Def.) A *configuration* C for a PDA M is a triple $C = (q, u, \alpha)$ where $q \in Q$, $u \in \Sigma^*$, and $\alpha \in \Gamma^*$.

1. We say that the configuration (q, u, α) *yields* the configuration (p, v, β) *in one move*, and write $(q, u, \alpha) \vdash_M (p, v, \beta)$, if there is a transition $\delta(q, u, \alpha) = (p, \beta)$. More exactly, we have $(q, u, X\gamma) \vdash_M (p, v, \xi\gamma)$, for $u = \sigma v$, $\sigma \in (\Sigma \cup \{\epsilon\})$,[22] and where if $\alpha = X\gamma$ for some $X \in \Gamma$ and some $\gamma \in \Gamma^*$, then $\beta = \xi\gamma$ for some string ξ for which $(p, \xi) \in \delta(q, \sigma, X)$.

2. A *computation* for a PDA M is a finite sequence of configurations $C_0, C_1, ..., C_n$ such that $C_{i-1} \vdash_M C_i$, $1 \leq i \leq n$.

3. A configuration C yields a configuration C' if there is a computation of C' from C in n moves, denoted by $C \vdash_M^n C'$, or in zero or more moves, denoted by $C \vdash_M^* C'$.

This can be restated in terms of the transition function.

---

[21] Alternatively, one can consider a transition relation $\Delta = Q \times (\Sigma \cup \{\epsilon\}) \times \Gamma \times Q \times \Gamma^*$.

[22] Clearly, $u = v$ if $\sigma = \epsilon$. Alternatively, we can write $(q, uv, X\gamma) \vdash_M (p, v, \xi\gamma)$.

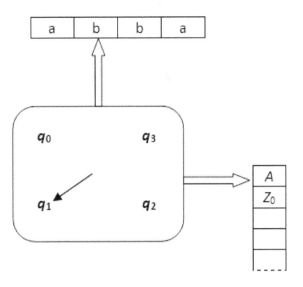

Figure 4.2.1.: Computer model for a PDA.

4.2.4. (Def.) Given a PDA M, we write

$$\delta(q, a, Z) = \{(p_1, \alpha_1), (p_2, \alpha_2), ..., (p_n, \alpha_n)\}$$

where $q, p_{1 \leq i \leq n} \in Q$, $a \in \Sigma$, $Z \in \Gamma$, and $\alpha_{1 \leq i \leq n} \in \Gamma^*$, to indicate that in state q, reading input symbol a, and with Z as the top stack symbol, M can enter state p_i, replace symbol Z by string α_i and advance the input head one symbol.[23] We write

$$\delta(q, \epsilon, Z) = \{(p_1, \alpha_1), (p_2, \alpha_2), ..., (p_n, \alpha_n)\}$$

to indicate that M at state q and with Z as the top symbol on the stack can enter any state p_i and replace Z by α_i independently of the input symbol being read. Note that in this case the head does not advance.

By convention, the leftmost symbol of α_i is placed highest, and the rightmost symbol of α_i is placed lowest, on the stack.

4.2.5. (Def.) Let there be given a PDA M. An *accepting configuration* of M is any configuration in which the state $p \in A$, and we

---

[23]It is not possible to choose state p_i and string α_j such that $i \neq j$ in a single move.

write[24]

$$(q_0, uv, Z_0) \vdash_M^* (p, v, \alpha).$$

Example 4.2.1. Recall the CFL $L = \{a^m b^m | m \geq 0\}$ of Example 3.3.1. The PDA for L is $M = (Q, \Sigma, \Gamma, q_0, A, Z_0, \delta)$ where $Q = \{q_0, q_1, q_2, q_3\}$, $A = \{q_0, q_3\}$, $\Sigma = \{a, b\}$ and the transitions are as follows:

State $q \in Q$	Input $(a, b \in \Sigma) \cup \{\epsilon\}$	Stack symbol $A, Z_0 \in \Gamma$	Move(s)
q_0	a	Z_0	(q_1, AZ_0)
q_1	a	A	(q_1, AA)
q_1	b	A	(q_2, ϵ)
q_2	b	A	(q_2, ϵ)
q_2	ϵ	Z_0	(q_3, Z_0)

The sequence of configurations that results in the acceptance of the string $aabb$ is:

$$q_0, aabb, Z_0 \vdash q_1, abb, AZ_0 \vdash q_1, bb, AAZ_0 \vdash q_2, b, AZ_0$$

$$\vdash q_2, \epsilon, Z_0 \vdash q_3, \epsilon, Z_0$$

This is translated in terms of δ as:

$$\begin{aligned}
\delta(q_0, a, Z_0) &= \{(q_1, AZ_0)\} \\
\delta(q_1, a, A) &= \{(q_1, AA)\} \\
\delta(q_1, b, A) &= \{(q_2, \epsilon)\} \\
\delta(q_2, b, A) &= \{(q_2, \epsilon)\} \\
\delta(q_2, \epsilon, Z_0) &= \{(q_3, Z_0)\}
\end{aligned}$$

4.2.6. (Def.) The state diagram $D = \vec{\mathfrak{D}}(M)$ of a PDA M is a labeled digraph as for a FA (cf. Def. 4.1.6, items 1 and 3) such that for each transition $\delta(q, u, X) = (p, \alpha)$ there is an arc from vertex q to vertex p labeled "$u; X/\alpha$" (also: $u, X/\alpha$), interpreted as "read u; replace X by α on the stack"

Example 4.2.2. We can actually simplify the PDA in Example 4.2.1 by making the set $Q = \{q_0, q_1, q_2\}$ and $A = \{q_2\}$. Figure 4.2.2 shows this PDA accepting (by final state) the language $L(M) = \{a^m b^m | m \geq 0\}$.

---

[24]Note that only u has been accepted, not the input string uv, and the stack is not empty. Thus, this is not a terminal accepting configuration. We shall shortly specify terminal accepting configurations in PDAs.

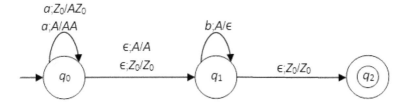

Figure 4.2.2.: A PDA M accepting $L(M) = \{a^m b^m | m \geq 0\}$.

4.2.2. Acceptance modes by PDAs

4.2.7. (Def.) A string w is *accepted* by a PDA M if, starting in state q_0 at the first symbol, the transition sequence of M terminates in two possible ways:

1. Termination in an accepting state $q_f \in A$. We denote this by

$$(q_0, w, Z_0) \vdash_M^* (q_f, \epsilon, \alpha)$$

where $\alpha \in \Gamma^*$. Accordingly, we have the *language accepted by final state*, denoted by $L(M)$, defined as the language

$$L(M) = \{w \in \Sigma^* | (q_0, w, Z_0) \vdash_M^* (q_f, \epsilon, \alpha)\}.$$

2. Termination in an empty stack after M has read the last symbol. We denote this by

$$(q_0, w, Z_0) \vdash_M^* (q, \epsilon, \epsilon)$$

where $q \in Q$. Accordingly, we have the *language accepted by empty (or null) stack*, denoted by $N(M)$, defined as the language

$$N(M) = \{w \in \Sigma^* | (q_0, w, Z_0) \vdash_M^* (q, \epsilon, \epsilon)\}.$$

The first mode of acceptance uses the internal memory (state), whereas the second uses the external memory, i.e. the stack. Unless it is necessary to specify that an accepted language is of the $L(M)$ or $N(M)$ kind, we shall designate a language accepted by a PDA M indifferently by $L(M)$. The following theorem supports this simplification:

Theorem 4.2.1. *For each PDA M, one can construct a PDA M' such that $L(M) = N(M')$, and vice-versa $N(M) = L(M')$.*

Proof: (Sketch) We have to show that (I) given a PDA M that accepts a language L by final state, we can construct a PDA M' that simulates M by accepting L by empty stack, and (II) given a PDA M that accepts L by empty stack, we can construct a PDA M' that simulates M by accepting L by final state.

(I) The idea is to let M' have the option to erase its stack whenever M enters a final state. For this end, we provide M' with a state q_e. Moreover, we provide M' with a bottom-of-stack marker X_0 intended to bar M' from accidentally accepting should M empty its stack without entering a final state. Let $M = (Q, \Sigma, \Gamma, q_0, Z_0, A, \delta)$. Now, let

$$M' = \left(Q \cup \left\{ q_0', q_e \right\}, \Sigma, \Gamma \cup \{X_0\}, q_0', X_0, \emptyset, \delta' \right)$$

where δ' is defined as follows: (1) $\delta'\left(q_0', \epsilon, X_0 \right) = \{(q_0, Z_0 X_0)\}$; (2) for all $q \in Q$, all $a \in \Sigma \cup \{\epsilon\}$, and all $Z \in \Gamma$, $\delta'(q, a, Z)$ includes the elements of $\delta(q, a, Z)$; (3) for all $q \in A$ and $Z \in \Gamma \cup \{X_0\}$, $\delta'(q, \epsilon, Z)$ contains (q_e, ϵ); (4) for all $Z \in \Gamma \cup \{X_0\}$, $\delta'(q_e, \epsilon, Z)$ contains (q_e, ϵ). Figure 4.2.3.1 shows a schematic state diagram of this simulation.

(II) The idea is to make M' detect when M empties its stack, entering a final state when and only when this occurs, so that no additional symbol is "consumed." M' detects that M has emptied its stack when a stack symbol X_0 appears. Let $M = (Q, \Sigma, \Gamma, q_0, Z_0, \emptyset, \delta)$. Now, we let

$$M' = \left(Q \cup \left\{ q_0', q_f \right\}, \Sigma, \Gamma \cup \{X_0\}, q_0', X_0, \{q_f\}, \delta' \right)$$

where δ' is defined as follows: (1) $\delta'\left(q_0', \epsilon, X_0 \right) = \{(q_0, Z_0 X_0)\}$; (2) for all $q \in Q$, all $a \in \Sigma \cup \{\epsilon\}$, and all $Z \in \Gamma$, we have $\delta'(q, a, Z) = \delta(q, a, Z)$; (3) for all $q \in Q$, $\delta'(q, \epsilon, X_0)$ contains (q_f, ϵ). Figure 4.2.3.2 shows a schematic state diagram of this simulation.

Now, let I.(1)–(4) and II.(1)–(3) be actually rules and let x be in $L(M)$ or $N(M)$, accordingly. For case I, if $x \in L(M)$, then for some $q \in A$ we have $(q_0, x, Z_0) \vdash_M^* (q, \epsilon, \alpha)$. Now we consider M' with input x: By rule I.(1),

$$\left(q_0', x, X_0 \right) \vdash_{M'}^* (q_0, x, Z_0 X_0).$$

Do the same (i.e. give the configurations and computations) for rules I.(2)–(4). Then work the other way round. Do the same for case II. **QED**

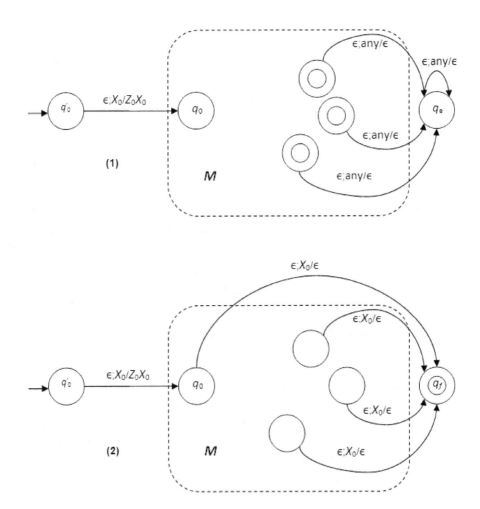

Figure 4.2.3.: Proving $L(M) = N(M)$.

4.2.3. Equivalence between CFLs and PDAs

We began this Section by stating that there is an equivalence between CFLs and PDAs. Theorems 4.2.2-3 below phrase this in a formal way. The proofs of both theorems are highly convoluted, and we leave them as exercises, providing only the essential ideas behind them. The examples that follow the proof sketches provide further clues for the complete proofs. Importantly, from these proofs one can extract algorithms for, (i) given a CFG G, constructing the corresponding PDA M such that we have the CFL $L = L(M)$ or $L = N(M)$, or (ii) given a CFL L and a PDA M, producing the equivalent CFG G such that we have $L = L(M)$ or $L = N(M)$. We give an algorithm for the former and leave the algorithm for the latter as an exercise.

Theorem 4.2.2. *If L is a CFL, then there is some PDA M such that $L = L(M)$.*

Proof: (Idea) If L is a CFL, then there is a CFG $G = (V, T, S, P)$ that generates it. Let $w \in L(G)$. Then, for S the start symbol and w there is a derivation $S \overset{*}{\underset{G}{\Longrightarrow}} w$ each step of which yields an intermediate string of variables and terminals. In particular, there is a leftmost derivation $S \overset{*}{\underset{G}{\Longrightarrow}}_l w$ and $L = L(M)$. Let there be given the PDA $M = (Q, \Sigma, \Gamma, q_0, A, Z_0, \delta)$ such that $\Sigma = T$ and $\Gamma = V \cup \{Z_0\}$. Given input w, M starts by writing S on its stack and then goes through a sequence of intermediate strings, non-deterministically selecting at each step a production for a particular variable and making the corresponding substitutions. M eventually arrives at a string w' with only terminals; if $w' = w$, then M accepts $L(G)$. M needs the feature of being able to store the intermediate strings; the stack requires an adaptation for this, as an intermediate string can have both variables and terminals, but M needs to detect a variable to make the corresponding substitution. The solution is to keep only a part of the intermediate string on the stack, namely the part starting with the leftmost variable symbol; terminal symbols anteceding this variable symbol are matched with symbols in the input string directly. In this way, the symbol at the top of the stack is always associated to a variable in an intermediate string, and the derivation is a leftmost derivation. **QED**

The idea for the proof of Theorem 4.2.2 can be summarized as follows: Given a CFG $G = (V, T, S, P)$, we need to construct a PDA M that "guesses" the leftmost derivations for strings $w \in (V \cup T)^*$ and checks their correctness. This is the basis for an algorithm to convert a CFG G into a PDA M (see Algorithm 4.5). Note in Algorithm 4.5 that the output PDA, which is non-deterministic, has invariably only three states: the initial state q_0, the final accepting state q_2, and state q_1 that concentrates all the processing of the strings of $L(G) = L(M)$. M starts by placing the symbol S on top of the stack (Step 1). Step 2.a of this algorithm makes it so that PDA M includes all the productions of G and Step 2.b tackles the matching between the input string and the stack, namely by popping off the matching terminals from the latter. M accepts a string $w \in L(G)$ by terminating in accepting state q_2; in order to make M accept by emptying the stack in Step 3 we simply define the transition

$$\delta(q_1, \epsilon, Z_0) = (q_2, \epsilon)$$

thus obtaining the PDA

$$M = (\{q_0, q_1, q_2\}, \Sigma = T, \Gamma = V \cup T \cup \{Z_0\}, q_0, \emptyset, Z_0, \delta)$$

such that $L(G) = N(M)$. Furthermore, Algorithm 4.5 outputs a PDA M such that $\Gamma_M = V \cup T \cup \{Z_0\}$, but, as stated in the sketch of the proof of Theorem 4.2.2, it is possible to construct a PDA M such that $\Gamma_M = V \cup \{Z_0\}$; this requires the productions to be in GNF and we leave this algorithm as an exercise.

Example 4.2.3. We apply Algorithm 4.5 to the CFG G in Example 3.3.6, obtaining the PDA with the following transitions:

$$
\begin{aligned}
\delta(q_0, \epsilon, Z_0) &= \{(q_1, SZ_0)\} \\
\delta(q_1, \epsilon, S) &= \{(q_1, aAB)\} \\
\delta(q_1, \epsilon, A) &= \{(q_1, Bba)\} \\
\delta(q_1, \epsilon, B) &= \{(q_1, bB), (q_1, c)\} \\
\delta(q_1, a, a) &= \{(q_1, \epsilon)\} \\
\delta(q_1, b, b) &= \{(q_1, \epsilon)\} \\
\delta(q_1, c, c) &= \{(q_1, \epsilon)\} \\
\delta(q_1, \epsilon, Z_0) &= \{(q_2, Z_0)\}
\end{aligned}
$$

The computation ending in the acceptance of the string $acbabc$ is as follows (the processed substrings are underlined; we omit the subscript M in $\vdash$):[25]

---

[25] See Figure 3.3.1 for the parse tree.

Algorithm 4.7 Conversion of a CFG G into a PDA M

Input: A CFG $G = (V, T, S, P)$ with productions of the form

$$\alpha \rightarrow \beta_1 \,|\, \beta_2 \,|\, ... \,|\, \beta_n$$

where $\alpha \in V$ and $\beta_i \in (V \cup T)^*$
Output: A PDA

$$M = (\{q_0, q_1, q_2\}, \Sigma = T, \Gamma = V \cup T \cup \{Z_0\}, q_0, \{q_2\}, Z_0, \delta)$$

such that $L(M) = L(G)$

START

1. Define the starting transition of M:

$$\delta(q_0, \epsilon, Z_0) = \{(q_1, SZ_0)\}$$

2. If the top stack symbol is

    a) a variable A, then define the transition

    $$\delta(q_1, \epsilon, A) = \{(q_1, \beta_1), ..., (q_1, \beta_n)\}.$$

    Do this for all the variables in V_G.

    b) a terminal a, then define the transition

    $$\delta(q_1, a, a) = \{(q_1, \epsilon)\}.$$

    Do this for all the terminals in T_G.

3. Define the final transition of M:

$$\delta(q_1, \epsilon, Z_0) = \{(q_2, Z_0)\}$$

TERMINATE

$$
\begin{array}{rcl}
q_0, acbabc, Z_0 & \vdash & q_1, acbabc, SZ_0 \\
& \vdash & q_1, acbabc, aABZ_0 \\
& \vdash & q_1, \underline{a}cbabc, ABZ_0 \\
& \vdash & q_1, \underline{a}cbabc, BbaBZ_0 \\
& \vdash & q_1, \underline{a}cbabc, cbaBZ_0 \\
& \vdash & q_1, \underline{ac}babc, baBZ_0 \\
& \vdash & q_1, \underline{acb}abc, aBZ_0 \\
& \vdash & q_1, \underline{acba}bc, BZ_0 \\
& \vdash & q_1, \underline{acba}bc, bBZ_0 \\
& \vdash & q_1, \underline{acbab}c, BZ_0 \\
& \vdash & q_1, \underline{acbab}c, cZ_0 \\
& \vdash & q_1, \underline{acbabc}, Z_0 \\
& \vdash & q_2, \epsilon, Z_0
\end{array}
$$

The PDA obtained in Example 4.2.3 by the application of Algorithm 4.5 and corresponding to leftmost derivations is called a *top-down PDA*. (Figure 4.2.4.1 shows this PDA.) It is also possible to construct a *bottom-up PDA*, corresponding to rightmost derivations (Fig. 4.2.4.2). We leave the algorithm for the latter as an exercise.

We now address the equivalence of CFLs with PDAs by focusing on the conversion of a PDA M into a CFG G. We do it for $L(G) = N(M)$ and leave the adaptation for $L(G) = L(M)$ as an exercise.

Theorem 4.2.3. *If, given a PDA M and a language L, $L = N(M)$, then L is a CFL.*

Proof: (Sketch) We now need a CFG G that simulates the moves of M. In particular, we need a leftmost derivation in G of some string x to be a simulation of M when given input x. Because this is a leftmost derivation, the processed prefix is the terminal part of x, to the right of which lies the variable part. Thus, just an in the proof of Theorem 4.2.2, we require that the symbols in the stack of M be matched to the unprocessed suffixes of x; when the stack is empty, x is a string of terminals. To this end, we need special variables. Let $M = (Q, \Sigma, \Gamma, q_0, Z_0, \emptyset, \delta)$ be a PDA. We need a grammar $G = (V, T, S, P)$ where $T = \Sigma \cup \{\epsilon\}$ and V is a set of objects of the form $[qAp]$ for $A \in \Gamma$ and $q, p \in Q$. The productions in P are of the form

$$S \to [q_0 Z_0 q]$$

for every $q \in Q$, and

$$[qAq_{m+1}] \to a \, [q_1 B_1 q_2] \, [q_2 B_2 q_3] \ldots [q_m B_m q_{m+1}]$$

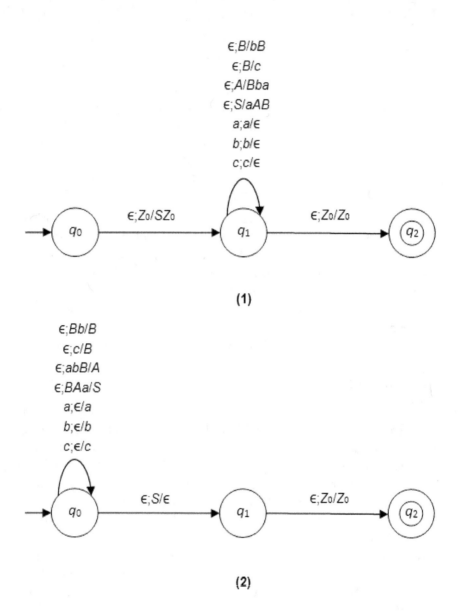

Figure 4.2.4.: Top-down (1) and bottom-up (2) PDAs.

for every $q, q_1, q_2, ...q_{m+1} \in Q$, every $a \in \Sigma \cup \{\epsilon\}$, and $A, B_1, B_2, ...B_m \in \Gamma$, such that $\delta(q, a, A) \supseteq (q_1, B_1 B_2...B_m)$. If $m = 0$, then we have $[qAq_1] \to a$. The idea is to have

$$[qAp] \overset{*}{\underset{G}{\Longrightarrow}}_l x \text{ iff } (q, x, A) \vdash_M^* (p, \epsilon, \epsilon).$$

That is, we want $[qAp]$ to derive x in a leftmost derivation if and only if x causes M to erase an A from its stack by a sequence of zero or more moves that starts in state q and ends in state p; at each move, the stack content is increased or decreased by a single symbol, until it is wholly empty at state p.

($\Rightarrow$) First we want to prove that

$$\text{if } (q, x, A) \vdash_M^i (p, \epsilon, \epsilon), \text{ then } [qAp] \overset{*}{\underset{G}{\Longrightarrow}}_l x.$$

The proof is by induction on i. If $i = 1$, then $\delta(q, x, A) \supseteq (p, \epsilon)$, and thus $([qAp] \to x) \in G$. For $i > 1$, let $x = ay$, so that we have the computation

$$(q, ay, A) \vdash (q_1, y, B_1 B_2...B_n) \vdash_M^{i-1} (p, \epsilon, \epsilon).$$

Let $y = y_1 y_2...y_n$, where each y_j causes B_j to be popped off the stack, so that we have (how?)

$$[qAp] \overset{*}{\underset{G}{\Longrightarrow}}_l ay_1 y_2...y_n = x.$$

($\Leftarrow$) We now want to prove that

$$\text{if } [qAp] \overset{i}{\underset{G}{\Longrightarrow}}_l x, \text{ then } (q, x, A) \vdash_M^* (p, \epsilon, \epsilon).$$

The proof is again by induction on i. (We leave the details as an exercise. Hint: write $x = ax_1 x_2...x_n$ so that the first move of M is $(q, x, A) \vdash_M (q_1, x_1 x_2...x_n, B_1 B_2...B_n)$.)

Finally, if we let $A = Z_0$ and $q = q_0$, then we obviously have

$$[q_0 Z_0 p] \overset{*}{\underset{G}{\Longrightarrow}}_l x \text{ iff } (q_0, x, Z_0) \vdash_M^* (p, \epsilon, \epsilon)$$

and thus

$$S \overset{*}{\underset{G}{\Longrightarrow}}_l x \text{ iff } (q_0, x, Z_0) \vdash_M^* (p, \epsilon, \epsilon).$$

Hence, $x \in L(G)$ if and only if $x \in N(M)$. **QED**

Example 4.2.4. Let δ as given below be the transition function for the PDA $M = (\{q_0, q_1\}, \{a, b\}, \{A, Z_0\}, q_0, Z_0, \emptyset, \delta)$:

$$
\begin{aligned}
\delta(q_0, a, Z_0) &= \{(q_0, AZ_0)\} \\
\delta(q_0, a, A) &= \{(q_0, AA)\} \\
\delta(q_0, b, A) &= \{(q_1, \epsilon)\} \\
\delta(q_1, b, A) &= \{(q_1, \epsilon)\} \\
\delta(q_1, \epsilon, A) &= \{(q_1, \epsilon)\} \\
\delta(q_1, \epsilon, Z_0) &= \{(q_1, \epsilon)\}
\end{aligned}
$$

The construction of the CFG G that generates $N(M)$ follows the following steps: Begin by setting the set V with the objects of the form $[q_i A q_j]$, $i, j = 0, 1$. Next, determine the productions with S as an antecedent. In this case, we have the productions:

$$S \to [q_0, Z_0, q_0]$$

$$S \to [q_0, Z_0, q_1]$$

Then, work out the productions for $[q_i Z_0, q_j]$ required by each transition. For instance, for the first transition we need the following productions:

$$[q_0, Z_0, q_0] \to a\,[q_0, A, q_0]\,[q_0, Z_0, q_0]$$

$$[q_0, Z_0, q_0] \to a\,[q_0, A, q_1]\,[q_1, Z_0, q_0]$$

$$[q_0, Z_0, q_1] \to a\,[q_0, A, q_0]\,[q_0, Z_0, q_1]$$

$$[q_0, Z_0, q_1] \to a\,[q_0, A, q_1]\,[q_1, Z_0, q_1]$$

For the transition $\delta(q_1, b, A) = \{(q_1, \epsilon)\}$, we need the production:

$$[q_0, A, q_1] \to b$$

Determine then the variables that are superfluous, i.e. variables for which there are no productions or from which no terminal string can be derived. Delete these variables. *Et voilà!* We leave the whole computation as an exercise. When the CFG has been computed, rename the objects of the form $[q_i A q_j]$ as A, etc.

4.2.4. CFLs accepted by deterministic PDAs

4.2.4.1. Deterministic PDAs

As said above, the CFLs accepted by a deterministic PDA constitute an important subset of $\mathscr{CFL}$. We now focus on this topic.

4.2.8. (Def.) An automaton $M = (Q, \Sigma, \Gamma, q_0, Z_0, A, \delta)$ is said to be a *deterministic PDA* (DPDA) if the following conditions are satisfied:

1. For every $q \in Q$, every $a \in \Sigma \cup \{\epsilon\}$, and every $X \in \Gamma$, we have $|\delta(q, a, X)| \leq 1$.

2. For every $q \in Q$, every $a \in \Sigma$, and every $X \in \Gamma$, if $|\delta(q, \epsilon, X)| \neq \emptyset$, then $|\delta(q, a, X)| = \emptyset$.

A language L is called a *deterministic CFL* (DCFL) if there is a DPDA accepting it.

Condition 1 above hinders there being a choice on the same input symbol (including ϵ), whereas condition 2 hinders there being a choice between an ϵ-transition and a transition using the next input. Because there are now no choices, the transitions are written simply

$$\delta(q, a, X) = (p, \alpha).$$

The following proposition specifies a *normal form* for the DPDAs; the only stack operations of a DPDA are erasing the top symbol or pushing a symbol. The proofs for conditions 1 and 2 are left as exercises.

4.2.9. (Prop.) Every DCFL L is a $L(M)$ for a DPDA M such that if $\delta(q, a, X) = (p, \alpha)$, then

1. $|\alpha| \leq 2$, and

2. $\alpha = \epsilon$, $\alpha = X$, or $\alpha = YX$.

Proof: (Sketch) With respect to condition 1, we want M to push only one symbol per move. So, if $\delta(q, a, X) = (r, \alpha)$ and $\alpha > 2$, let $\alpha = Y_1 Y_2 ... Y_n$, $n \geq 3$, and create states $p_1, p_2, ..., p_{n-2}$. These are non-accepting states. Define then $\delta(q, a, X) = (p_1, Y_{n-1} Y_n)$. What else do we need so that, in state q, on input a, X is at the top of the stack, this DPDA still replaces X with α and then enters state r, but now does so in $n - 1$ moves? As for condition 2, let M' be a DPDA satisfying condition 1. We need some DPDA M to simulate M'. Define M and δ so that it can be shown by induction on the number of moves that

$$\left(q_0', w, X_0 \right) \vdash^*_{M'} (q, \epsilon, X_1 X_2 ... X_n)$$

if and only if

$$\left(\left[q_0' X_0 \right], w, Z_0 \right) \vdash^*_{M} ([q X_1], \epsilon, X_2 X_3 ... X_n Z_0)$$

and $L(M) = L(M')$. **QED**

Further important results for DCFLs are as follows.

4.2.10. (Prop.) The class of DCFLs is closed under complementation.

Proof: (Idea) We need a DPDA that reads the entire input string and whose accepting states can only be reading states; then, we swap acceptance and non-acceptance with respect to these states. **QED**

4.2.11. (Prop.) The class of DCFLs is *not* closed under (i) union, (ii) concatenation, or (iii) Kleene closure.

Proof: (Sketch) Let $L_1 = \{a^i b^i c^j | i, j \geq 0\}$ and $L_2 = \{a^i b^j c^j | i, j \geq 0\}$. For (i), $L_1 \cup L_2$ is equivalent to $L_3 = \{a^i b^j c^k | i \neq j, j \neq k\}$, but L_3 is not a DCFL (why?). (ii) Show why $L_4 = 0L_1 \cup 0L_2$ is not a DCFL. (iii) $L_5 = \{0\} \cup (0L_1 \cup L_2)$ is a DCFL, but $(L_5)^*$ is not (why?). **QED**

4.2.12. (Prop.) Let L_1 be a DCFL and L_2 a regular language. Then, the following problems are decidable:

1. $L_1 \overset{?}{=} L_2$.

2. $L_2 \overset{?}{\subseteq} L_1$.

3. $\overline{L_1} \overset{?}{=} \emptyset$.

4. $L_1 \overset{?}{\in} \mathcal{RGL}$.

5. $\overline{L_1} \overset{?}{\in} \mathcal{CFL}$.

Proof: Left as an exercise.

4.2.13. (Prop.) Let L_1, L_2 be DCFLs. Then, the following problems are undecidable:

1. $(L_1 \cap L_2) \overset{?}{\in} \mathcal{DCFL}$.

2. $(L_1 \cap L_2) \overset{?}{\in} \mathcal{CFL}$.

3. $(L_1 \cap L_2) \overset{?}{=} \emptyset$.

4. $(L_1 \cup L_2) \overset{?}{\in} \mathscr{DCFL}$.

5. $L_1 \overset{?}{\subseteq} L_2$.

Proof: Left as an exercise.

4.2.4.2. LR(k) grammars

The simplest way to define a DCFL is to say that it is generated by a CFG with restrictions. In particular, the restricted CFGs known as LR(k) grammars generate *exactly* the DCFLs. It will prove useful to know that *LR(k) grammar* stands for "left-to-right scan of the input producing a rightmost derivation and using k symbols of look-ahead on the input." We elaborate on LR(0) and LR(1) grammars to the extent considered relevant in this book; the reader wishing more depth of treatment of these grammars–and of parsing in general–can consult, for instance, Sippu & Soisalon-Soininen (1990) and Grune & Jacobs (2010).

When discussing ambiguity in CFLs (cf. Section 3.3.1.5), we spoke of a convention that favors leftmost over rightmost derivations. So, the rightmost derivation of the LR(k) grammars may appear as surprising. In fact, the derivation of such a grammar is actually a *reduction*, so that a leftmost reduction is a rightmost derivation.

4.2.14. (Def.) Let u, v be strings of terminals and variables such that there is a derivation $u \overset{*}{\Longrightarrow} v$. We say that v *is reducible to* u, and write $v \overset{*}{\hookrightarrow} u$, if there is a sequence

$$v = v_1 \hookrightarrow v_2 \hookrightarrow \ldots \hookrightarrow v_m = u$$

of *reduction steps* that is a *reduction from v to u*. The string u is called the *reducing string*. A *reduction from v* is a reduction from v to the start variable, i.e.

$$v = v_1 \hookrightarrow v_2 \hookrightarrow \ldots \hookrightarrow v_m = S.$$

We say that a reduction from v to u is a *leftmost reduction*, written $v \overset{*}{\hookrightarrow}_l u$, if each reducing string $v_m, v_{m-1}, \ldots, v_1$ is reduced only after all the other reducing strings that lie to its left. In particular, we have

$$v \overset{*}{\hookrightarrow}_l u \text{ whenever } u \overset{*}{\Longrightarrow}_r v.$$

Informally, whereas a CFG G is a collection of derivation rules that generate strings in a top-down, leftmost derivation, a LR grammar G' is

207

a collection of reductions that generate strings in a bottom-up, rightmost derivation. Each reduction step is an inverted substitution: A string of variables and terminals in the consequent of a production is replaced by the variable in the antecedent.

Example 4.2.5. Figure 4.2.5 shows the partial parse trees and the final parse tree for the LR parsing of the string *acbabc* generated by the CFG G of Example 3.3.6. The number below the trees corresponds to the move by the PDA.

In order to approach these grammars in an adequate depth some more definitions are required.

4.2.15. **(Def.)** Let $u \in L(G)$, G is a CFG, and let v_i occur in a leftmost reduction of u. Let $v_i \hookrightarrow v_{i+1}$ be a reduction step, and let further $v_i = xyz$ and $v_{i+1} = xAz$, so that we have

$$v_i = \underbrace{x_1...x_k}_{x}\underbrace{y_1...y_l}_{y}\underbrace{z_1...z_n}_{z} \hookrightarrow \underbrace{x_1...x_k}_{x}A\underbrace{z_1...z_n}_{z} = v_{i+1}$$

where x, y are strings of variables and terminals, z is a string of terminals, and

$$S \overset{*}{\underset{G}{\Longrightarrow}}_r xAz \underset{G}{\Longrightarrow}_r xyz.$$

Then we say that the reducing substring y in v_i is a *valid string* and we call y, together with the production $A \to y$, *the handle of* v_i if G is unambiguous (otherwise, i.e. if G is ambiguous, we speak of *a handle of* v_i). Let now $xyz = u$; a *viable prefix* of u is any prefix of u that ends no farther right than the right end of the handle of u.

Handles are important for the definition of DCFLs, because when we know the handle of a string, we know exactly what the next reducing step is.

Example 4.2.6. We introduce the CFL known as *balanced parentheses* (BP). Clearly, if the number of parentheses is to be balanced, i.e. if the number of right parentheses must match the number of left parentheses, then this must be an unambiguous CFL. Let BP be generated by the CFG $G_{BP} = (\{S, S_1, A\}, \{[,], \dagger\}, S_1, P)$ with the following set of production rules:

$$P = \left\{ \begin{array}{c} S_1 \to S\dagger \\ S \to SA \mid A \\ A \to [S] \mid [] \end{array} \right\}$$

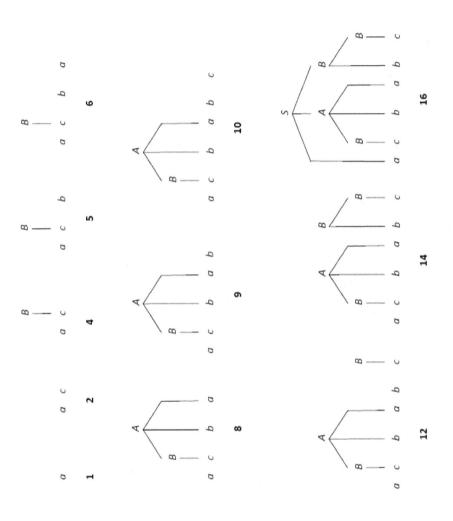

Figure 4.2.5.: LR partial trees (1-14) and final parse tree of the string *acbabc*.

We have the following rightmost derivation in G_{BP}:

$$S_1 \Longrightarrow S\dagger \Longrightarrow SA\dagger \Longrightarrow S[S]\dagger$$

The right-sentential form (cf. Def. 3.1.11.4) is $S\,[S]\,\dagger$ and its handle is $[S]$. The viable prefixes of this right-sentential form are ϵ, S, $S[$, $S[S$, and $S\,[S]$. The symbol $\dagger$ denotes an end marker (cf. next Definition).

4.2.16. (Def.) Let $\dagger$ denote an *end marker* to a string. For any language L, we define the *end-marked language* $L\dagger$ as:

$$L\dagger = \{w\,\dagger \,|w \text{ is in } L\}$$

4.2.17. (Def.) A language L is said to have the *prefix property* if, whenever w belongs to L, no proper prefix of w is in L.

Introducing an end marker in a DCFL converts it into a DCFL with the prefix property.

4.2.18. (Prop.) L is a DCFL if and only if $L\dagger$ is a DCFL.

Proof: (Sketch) ($\Rightarrow$) Let $M = (Q, \Sigma, \Gamma, q_0, A, \delta)$ be a DPDA that recognizes L. We can construct a DPDA $M_\dagger = (Q, \Sigma \cup \{\dagger\}, \Gamma, q_0, A, \delta)$ that recognizes $w\dagger$ by simulating M reading $w = a_1 a_2 ... a_n$. When $M_\dagger$ reaches $\dagger$, $M_\dagger$ accepts w if M entered an accepting state at reading the terminal symbol a_n.

($\Leftarrow$) Given a DPDA $M_\dagger = (Q, \Sigma \cup \{\dagger\}, \Gamma, q_0, A, \delta)$, we can construct a DPDA $M' = \left(Q', \Sigma, \Gamma', q_0', A', \delta'\right)$ that simulates $M_\dagger$ when this reads its input string $w\dagger$. M' needs to determine, before reading each input symbol a_i, whether $M_\dagger$ would accept if $a_i = \dagger$, in which case M' would enter an accepting state. In order to do this we must set $\Gamma' = \Gamma \cup 2^Q$ (why?). **QED**

4.2.19. (Def.) Let $G = (V, T, S, P)$ be a CFG. An *item* (also: *dotted rule*) for G is any production in P with the symbol **.** anywhere in the consequent. For a production $A \rightarrow v_1 v_2 ... v_k$ with k symbols in the consequent, there are $k+1$ productions:

$$A \rightarrow .v_1 v_2 ... v_k$$

$$A \rightarrow v_1 . v_2 ... v_k$$

$$\vdots$$

$$A \rightarrow v_1 v_2 ... v_k.$$

For a production of the form $A \to \epsilon$ we have the item $A \to {\boldsymbol .}$. An item $A \to x {\boldsymbol .} y$ is said to be *valid* for a viable prefix u if there is a derivation

$$S \underset{G}{\overset{*}{\Longrightarrow}}_r vAz \underset{G}{\Longrightarrow}_r vxyz$$

and $vx = u$. An item is *complete* if ${\boldsymbol .}$ is the rightmost symbol in it.

Example 4.2.7. Let us consider G_{BP} of Example 4.2.6. The following are items for G_{BP}:

$$
\begin{array}{lll}
S_1 \to {\boldsymbol .}S\dagger & S \to {\boldsymbol .}SA & A \to {\boldsymbol .}[S] \\
S_1 \to S{\boldsymbol .}\dagger & S \to S{\boldsymbol .}A & A \to [{\boldsymbol .}S] \\
S_1 \to S\dagger{\boldsymbol .} & S \to SA{\boldsymbol .} & A \to [S{\boldsymbol .}] \\
& S \to {\boldsymbol .}A & A \to [S]{\boldsymbol .} \\
& S \to A{\boldsymbol .} & A \to {\boldsymbol .}[] \\
& & A \to [{\boldsymbol .}] \\
& & A \to []{\boldsymbol .}
\end{array}
$$

Consider the right-sentential form $[]\dagger \in L(G_{BP})$. We have the rightmost derivation (we omit the subscript G_{BP}):

$$S_1 \overset{*}{\Longrightarrow}_r A\dagger \Longrightarrow_r []\dagger$$

The following items are valid for the corresponding viable prefixes: $A \to []{\boldsymbol .}$ for $[]$, $A \to [{\boldsymbol .}]$ for $[$, and $A \to {\boldsymbol .}[]$ for ϵ.

Complete items allow us to proceed backwards from a string of terminals w to S by passing through the intermediate right-sentential forms. In particular, if we see valid items as states of some FA M, then the complete items are the accepting states of M. Obviously, for any CFG G the sets of valid items for each viable prefix are regular sets. M is actually a NDFA, but by means of subset construction (cf. Algorithm 4.2) we can convert M into a DFA. We formalize this.

4.2.20. (Def.) Let $M = (Q - \{q_0\}, V \cup T, q_0, A, \delta)$, where $Q - \{q_0\}$ is a set of items for some CFG $G = (V, T, S, P)$, be a NDFA. Define δ as follows:

1. $\delta(q_0, \epsilon) = \{S \to {\boldsymbol .}u \mid (S \to u) \in P\}$

2. $\delta(A \to u {\boldsymbol .} Bv, \epsilon) = \{B \to {\boldsymbol .}y \mid (B \to y) \in P\}$

3. $\delta(A \to u {\boldsymbol .} Xv, X) = \{A \to uX {\boldsymbol .} v\}$

211

Then, M recognizes the viable prefixes for G.

Example 4.2.8. Figure 4.2.6 shows the NDFA M_{BP} for the CFG G_{BP}.

4.2.21. (Def.) A grammar G is said to be a *LR(0) grammar* if

1. the start symbol does not occur anywhere in the consequent of any item, and

2. for every viable prefix $u \in G$, whenever $A \to v.$ is a complete item valid for u, then no other complete item nor an item ending in $.z$, for z a terminal or a string of terminals, is valid for u.

Theorem 4.2.4. *Let L be a language. If $L = L(G)$ for G a LR(0) grammar, then $L = N(M)$ for M a DPDA.*

Proof: (Sketch) Given G, construct a DFA F that recognizes G's viable prefixes. Let now M be a DPDA whose stack symbols are the symbols of G and the states of F. M has a start state q and states used to make reductions by sequences of moves of the form

$$[q, s_0 X_1 ... s_{k-1} X_k s_k, w] \vdash^* \left[q, s_0 X_1 ... s_{i-1} X_i s_i A \underbrace{s}_{=\delta(s_i, A)}, w \right]$$

where $X_1 ... X_k w$ is a right-sentential form, $X_1 ... X_k$ is a viable prefix on the stack, and $s_0 X_1 ... s_{k-1} X_k s_k$, $s_i = \delta_F(q_0, X_1 ... X_i)$, is the complete stack contents, with s_k the top state giving the valid items for $X_1 ... X_k$. The new configurations $[q, \alpha, w]$ are synonymous with (q, w, α^R).

The claim is that, starting with $w \in L(G)$ on the input tape and only s_0 on the stack, M constructs a rightmost derivation for w in reverse order. The workings of M are as follows. Let us visualize the stack when the input tape has $X_1 ... X_k w$:

s_k	✓ Top of the stack State of F recognizing the viable prefix $X_1 ... X_k$
X_k	
s_{k-1}	State of F recognizing the viable prefix $X_1 ... X_{k-1}$
$\vdots$	
X_1	
s_0	State of F recognizing w

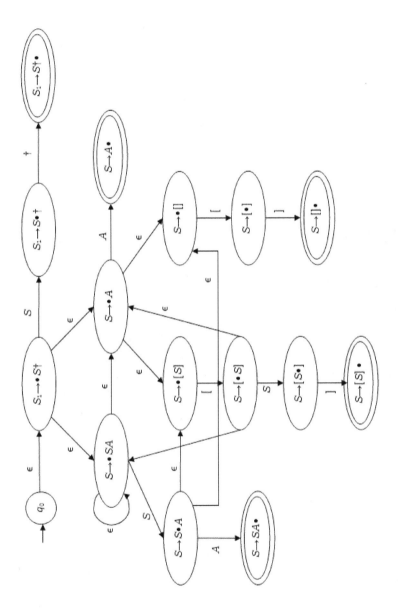

Figure 4.2.6.: NDFA recognizing the viable prefixes for the CFG of Balanced Parentheses.

Let now s_k contain the complete item $A \to \alpha..$ Then, $A \to \alpha.$ is valid for $X_1...X_k$ and

$$X_1...X_i \underbrace{X_{i+1}...X_k}_{\alpha}$$

i.e. α is a suffix. Given the derivation

$$S \overset{*}{\Rightarrow}_r \underbrace{X_1...X_i Aw}_{z} \Rightarrow_r X_1...X_k w$$

to obtain the right-sentential form z we reduce α to A and replace $X_{i+1}...X_k$ on top of the stack by A and the correct covering state, so that we have the following stack:

	✓ Top of the stack
s	State of F recognizing the viable prefix $X_1...X_i A$
A	
X_i	
s_{i-1}	State of F recognizing the viable prefix $X_1...X_{i-1}$
$\vdots$	
X_1	
s_0	

Actually, what was replaced by As on top of the stack now was $s_i X_{1+1}...s_{k-1}X_k s_k$, so there was a series of pop moves before the pushing of A onto the stack. Let now s_k contain only incomplete items. Then, the right-sentential form $X_1...X_k w$ cannot be formed by means of a reduction (why?) and we simply shift the next input symbol onto the stack.

When the top state on the stack is $\{S \to \alpha.\}$, M pops its stack (why?), accepting. Thus, $L(G) = N(M)$. **QED**

Corollary 4.2.5. *Every LR(0) grammar is unambiguous.*

Proof: Follows immediately from the above proof. **QED**

Theorem 4.2.6. *A language L has a LR(0) grammar if and only if L is a DCFL with the prefix property.*

Proof: Left as an exercise. Hints: For the $\Rightarrow$-direction, if L is a DCFL, then there is a DPDA M' such that $L = L(M')$. Knowing the behavior of M', we can construct a DPDA M such that $L = L(G_M)$. For the $\Leftarrow$-direction, start from Theorem 4.2.4.

Corollary 4.2.7. *L† has a LR(0) grammar if and only if L is a DCFL.*

Proof: Left as an exercise.

Our elaboration above on LR(0) grammars was carried out having in mind not the importance of these grammars per se (very few grammars are actually LR(0) grammars), but the fact that the LR(1) grammars are extensions of the former. LR(1) grammars are extremely important because they include the syntax of most programming languages yet are restrictive enough to have efficient parsers. In fact, for any LR(k) grammar there is an equivalent LR(1) grammar. Importantly, all and only the DCFLs have LR(1) grammars. We need a new definition before we begin discussing LR(1) grammars:

4.2.22. (Def.) A *look-ahead set* $\dot{T}$ is a set consisting of terminals and/or the symbol † that denotes the right end of a string.

A LR(1) grammar extends a LR(0) grammar in the following way: A LR(1) item is a LR(0) item followed by a look-ahead set $\dot{T}$.

4.2.23. (Def.) A *LR(1) item* is an item of the form

$$A \to u \cdot v, \dot{T}$$

where u, v are strings of variables and/or terminals and $\dot{T} = \{a_1, ..., a_n\}$ is a look-ahead set. We say that the LR(1) item $A \to u \cdot v, \{a\}$ is valid for viable prefix y if there is a rightmost derivation

$$S \overset{*}{\Longrightarrow}_r wAz \Longrightarrow_r wuvz$$

where $wu = y$, and either (i) a is the first symbol of y, or (ii) $y = \epsilon$ and $a = †$. We say that the LR(1) item $A \to u \cdot v, \{a_1, ..., a_n\}$ is valid for y if for each i, $A \to u \cdot v, \{a_i\}$ is valid for y.

4.2.24. (Def.) Let I be a set of items valid for some prefix. A grammar G is said to be a *LR(1) grammar* if

1. the start symbol occurs on no consequent of an item in I, and

2. whenever I contains some complete item $A \to u \cdot, \{a_1, ..., a_n\}$, then (i) no a_i occurs immediately to the right of the dot on any item of I, and (ii) if $B \to v \cdot, \{b_1, ..., b_m\}$ is another complete item in I, then $a_i \neq b_j$ for any $1 \leq i \leq n$ and $1 \leq j \leq m$.

The set of LR(1) items constitutes the states of a NDFA M that recognizes viable prefixes. The computation of the set of valid items for each prefix is carried out by converting M into a DFA M'. The transitions of M are defined as follows:

4.2.25. (Def.) Let $M = (Q - \{q_0\}, V \cup T, q_0, A, \delta)$, where $Q - \{q_0\}$ is a set of items for some CFG $G = (V, T, S, P)$, be a NDFA. Define δ as follows:

1. $\delta([A \to u \centerdot Xv, \{a_1, ..., a_n\}], X) = \{A \to uX \centerdot v, \{a_1, ..., a_n\}\}$

2. $\delta([A \to u \centerdot Bv, \{a_1, ..., a_n\}], \epsilon) = \{B \to \centerdot y, \dot{T} \mid (B \to y) \in P \text{ and } \ddot{T}\}$,
   where $\dot{T}$ is $\dot{T}$ such that $b \in \dot{T}$ if and only if either

   a) v derives a terminal string beginning with b, or
   b) $v \overset{*}{\Longrightarrow} \epsilon$ and $b = a_i$ for some $1 \leq i \leq n$

3. $\delta(q_0, \epsilon) = \{[S \to \centerdot u, \{\dagger\}] \mid (S \to u) \in P\}$

Example 4.2.9. We leave the construction of a NDFA M for LR(1) items and the conversion of this into a DFA M' as an exercise.

Exercises

Exercise 4.2.1. Design PDAs that accept the following languages:

1. $N(M) = \{a^n b^m a^n \mid m, n \geq 1\}$.

2. $L(M) = \{a^n b^m a^n \mid m, n \geq 1\}$.

3. $N(M) = \{a^m b^m c^n \mid m, n \geq 1\}$.

4. $N(M) = \{ww^R \mid w \in \{a, b\}^+\}$.

5. $L(M) = \{0^m 1^n \mid m > n\}$.

6. $L(M) = \{a^n b^n \mid n \geq 0\} \cup \{a\}$.

7. $L(M) = \{w \in \{a, b\}^* \mid |w|_a = |w|_b\}$.

Exercise 4.2.2. Let the PDA $M = (Q, \Sigma, \Gamma, q_0, Z_0, A, \delta)$ with $|Q| = 3$, $\Sigma = \{a, b\}$, $\Gamma = \{A, B, Z_0\}$, and $A = \{q_2\}$ be given. The following are the transitions by M accepting the language L:

$$\begin{array}{rcl}
\delta\left(q_0, a, Z_0\right) & = & \{(q_1, A), (q_2, \epsilon)\} \\
\delta\left(q_0, b, Z_0\right) & = & \{(q_1, B), (q_2, \epsilon)\} \\
\delta\left(q_1, a, A\right) & = & \{(q_1, B)\} \\
\delta\left(q_1, a, B\right) & = & \{(q_1, B)\} \\
\delta\left(q_1, a, B\right) & = & \{(q_2, \epsilon)\} \\
\delta\left(q_1, b, A\right) & = & \{(q_1, B)\} \\
\delta\left(q_1, b, B\right) & = & \{(q_1, B)\} \\
\delta\left(q_1, b, B\right) & = & \{(q_2, \epsilon)\}
\end{array}$$

1. Determine L.

2. Draw the state diagram of M.

Exercise 4.2.3. The PDA $M = (Q, \Sigma, \Gamma, q_0, Z_0, A, \delta)$ with $|Q| = 4$, $\Sigma = \{a, b\}$, $\Gamma = \{X, Y, Z_0\}$ and $A = \{q_3\}$ accepts the language $L(M) = \{u \in \Sigma^* | u = ww^R\}$. Figure 4.2.7 shows the state diagram of this PDA with incomplete labels on the arcs.

1. Fill in the gaps in the labels.

2. Give the computation by this PDA when given the input string $abba$.

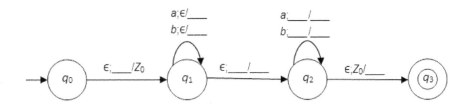

Figure 4.2.7.: A PDA accepting $L(M) = \{u \in \Sigma^* | u = ww^R\}$.

Exercise 4.2.4. Determine the languages accepted by the PDAs 1-4 of Figure 4.2.8.

Exercise 4.2.5. Given the language $L = \{u \in \Sigma^* | u = wcw^R\}$ with $\Sigma = \{a, b, c\}$, $c \notin w$:

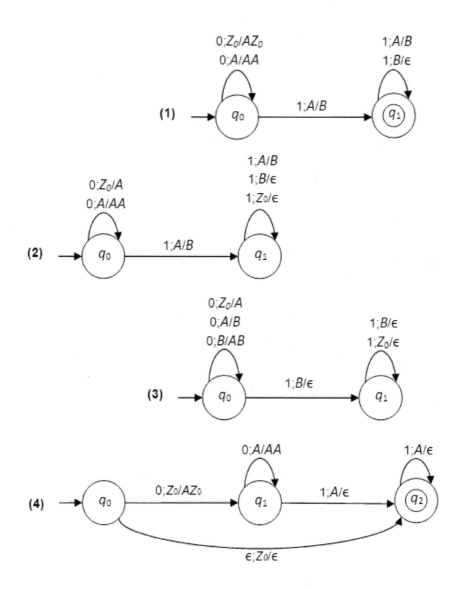

Figure 4.2.8.: Pushdown automata.

1. Design a CFG G for L with $V = \{S\}$ and $T = \{a, b, c\}$.

2. Comment on the behavior of a PDA M accepting L.

Exercise 4.2.6. Consider Theorem 4.2.1.

1. Complete its proof.

2. From the (complete) proof of this theorem extract an algorithm for (i) finding an equivalent $N(M)$ given some $L(M)$, and (ii) finding an equivalent $L(M)$ given some $N(M)$.

Exercise 4.2.7. Given $M = (Q, \{a, b\}, \{Z_0, A\}, q_0, Z_0, \{q_3\}, \delta)$, M is a PDA with δ given as below, construct the equivalent PDA M' that accepts by empty stack.

$$
\begin{array}{rcl}
\delta(q_0, a, Z_0) & = & \{(q_1, AZ_0)\} \\
\delta(q_0, \epsilon, Z_0) & = & \{(q_3, Z_0)\} \\
\delta(q_1, a, A) & = & \{(q_1, AA)\} \\
\delta(q_1, b, A) & = & \{(q_2, \epsilon)\} \\
\delta(q_2, b, A) & = & \{(q_2, \epsilon)\} \\
\delta(q_2, \epsilon, Z_0) & = & \{(q_3, Z_0)\}
\end{array}
$$

Exercise 4.2.8. Consider top-down and bottom-up parsing of CFGs.

1. In converting a CFG G into a PDA M, it is possible to have $\Gamma_M = (V_G \cup Z_0) - T_G$. Make the necessary changes in Algorithm 4.7 to obtain a PDA M with a terminal-free stack.

2. Design an algorithm to convert a CFG G into a bottom-up PDA M. (Hint: Figure 4.2.4.2.).

3. Give the computation of the bottom-up PDA corresponding to the CFG of Example 3.3.6 for the string $acbabc$.

Exercise 4.2.9. Consider the language $L = \{a^n b^m \mid n \le m \le 2n\}$.

1. Give the transition table of a PDA M accepting L.

2. Describe M's behavior.

Exercise 4.2.10. Construct a PDA M that corresponds to the CFGs with the following production sets:

1.
$$P = \left\{ \begin{array}{c} S \to aABB \,|\, aAA \\ A \to aBB \,|\, a \\ B \to bBB \,|\, A \end{array} \right\}$$

2.
$$P = \{S \to aSbb \,|\, aab\}$$

3.
$$P = \left\{ \begin{array}{c} S \to aAA \,|\, A \\ A \to aS \,|\, bS \,|\, a \end{array} \right\}$$

4.
$$P = \left\{ \begin{array}{c} S \to b \,|\, d \,|\, aSB \,|\, bA \\ A \to bA \,|\, b \\ B \to c \end{array} \right\}$$

Exercise 4.2.11. Consider Theorem 4.2.3.

1. From the (complete) proof of this theorem extract an algorithm for, given a PDA M and a CFL L, producing the CFG G such that $L = N(M)$.

2. Adapt the algorithm obtained above for $L = L(M)$.

Exercise 4.2.12. Solve the exercise proposed in Example 4.2.4.

Exercise 4.2.13. Consider the language L of all the palindromes over $\Sigma = \{a, b\}$.

1. Design a PDA that accepts L.

2. Show that L cannot be accepted by a DPDA.

Exercise 4.2.14. Convert the NDFA M_{BP} of Example 4.2.8 into a DFA.

Exercise 4.2.15. Is G_{BP} a LR(0) grammar? Justify your answer.

Exercise 4.2.16. Do the exercise proposed in Example 4.2.9.

Exercise 4.2.17. Let there be given a CFG G with the following production set:

$$P = \left\{ \begin{array}{c} S \to A \\ A \to BA \,|\, \epsilon \\ B \to aB \,|\, b \end{array} \right\}$$

1. Determine the language generated by G.

2. Construct the NDFA recognizing the LR(1) items of G.

3. Convert the obtained NDFA into a DFA.

Exercise 4.2.18. Prove (Complete the proof of) the theorems and propositions in this Section that were left as an exercise (with a sketchy proof, respectively).

Exercise 4.2.19. Comment on the practical importance of Proposition 4.2.10.

Exercise 4.2.20. Let L_1 be a DCFL and L_2 a regular language. Show that (i) $L_3 = L_1 \cap L_2$ and (ii) $L_3 = L_1 - L_2$ is a DCFL. (Hint: You will need a DPDA M_1 and a (D)FA M_2.)

Exercise 4.2.21. A *two-way PDA* (abbrev.: 2PDA) is a PDA whose read-only head can move to both the left and the right.

1. Give a formal definition of a 2PDA.

2. Describe the main aspects of its behavior when accepting a string.

3. Are 2PDAs equivalent to PDAs?

4. Find applications for a 2PDA.

5. Do the 2PDAs change the class $\mathscr{CFL}$?

Exercise 4.2.22. A *pushdown transducer* is a PDA that prints symbols at each move.

1. Give a formal definition of a pushdown transducer.

2. Describe the main aspects of its computation.

3. Find applications for a pushdown transducer.

Exercise 4.2.23. Just like the LR grammars, *LL grammars* constitute a deterministic subset of $\mathscr{CFL}$.

1. Give a formal definition of:

    a) a LL grammar.

    b) a LL(k) grammar.

    c) a LL(*) parser.

2. Show that LL(k) grammars and LR(k) grammars are equivalent.

3. Give applications for these grammars.

Exercise 4.2.24. The PDA of Figure 4.2.9 was designed to accept the language $L = \left\{ 0^n \, (12)^{2n} \, a^{3m} \,|\, n \geq 0, m > 0 \right\}$.

1. Simulate its behavior over the input strings:

    a) *aaaaaaaa*

    b) *0012121212aaa*

    c) *000012121212aaaaaaa*

2. Is the design optimal or can/should it be improved?

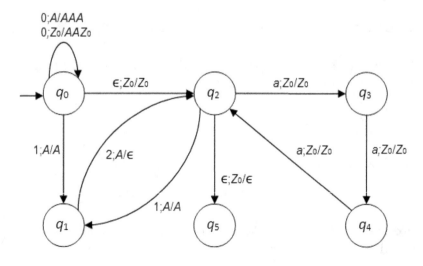

Figure 4.2.9.: A PDA for $L = \left\{ 0^n \, (12)^{2n} \, a^{3m} \,|\, n \geq 0, m > 0 \right\}$.

4.3. Turing machines

The Turing machine, so coined after its conceiver A. Turing (cf. Turing, 1937), provides the most encompassing and most powerful model of computation; so much so that it actually is at the root of the modern digital computer (see Introduction). This particular automaton is equivalent, in definitional terms, to the fundamental notion of a computable function (see next Chapter). This, in turn, is connected to the RELs in the sense that a Turing machine can enumerate their elements, an action that equates with accepting these languages. Thus, in the same way that finite-state machines are associated with regular languages and PDAs are so with CFLs, Turing machines are associated with RELs.

4.3.1. Basic aspects of Turing machines

4.3.1. (Def.) A *Turing machine* (TM) is a 7-tuple

$$M_T = (Q, \Gamma, \#, \Sigma, q_0, A, \delta)$$

where Q is a finite set of states, Γ is the *tape alphabet*, $\# \in \Gamma$ is the *blank symbol*, $\Sigma \subseteq (\Gamma - \#)$ is the *input alphabet*, $A \subseteq Q$ is the set of *accepting states*, and $\delta : (Q \times \Gamma) \longrightarrow (Q \times \Gamma \times \{L, R\})$, where L, R denote direction (left and right, respectively), is the *transition function*.

There are (many) variations to this definition. For instance, we may have $\# \in \Sigma$. In particular, we can consider two *halting states*, to wit, q_a and q_r for acceptation and rejection, respectively, so that the transition function is $\delta : (Q \times \Gamma) \longrightarrow ((Q \cup \{q_a, q_r\}) \times \Gamma \times \{L, R\})$. Also alternatively, the set A may be empty, acceptation being the case when the machine processes a string completely, or computes a function, and no more subsequent moves are specified. Another variation is the addition of a stop or no-action symbol, S or N, respectively, to $\{L, R\}$. However, these variations do not change the computing power of a Turing machine.

As said above, a Turing machine is a surprisingly parsimonious machine if we take into consideration its computational power. Its computer model reflects this parsimony and the examples and exercises below illustrate its computational power.

4.3.2. (Def.) The *computer model* for a Turing machine $M_T = (Q, \Gamma, \#, \Sigma, q_0, A, \delta)$ consists simply of (i) a control box programmed by δ equipped with (ii) a read-and-write head. This head reads an input string starting on the left of an input tape that is infinite to the right (or to both sides; cf. Fig. 4.3.1).[26] When the machine reads a symbol a while in state q, it switches into state p, replaces symbol $a \in \Gamma$ by symbol $b \in \Gamma$, and moves one tape cell in direction $D = \{L, R\}$, so that we have

$$\delta (q, a) = (p, b, D).$$

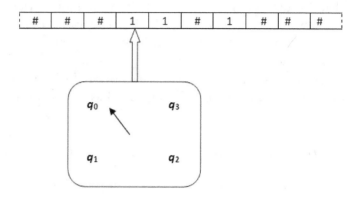

Figure 4.3.1.: Computer model for a Turing machine.

Note how the computer model for a Turing machine is basically that for a FA (cf. Def. 4.1.3) with the differences that the input tape is infinite to the right (or to both the right and the left) and the reading head is also a delete/write-head. Figure 4.3.1 shows the computer model of a Turing machine in which the tape is infinite to both the right and the left sides of the input string; the current content on the tape is ...#11#1#... and the machine is (possibly back) in state q_0.

4.3.3. (Def.) A *configuration* for a Turing machine M_T is a pair $C = (q, u\underline{a}v)$ indicating that M_T is in state q with the present tape string $u\underline{a}v$ and reading the symbol a.

1. The M_T configuration $(q, u\underline{a}v)$ *yields* the configuration $(p, x\underline{b}y)$ *in one step* (or *move*), denoted by

$$\underbrace{(q, u\underline{a}v)}_{C_i} \vdash_T \underbrace{(p, x\underline{b}y)}_{C_{i+1}}$$

if and only if the transition $\delta (q, a)$ changes configuration $(q, u\underline{a}v)$ to configuration $(p, x\underline{b}y)$.

---

[26]Note that this feature does not change the computing power of the Turing machine.

2. A *starting configuration* C_0 for M_T is a configuration of the form $(q_0, \epsilon \underline{a} v)$, or $(q_0, \#\underline{a} v)$, indicating that a is the symbol in the left-most cell of the input tape or string, respectively.

3. An *accepting configuration* C_n for M_T has the form $(q, u \underline{a} v)$ indicating that uav is the output, the read-and-write head is positioned at a, and $q \in A$ or $q = q_a$. If $q = q_r$ in C_n, then $(q, u \underline{a} v)$ is a *rejecting configuration*.

4. A *hanging configuration* C_n for M_T is a configuration of the form $(q, \epsilon \underline{a} v)$ such that the transition function $\delta(q, a)$ instructs the machine to move left (i.e. off the tape), or any configuration from which the machine is instructed to make an impossible move.

5. We write $C_i \vdash_T^n C_j$ or $C_i \vdash_T^* C_j$, $i, j = 0, 1, ..., n$, to denote that there is a sequence of $n \geq 1$ or $n \geq 0$ moves, respectively, taken by M_T to go from configuration C_i to configuration C_j.

6. A *computation* for a Turing machine M_T on input $w \in \Sigma^*$ is any of four possibilities:

   a) A finite sequence $C_0, C_1, ..., C_n$ of configurations (where possibly $n = 0$) such that

   $$\underbrace{q_0, w}_{C_0} \vdash_T^* \underbrace{q_i, z}_{C_n}$$

   where $q_i \in A$ or $q_i = q_a$ and $z \in \Gamma^*$, and C_n is an accepting configuration;

   b) A finite sequence $C_0, C_1, ..., C_n$ of configurations (where possibly $n = 0$) such that

   $$\underbrace{q_0, w}_{C_0} \vdash_T^* \underbrace{q_i, z}_{C_n}$$

   where $q_i \notin A$ or $q_i = q_r$ and $z \in \Gamma^*$, and C_n is a rejecting configuration;

   c) A finite sequence $C_0, C_1, ..., C_n$ of configurations (where possibly $n = 0$) such that

   $$\underbrace{q_0, w}_{C_0} \vdash_T^* \underbrace{q_i, z}_{C_n}$$

   where $q_i \notin A$ and $z \in \Gamma^*$, and C_n is a hanging configuration;

    d) An infinite sequence $C_0, C_1, \ldots$ of configurations such that

$$\underbrace{q_0, w}_{C_0} \vdash_T^* \infty.$$

7. An infinitely repeated computation $C_i \vdash_T^n C_i$, $n \geq 2$, is an *infinite loop*. In practical terms, we have $C_0 \vdash_T^* \infty$.[27]

8. A string $w \in \Sigma^*$ is accepted by the Turing machine M_T if M_T *halts* on input w and accepts w, i.e. if we have

$$q_0, w \vdash_T^* q_i, z$$

for some $q_i \in A$ (or $q_i = q_a$) and $z \in \Gamma^*$. Otherwise, if M_T *halts* but does not accept w (for instance, we have $q_0, w \vdash_T^* q_r, z$), then w is rejected by M_T.[28] A language $L \subseteq \Sigma^*$ is accepted by a Turing machine M_T if

$$L = L(M_T) = \{w \in \Sigma^* | M_T \text{ accepts } w\}.$$

9. A language L is *Turing-machine acceptable* if there is a Turing machine M_T that accepts it.

    In order to define a transition table for a Turing machine the following definition is required:

4.3.4. (Def.) A $m \times n$ *Turing machine* M_T is a Turing machine with m states and n symbols.

4.3.5. (Def.) A *transition table* for a $m \times n$ Turing machine M_T is a table with m rows and n columns such that the entry in row q and column a is $\delta(q, a)$.

    Just like finite-state machines and PDAs, Turing machines can be defined by means of state diagrams.

4.3.6. (Def.) Given a Turing machine M_T, its state diagram is a labeled digraph $D = \vec{\mathfrak{D}}(M_T)$ as for a FA such that for each transition $\delta(q, a) = (p, b, D)$ there is an arc from vertex q to vertex p labeled with "a/bD," read "if M_T reads symbol a, then it replaces a by b and moves in direction D."

---

[27] This explains why an infinite sequence (Def. 4.3.3.6.d) is more often than not called an infinite loop, when in fact no loop proper is the case.

[28] It is important to notice here that a TM can *halt* in either an accepting or a rejecting state. Contrast this with the cases when a TM does *not* halt (cf. Defs. 4.3.3.6.d and 4.3.3.7).

Clearly, if there is a label of the form "a/aD," then M_T leaves a untouched and minds only the direction instruction.

Example 4.3.1. Figure 4.3.2 shows the state diagram of the Turing machine in Example 4.3.2 below.

4.3.2. Turing machines computing functions

Recall that Turing machines also compute functions, besides recognizing formal languages.[29] We begin by showing how Turing machines compute functions, because their behavior appears more intuitive here than when recognizing languages. However, programming a Turing machine for any but the most basic functions is typically a daunting task.[30] We thus stick to very basic functions from positive integers to positive integers.

4.3.7. (Def.) We say that a Turing machine M_T *defines* a function $f(x) = y$ for strings $x, y \in \Sigma^*$ and some $q_i \in A$ (or some $q_i = q_a$) if

$$q_0, x \vdash_T^* q_i, y.$$

Example 4.3.2. The following is the transition table for a Turing machine $M_T = (\{q_0, q_1, q_2, q_3\}, \{1, \#\}, \#, \{1\} \cup \{\#\}, q_0, \{q_3\}, \delta)$ adding two positive integers (the integers are represented in unary notation $1^n = \underbrace{111...1}_{n}$; e.g. $1^3 = 111 = 3$):

	1	#
q_0	$q_0 1R$	$q_1 1R$
q_1	$q_1 1R$	$q_2 \#L$
q_2	$q_3 \#R$	–
q_3	–	–

On input $11\#111\#\#...$, M_T behaves as follows (we omit the subscript T in $\vdash$ and the commas between states and strings):[31]

$$q_0 1\underline{1}\#111\# \vdash q_0 1\underline{1}\#111\# \vdash q_0 11\underline{\#}111\# \vdash q_1 111\underline{1}11\# \vdash q_1 11111\underline{1}\#$$

$$\vdash q_1 11111\underline{1}\# \vdash q_1 111111\underline{\#} \vdash q_2 11111\underline{1}\# \vdash q_3 11111\#\underline{\#}$$

---

[29] As we shall see, these are actually one and the same thing for Turing machines.
[30] See Example 4.3.3 below.
[31] In this input string, we have $\Sigma = \{1\} \cup \{\#\}$ because the symbol # between 1s is part of the string, whereas the symbol # after the final 1 simply indicates the first empty cell after the input string.

$$\approx q_0 11\#111\#\vdash^8 q_3 11111\#$$

The behavior of the machine is as follows: Given the input $11\#111\#\#...$, which corresponds to the two integers 2 and 3, in order to add both strings M_T has firstly, after reading the two initial 1s, to delete the blank space between them, replace it with 1, and then keep moving right until it finds the last symbol 1 and the first empty cell after it; M_T moves one cell to the left, deletes this 1, moves to the right and halts in an accepting state. The output string is 11111 followed by infinitely many blank symbols. Figure 4.3.2 shows the state diagram of this M_T. More formally, we say that M_T defines the function $f(m,n) = m+n$, $m, n \in \mathbb{Z}^+$, for an arbitrary input string $1^m\#1^n$ if

$$q_0, 1^m\#1^n \vdash_T^{(m+n)+3} q_3, 1^m 1^n.$$

Finally, because there are no transitions from state q_3 we can simply consider it as a halting state for acceptance q_a; this allows us to simplify the transition table as follows:

	1	#
q_0	$q_0 1R$	$q_1 1R$
q_1	$q_1 1R$	$q_2 \#L$
q_2	$q_a \#R$	$-$

We can then write the computation

$$q_0, 1^m\#1^n \vdash_T^{(m+n)+3} q_a, 1^m 1^n$$

where termination in an accepting state is made explicit.

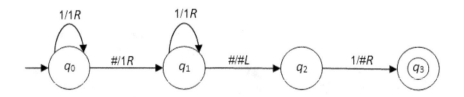

1/1R   1/1R

q_0 #/1R q_1 #/#L q_2 1/#R q_3

Figure 4.3.2.: A Turing machine that computes the function $f(m, n) = m + n$ for $m, n \in \mathbb{Z}^+$.

We conclude this brief discussion of Turing machines computing functions with an illustration of the statement above that it can be quite challenging to program a Turing machine for even very elementary functions.

Example 4.3.3. Figure 4.3.3 shows the state diagram of a Turing machine that computes the function $f(m, n) = 2m + 3n$ for $m, n \in \mathbb{Z}^+$. Figure 4.3.4 shows the program in a notation that can be implemented in the Turing machine simulator to be found at http://ironphoenix.org/tril/tm/. In this specific simulator:

- We use a tape alphabet $\{0, 1\}$ with the additional symbol X, i.e. $\Gamma = \{0, 1\} \cup X$;

- on the tape file only 1 or 0 can be found initially;

- if there is no 1 or X on a cell, then there is a 0;

- state q_0 in the state diagram (Fig. 4.4.3) corresponds to state 1 in the program, state q_1 to state 2, etc.;

- right is denoted by $>$ and left by $<$;

- the initial string on the tape is $1^m\_1^n$, where $\_$ denotes a blank cell.

The program can be easily adapted to any other simulator.

4.3.3. Turing machines accepting languages

4.3.3.1. Turing machines and unrestricted grammars

As said above, Turing machines are also associated to the RELs via unrestricted grammars.

Example 4.3.4. We show now a Turing machine accepting a language. We consider the language $L = \{0^n 1^n | n > 0\}$. A Turing machine M_T accepting this language has the following sets: $Q = \{q_0, q_1, q_2, q_3, q_4\}$, $\Sigma = \{0, 1\}$, $\Gamma = \{0, 1, X, Y, \#\}$, and $A = \{q_4\}$. The behavior of the machine is as follows: Given the input $0^n 1^n \#\#...$, M_T replaces the leftmost 0 by X, moving then right to the leftmost 1 and replacing it by Y; next, M_T moves left to the rightmost X, moves one cell to the leftmost 0, and repeats the cycle. If after changing a 1 to a Y the machine finds no more 0, it checks for any 0 left on the tape; if there is none, it accepts the input string. We show the transition table for M_T:

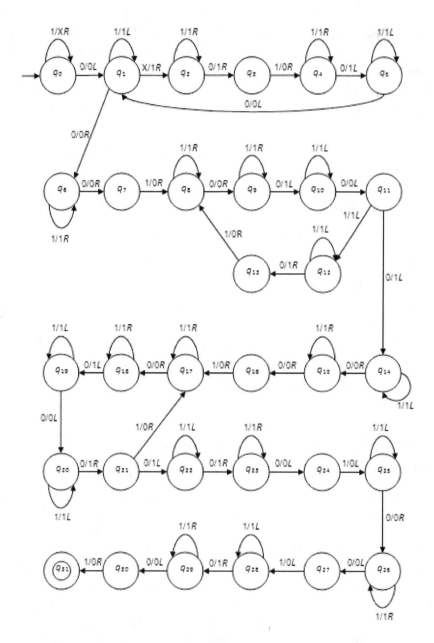

Figure 4.3.3.: Turing machine M_T that computes the function $f(m, n) = 2m + 3n$ for $m, n \in \mathbb{Z}^+$.

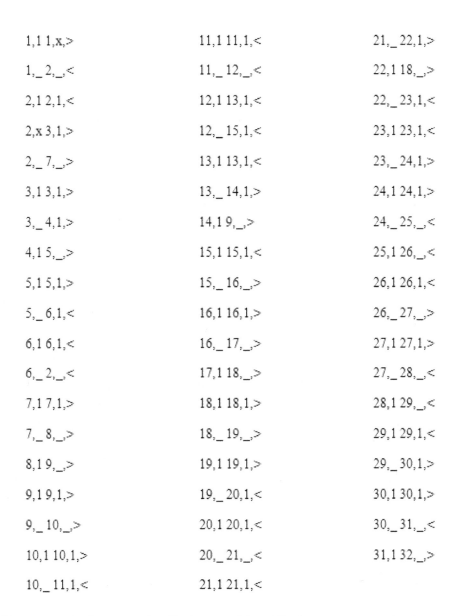

1,1 1,x,>	11,1 11,1,<	21,_ 22,1,>
1,_ 2,_,<	11,_ 12,_,<	22,1 18,_,>
2,1 2,1,<	12,1 13,1,<	22,_ 23,1,<
2,x 3,1,>	12,_ 15,1,<	23,1 23,1,<
2,_ 7,_,>	13,1 13,1,<	23,_ 24,1,>
3,1 3,1,>	13,_ 14,1,>	24,1 24,1,>
3,_ 4,1,>	14,1 9,_,>	24,_ 25,_,<
4,1 5,_,>	15,1 15,1,<	25,1 26,_,<
5,1 5,1,>	15,_ 16,_,>	26,1 26,1,<
5,_ 6,1,<	16,1 16,1,>	26,_ 27,_,>
6,1 6,1,<	16,_ 17,_,>	27,1 27,1,>
6,_ 2,_,<	17,1 18,_,>	27,_ 28,_,<
7,1 7,1,>	18,1 18,1,>	28,1 29,_,<
7,_ 8,_,>	18,_ 19,_,>	29,1 29,1,<
8,1 9,_,>	19,1 19,1,>	29,_ 30,1,>
9,1 9,1,>	19,_ 20,1,<	30,1 30,1,>
9,_ 10,_,>	20,1 20,1,<	30,_ 31,_,<
10,1 10,1,>	20,_ 21,_,<	31,1 32,_,>
10,_ 11,1,<	21,1 21,1,<	

Figure 4.3.4.: Program for Turing machine M_T that computes the function $f(m, n) = 2m + 3n$ for $m, n \in \mathbb{Z}^+$.

	0	1	X	Y	#
q_0	q_1XR	$-$	$-$	q_3YR	$-$
q_1	q_1OR	q_2YL	$-$	q_1YR	$-$
q_2	q_2OL	$-$	q_0XR	q_2YL	$-$
q_3	$-$	$-$	$-$	q_3YR	$q_4\#R$
q_4	$-$	$-$	$-$	$-$	$-$

The computation carried out by M_T given an input string 0011 is as follows (we omit the subscript T in $\vdash$ and the commas between states and strings):

$$q_0\underline{0}011 \vdash q_1X\underline{0}11 \vdash q_1X0\underline{1}1 \vdash q_2X\underline{0}Y1 \vdash q_2\underline{X}0Y1 \vdash q_0X\underline{0}Y1 \vdash q_1XX\underline{Y}1$$

$$\vdash q_2XX\underline{Y}Y \vdash q_2X\underline{X}YY \vdash q_0XX\underline{Y}Y \vdash q_3XXY\underline{Y} \vdash q_4XXYY\underline{\#}$$

Theorem 4.3.1. *For every UG G, there is a Turing machine M_T such that $L(M_T) = L(G)$.*

Proof: Left as an exercise. Hint: Describe a (non-deterministic)[32] Turing machine M_T that accepts $L(G)$. (Recall that a UG has productions of the form $\alpha \rightarrow \beta$, where $\alpha \in (V \cup T)^+, \beta \in (V \cup T)^*$, and $|V(\alpha)| \geq 1$.)

There are many variations to the computer model of the Turing machine above. In effect, there are Turing machines with $n > 1$ tapes, with a two-way infinite tape, with $k > 1$ heads, with a read-only input tape, etc. For our purposes, the distinction between a *deterministic* and a *non-deterministic* Turing machine is the most relevant.

4.3.8. (Def.) A Turing machine M_T is said to be *non-deterministic* (abbr.: NDTM) if, given a state q and a symbol a being read, the machine has a finite number of choices for the next move. Otherwise, i.e. if there is exactly one move for any pair (q, a), M_T is said to be *deterministic* (DTM).

Theorem 4.3.2. *If a language L is accepted by a NDTM M_{T1}, then it is accepted by some DTM Turing machine M_{T2}.*

Proof: Left as an exercise. (Hints: The transition function for M_{T1} must be $\delta : (Q \times \Gamma) \rightarrow 2^{(Q \times \Gamma \times \{L,R\})}$. M_{T2} requires a means to keep all of M_{T1}'s configurations on its tape, in order to simulate M_{T1}. Language acceptance must be addressed.)

---

[32]See below.

We now present the fundamental theorem associating UGs with RELs. The inverse of this theorem is far more difficult to prove, and we leave it as an optional exercise.

Theorem 4.3.3. *Given a UG G, if $L = L(G)$, then L is a REL.*

Proof: Design a NDTM M_T with two tapes, one (Tape 1) for the input string w and the other (Tape 2) for the sentential form $\alpha \in G$. Let $|\alpha| = n$. M_T initializes α to S and repeatedly (i) selects a position i in α, $1 \leq i \leq n$, (ii) selects a production $\beta \to \gamma$ of G, (iii) replaces β by γ if β begins in position i, and (iv) compares this new sentential form with the input on Tape 1: M_T accepts w if the two tapes match; otherwise, M_T returns to (i). Thus, only, and all, the sentential forms of G appear on Tape 2. Hence, $L(G) = L(M_T) = L$, L is a REL by Definition 3.4.1. **QED**

4.3.3.2. Linear-bounded automata: Special Turing machines for CSGs

Now that we have a good grasp of the Turing machines (for RELs), we can approach a particular type of Turing machine that is associated to the CSLs (cf. Def. 3.3.2).

4.3.9. (Def.) A *linear-bounded automaton* (LBA) is a non-deterministic Turing machine

$$M_{[\![T]\!]} = (Q, \Gamma, \#, \Sigma, q_0, A, \delta)$$

with two additional tape symbols $[\![,]\!] \in \Gamma$, called *left* and *right end-markers*, respectively.

4.3.10. (Def.) The *initial configuration* of a LBA $M_{[\![T]\!]}$ with input w is $q_0[\![w]\!] = q_0[\![w_1 w_2 ... w_n]\!]$. A string $w \in [(\Sigma - \{[\![,]\!]\})^* = \Sigma^\bullet]$ is accepted by a LBA $M_{[\![T]\!]}$ if it halts on input w, i.e. if we have the computation

$$q_0, [\![w]\!] \vdash^*_{[\![T]\!]} q_i, z$$

for some $q_i \in A$ and $z \in \Gamma^*$, $|z| \geq |w|$. A language $L \subseteq \Sigma^\bullet$ is accepted by a Turing machine $M_{[\![T]\!]}$ if

$$L = L(M_{[\![T]\!]}) = \{w \in \Sigma^\bullet | M_{[\![T]\!]} \text{ accepts } w\}.$$

The additional tape symbols $[\![,]\!] \in \Gamma$ around w cannot be printed over and the read-and-write head cannot move to the right of $]\!]$ nor to the left of $[\![$ during the computation. That is, no production in a CSG can be length-decreasing. Another way to put the above is to say that a LBA is a NDTM with a finite tape whose finiteness is determined by $cn + 2$, where c is a specific constant for each individual LBA, n is the length in tape cells of the input string w, and 2 corresponds to the cells for the left and right end-markers, one cell for each. This finiteness with respect to the tape places LBAs on the side of finite machines and PDAs, rather than on the side of the Turing machines, which have an infinite tape.

Theorem 4.3.4. *If $L \subseteq \Sigma^\bullet$ is a CSL, then there is a LBA that accepts L.*

Proof: We conceive a LBA M (abbreviating $M_{\llbracket T \rrbracket}$) with a second track on its input tape. On the input string $\llbracket w \rrbracket$ on its tape, M writes the symbol S below the leftmost symbol of w on a second track. If $w = \epsilon$, M rejects w. Otherwise, M proceeds by guessing a production and a position in the sentential form on the second track. Applying the production, M moves the part of the sentential form to the right whenever the sentential form increases in length, but stops in a rejecting state if the new sentential form is longer than w, as given the non-decreasing feature of CSG productions there can be no derivation $S \overset{*}{\Longrightarrow} \alpha \overset{*}{\Longrightarrow} w$ in which the sentential form α is longer than w. M rejects thus empty strings and productions in which the antecedent is longer than the consequent. In other words, M accepts only strings generated by a CSG and all strings generated by a CSG. **QED**

The use of two tape tracks allows for M to be operational with n cells instead of $2n$. In fact, by using k tracks a LBA M can simulate a computation of a Turing machine requiring kn cells, where kn is a linear bound on the input length. This explains the label "linear-bounded" for these automata.

4.3.4. The universal Turing machine

As a matter of fact, the variations above are to some extent superfluous, because there is a Turing machine capable of simulating any other Turing machine. In order to introduce this machine we require the notion of an encoding; this notion will prove relevant also in Sections below.

    4.3.11. (Def.) Let a Turing machine M_T be given; then, there is an *encoding function* $e : M_T \longrightarrow \{0, 1\}^*$ that is a unique description of M_T.[33] In detail, given a Turing machine M_T, a generic move $\delta(q_i, \sigma_j) =$

---

[33]Turing (1937) referred to this encoding that, for practical ends, just is the program of a Turing machine, as the *Standard Description*. Of course, a Turing machine just is its program, or Standard Description.

(q_k, σ_l, D_m) is *encoded* by the binary string

$$\xi = 0^i 10^j 10^k 10^l 10^m$$

and a *binary code* for M_T is

$$111 \; \text{code}_1 \; 11 \; \text{code}_2 \; 11...11 \; \text{code}_n \; 111 = \langle M_T \rangle$$

where every code_i has the form of ξ.

As said, this encoding is unique, i.e. every string ξ is interpreted as the code for at most one Turing machine, and a Turing machine has many codes.

4.3.12. (Def.) A *universal Turing machine* is a machine M_{TU} such that, given an arbitrary Turing machine M_T and $z \in \Gamma^* \subset M_T$, and an encoding function e, upon receiving an input string of the form $\xi^* = e(M_T) e(z) = \langle M_T, z \rangle$

1. M_{TU} accepts ξ^* if and only if M_T accepts z.[34]

2. M_{TU} produces output $\langle y \rangle$ if M_T accepts z and produces output y.

Example 4.3.5. Let $q_{i,k}$, $i, k \geq 0$, be coded as $\langle q_0 \rangle = 0$, $\langle q_1 \rangle = 00$, etc. Let the following be the binary coding for the tape symbols: $\langle 1 \rangle = 00$ and $\langle \# \rangle = 0$. Finally, encode the directions $\langle L \rangle = 0$ and $\langle R \rangle = 00$. Then, Figure 4.3.5 shows the encoding of the Turing machine $M_T = (\{q_0, q_1, q_2, q_3\}, \{1, \#\}, \#, \{1\}, q_0, \{q_3\}, \delta)$ of Example 4.3.2, as well as the encoding of this Turing machine with the input string $z = 11\#111$ with $\langle 1 \rangle = 1$ and $\langle \# \rangle = 0$, so that $\langle z \rangle = 110111$.

Exercises

Exercise 4.3.1. Given the transition tables and the tape strings, determine the computing behavior of each Turing machine and, if any, its output. Draw their state diagrams.

1. Tape string: 11; transition table:

	1	#
q_0	$q_0 1 R$	$q_1 \# L$
q_1	$q_2 \# R$	$q_1 1 R$
q_2	$q_2 \# R$	$q_a 1 R$

---

[34]Obviously, if $\Gamma \subseteq \{0, 1\}^*$, then for a string $z \in \Gamma^*$ we have $e(z) = \langle z \rangle = z$.

$$\langle M_T \rangle = 1110100101001001001100100100100110010010010101001001001100100100001010011$$

$$\langle M_T, z \rangle = 111010010100110101001001100100100100100100110010010001010110001001000010100111110111$$

Figure 4.3.5.: The encodings $\langle M_T \rangle$ and $\langle M_T, z \rangle$.

2. Tape string: 111; transition table:

	1	#
q_0	$q_1 \# R$	$q_5 \# L$
q_1	$q_1 1R$	$q_2 \# R$
q_2	$q_2 1R$	$q_3 1L$
q_3	$q_3 1L$	$q_4 \# L$
q_4	$q_4 1L$	$q_0 1R$
q_5	$q_5 1L$	$q_a \# R$

3. Tape string: 0011; transition table:

	0	1	#
q_0	$q_1 1R$	$q_1 0R$	–
q_1	$q_1 1L$	$q_1 0R$	$q_a \# L$

4. Tape string: 0000; transition table:

	0	a	b	#
q_0	$q_1 aR$	–	$q_a bR$	–
q_1	$q_1 0R$	–	$q_1 bR$	$q_2 bL$
q_2	$q_2 0L$	$q_0 aR$	$q_2 bL$	–

Exercise 4.3.2. Construct the state diagram of the Turing machine accepting the language L of Example 4.3.4.

Exercise 4.3.3. Design the following Turing machines:

1. M_T changes 0s into 1s and vice-versa given an input $w \in \{0,1\}^*$.

2. M_T computes the successor of a given positive integer in unary code.

3. M_T writes a 1 at the end of a string representing a positive integer in unary code if the integer is even, and writes a 0 otherwise.

4. M_T outputs the number of letters (in unary code) of a string over the alphabet $\Sigma = \{a, b, c\}$.

5. M_T computes the function $f(n) = 3n$ for an arbitrary positive integer n.

6. Given a string w over $\Sigma = \{a, b, c\}$ input as $\# w_1 w_2 ... w_n \#$:

   a) M_T outputs a copy of w.
   b) M_T outputs a copy of w^R.

7. M_T checks whether two strings x and y over $\Sigma = \{0, 1\}$, input as $x_1 x_2 ... x_n \# y_1 y_2 ... y_m$, are equal. M_T writes a Y if the two strings are equal, and a N otherwise.

8. Given a string over $\Sigma = \{0, 1\}$, M_T computes whether the number of occurrences of 1 in the string is equal to that of 0. M_T writes a Y if it is, and a N otherwise.

9. M_T accepts the language $L = \{w^n \in \{a\}^* \mid n \text{ is odd}\}$.

10. M_T accepts the language $L = \{a^n b^n \mid n \geq 1\}$.

11. M_T accepts the language $L = \{a^n b^n c^n \mid n \geq 1\}$.

12. M_T accepts the language $L = \{a^m b^n \mid m < n\}$.

Exercise 4.3.4. Design a Turing machine that computes the function

$$f(x, y) = \begin{cases} x - y & \text{if } x > y \\ 0 & \text{otherwise} \end{cases}.$$

Hint: You will need a combination of Turing machines (see Fig. 4.3.6).

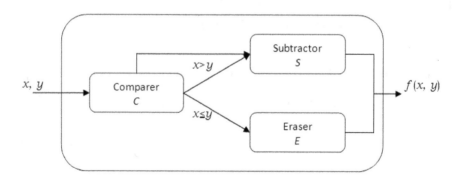

Figure 4.3.6.: A combination of Turing machines.

Exercise 4.3.5. For each of the Turing machines in Figure 4.3.7:

1. Define it formally.

2. Determine the function computed on the following input strings:

   a) 11 (Fig. 4.3.7.1).

   b) 111 (Fig. 4.3.7.2).

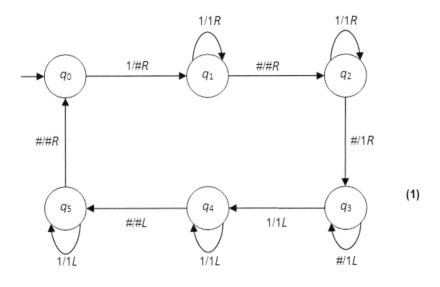

(1)

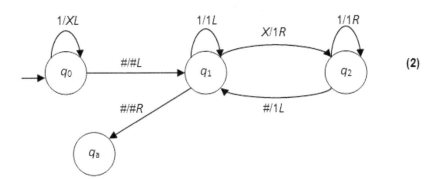

(2)

Figure 4.3.7.: Function-computing Turing machines.

3. Describe its behavior informally.

Exercise 4.3.6. Describe informally the behavior of the Turing machine in Example 4.3.3.

Exercise 4.3.7. Figures 4.3.8-10 show Turing machines accepting the languages $L = \{0^{2^n}|n \geq 0\}$, $L = \{w\#w|w \in \{0,1\}^*\}$, and $L = \{a^iba^j|0 \leq i < j\}$, respectively. For each machine:

1. Define it formally.

2. Trace its moves on the following input strings:

    a) 0000 (TM in Fig. 4.3.8).

    b) 000 (TM in Fig. 4.3.8).

    c) 001#001 (TM in Fig. 4.3.9).

    d) 001#100 (TM in Fig. 4.3.9).

    e) *baaa* (TM in Fig. 4.3.10).

    f) *abaa* (TM in Fig. 4.3.10).

    g) *aba* (TM in Fig. 4.3.10).

3. Describe its behavior informally.

Exercise 4.3.8. Identify the languages over $\Sigma = \{a, b, c\}$ accepted by the Turing machines M_1 (Fig. 4.3.11) and M_2 (Fig. 4.3.12) by testing them with the given inputs. Trace their moves for both acceptance and rejection.

1. *aaaabbcccc*

2. *aabbbcccccc*

3. *aabbcccc*

4. *aaabbbccc*

Exercise 4.3.9. Show that every Turing machine with $k > 1$ tapes can be simulated by a one-tape Turing machine.

Exercise 4.3.10. Give the universal TM encoding, with respective input string, of each of the Turing machines of Exercise 4.3.1.1-4.

Exercise 4.3.11. How many tapes is the universal TM of Definition 4.3.12 required to have? Explain why.

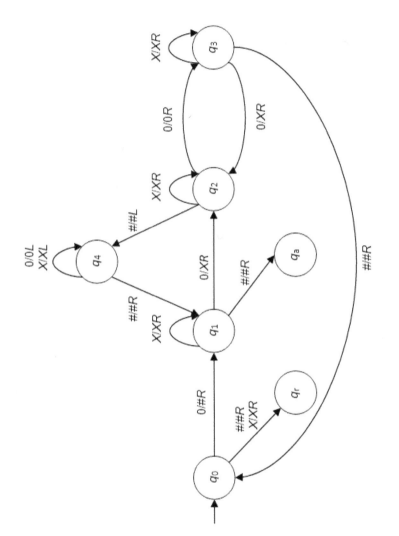

Figure 4.3.8.: Turing machine accepting $L = \{0^{2^n} | n \geq 0\}$.

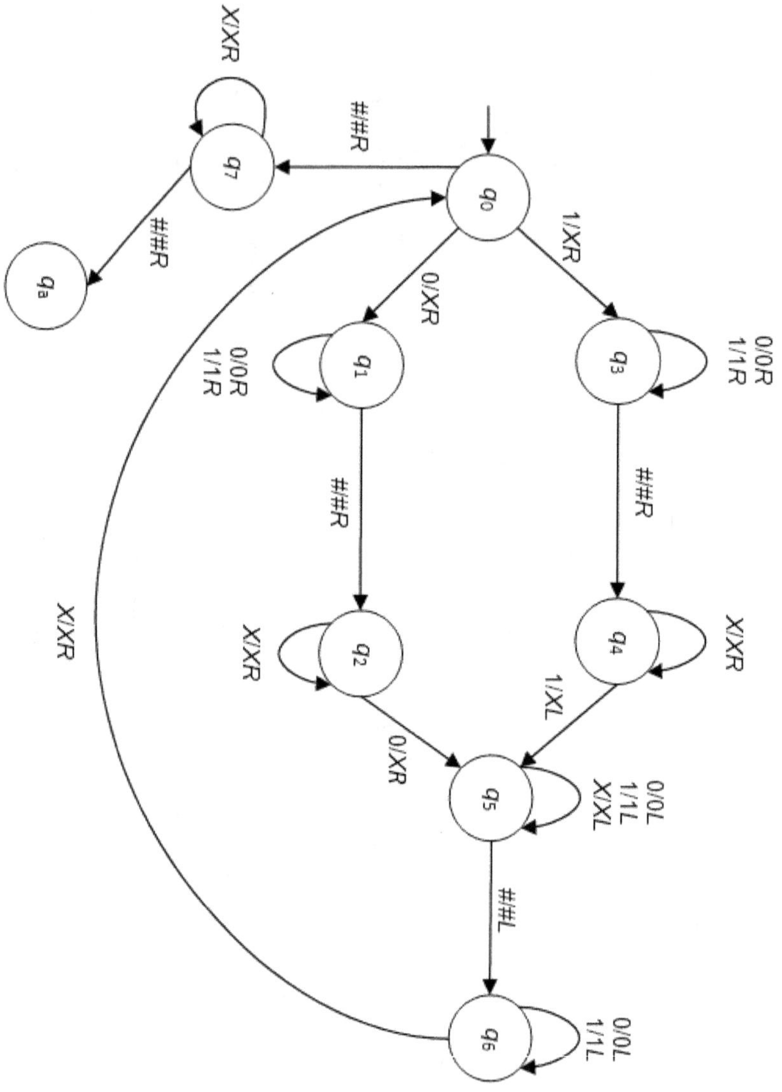

Figure 4.3.9.: Turing machine accepting $L = \{w\#w \mid w \in \{0,1\}^*\}$.

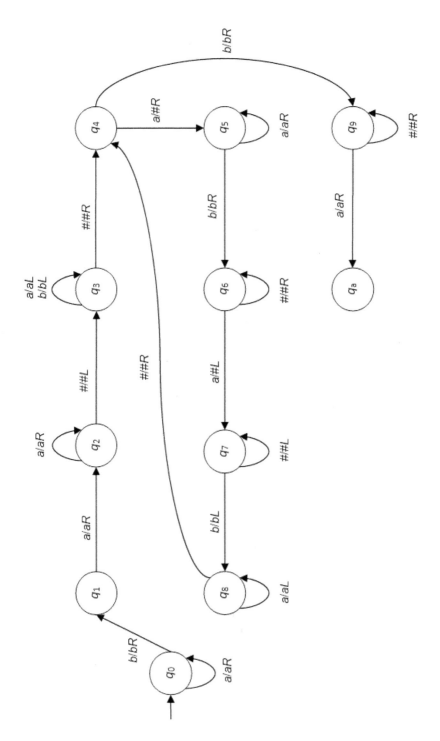

Figure 4.3.10.: Turing machine accepting $L = \{a^i ba^j \mid 0 \leq i < j\}$.

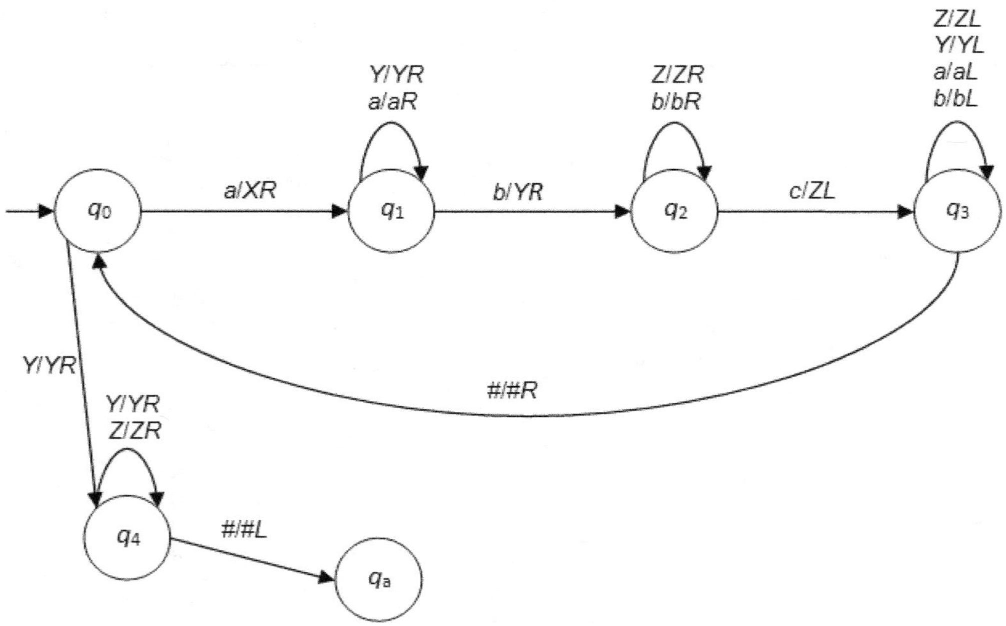

Figure 4.3.11.: Turing machine M_1 accepting a language over $\Sigma = \{a, b, c\}$.

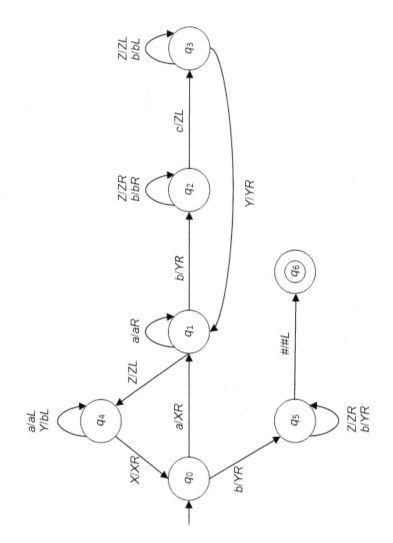

Figure 4.3.12.: Turing machine M_2 accepting a language over $\Sigma = \{a, b, c\}$.

Exercise 4.3.12. Reflect on the importance of the universal TM for the modern-day digital computer.

Exercise 4.3.13. Construct a LBA that accepts the CSL $L = \{a^n b^n c^n | n > 0\}$. (Cf. Exercise 3.4.10.)

Exercise 4.3.14. Prove Theorems 4.3.1-2.

4.4. The Chomsky hierarchy (II)

As seen above, the computation of both finite-state machines and PDAs has essentially to do with accepting or rejecting a language, whereas the computation of a Turing machine is more powerful: It also computes functions. By saying "is more powerful," we intend to express the fact that all Turing machines are finite automata and PDAs, though the reverse does not hold. In effect, Turing machines have an enhanced output capability with respect to these two other kinds of automata: They can decide membership in recursive sets. But they are also more powerful than the LBAs, as these accept only a subset of the RELs, i.e. the CSLs.

As a matter of fact, the CSLs are important in terms of the Chomsky hierarchy, because this class is strictly or properly contained in the class of the *recursive languages*. These, in turn, distinguish themselves from the RELs according to the following important definition (recall from Def. 4.3.3.8 that a Turing machine M_T with input alphabet Σ *accepts* a language $L \subseteq \Sigma^*$ if $L = L(M_T)$, and $L(M_T)$ is a REL):

4.4.1. (Def.) A Turing machine M_T *decides* a language L if M_T computes the characteristic function $\chi_L : \Sigma^* \longrightarrow \{0, 1\}$ defined as follows for some string x:

$$\chi_L(x) = \begin{cases} 1 & \text{if } x \in L \\ 0 & \text{otherwise} \end{cases}$$

L is a *recursive language* if there is a Turing machine M_T that decides L.

Theorem 4.4.1. *Every recursive language is recursively enumerable.*

Proof: Given a string $x \in \Sigma^*$ and a Turing machine M_T that decides $L \subseteq \Sigma^*$, on input x M_T halts and produces output 1 ($\chi_L(x) = 1$) or 0 ($\chi_L(x) = 0$); if the output is 1, accept, otherwise reject. **QED**

In fact, this calls for a definition of a special Turing machine:

4.4.2. (Def.) A Turing machine that halts on every input string x is called a *total Turing machine*.

It should be obvious why a total Turing machine is also called a *decider*. The following theorem establishes the equivalence between a total Turing machine and a recursive language.

Theorem 4.4.2. *If $L \subseteq \Sigma^*$ is accepted by a total Turing machine M_T, then L is a recursive language.*

Proof: M_T halts on every input string x. Then, the characteristic function $\chi_L(x) : \Sigma^* \longrightarrow \{0, 1\}$ constitutes an algorithm for deciding L in the following way: If M_T accepts x, return 1, otherwise, i.e. if M_T rejects x, then return 0. **QED**

In the next Chapter, we shall see more clearly how deciding a language is different from accepting a language. In the meantime, in Table 4.4.1 we show the *extended* Chomsky hierarchy with both the formal languages and the machines associated to them.[35] Just to complete the hierarchy first given in Section 3.5, we have

$$\mathscr{RGL}\,(3) \subset \mathscr{CFL}\,(2) \subset \mathscr{CSL}\,(1) \subset \mathscr{RL} \subset \mathscr{REL}\,(0)$$

where we abbreviate "recursive language" as RL. Note in Table 4.4.1 that there is no specific grammar associated to the recursive languages; in effect, no such grammar is known.

Exercises

Exercise 4.4.1. Show that if A and B are recursive sets, then $A \cup B$, $A \cap B$, and $\overline{A}$ are also recursive. (Hint: Begin with $\chi_{\overline{A}}(x) = 1 - \chi_A(x)$, x is a string.)

Exercise 4.4.2. Show that CSLs are closed under union, intersection, concatenation, and positive closure.

Exercise 4.4.3. A PDA with two stacks is known as a *two-stack pushdown automaton*. Explain why:[36]

1. It is as powerful as a Turing machine.

---

[35]N. Chomsky did not include the recursive languages in his hierarchy. Note that currently the Chomsky hierarchy is actually larger.

[36]Research hint: Révész (1991) contains a complete section on these PDAs; he calls these PDAs "two-pushdown automata."

Grammar	Language class	Computer Model
0 (UG)	Recursively enumerable ($\mathscr{REL}$)	Turing machines (TMs)
	Recursive ($\mathscr{RL}$)	Total TMs (Deciders)
1 (CSG)	Context-sensitive ($\mathscr{CSL}$)	Linear-bounded automata (LBAs)
2 (CFG)	Context-free ($\mathscr{CFL}$)	Pushdown automata (PDAs)
3 (Regular)	Regular ($\mathscr{RL}$)	Finite-state machines

Table 4.4.1.: The extended Chomsky hierarchy: Grammars, languages, and associated computer models.

2. A LBA is a restricted type thereof.

Exercise 4.4.4. A LBA is not as powerful as an unrestricted Turing machine. Explain why, expanding on the reason given above.

Exercise 4.4.5. Prove the following statement: Let $M_1, M_2, \ldots$ be an enumeration of some set of Turing machines halting on all inputs. Then, there is some recursive language that is not $L(M_i)$ for any i (M_i abbreviates M_{T_i}).

Exercise 4.4.6. Prove that there is a recursive language that is not a CSL. (Hint: Use the statement in Exercise 4.4.5.)

Exercise 4.4.7. Let there be given the following statement: If L is a REL, and its complement $\overline{L}$ is also a REL, then L ($\overline{L}$) is a recursive language.

1. Prove it.

2. Comment on its importance for the Chomsky hierarchy.

5. Computability and complexity

In this Chapter, we give the main aspects of the classical theory of computability and complexity, namely from the viewpoint of the Chomsky hierarchy. We refer the reader to Cooper (2003) and Bridges (1994), for instance, for more advanced and/or comprehensive discussions of computability and complexity theory.

5.1. The decision problem and Turing-decidability

It should be obvious by now that formal languages are at the very core of the classical theory of computation. In effect, whatever can be *classically* computed, can so only with and over a formal language. But this is still too general: In fact, whatever can be *classically* computed, can so only with and over *a language that is decidable*. In other words, we are speaking here of a language for which there is an algorithm for deciding whether an arbitrary string x belongs to the language. Thus, the question whether such an algorithm exists is paramount. This is known as the *decision problem*.

5.1.1. (Def.) Given an arbitrary string x and a language L, it is asked:

$$x \overset{?}{\in} L$$

i.e. does x belong to L? The *decision problem* consists in the following: *Is there an algorithm to answer the question $x \overset{?}{\in} L$?*

The decision problem is formulated in terms of set membership, and deciding with respect to a subset of a language whether or not a given string x belongs to it is in no way different from deciding with respect to a subset of the natural numbers whether a given number x is an element thereof.

5.1.2. (Def.) A set $S \subseteq \mathbb{N}$ is said to be *recursive, computable*, or *decidable* if there is an algorithm Ψ that terminates *after a finite amount of time* and correctly decides with respect to a given number x whether $x \in S$. More formally, $S \subseteq \mathbb{N}$ is a recursive (or computable or decidable) set if there is a total computable function $f : \mathbb{N} \longrightarrow \{0, 1\}$ such that for

251

a given number x we have $f(x) = 1$ if $x \in S$ and $f(x) = 0$ if $x \notin S$.

Hence, for a set to be classified as computable, it must be the case that algorithm Ψ *also* outputs the answer "No" whenever $x \notin S$. In the specific case of a formal language, *decidability* is formulated in the following way:

5.1.3. (Def.) A formal language L is said to be *(Turing-)decidable* if there is an algorithm guaranteed to determine whether an arbitrary string x belongs to L.

As seen above, this algorithm is the computation of the characteristic function $\chi_L(x) : \Sigma^* \longrightarrow \{0, 1\}$ by a total Turing machine. This explains why saying *decidable* just is the same as saying *Turing-decidable* with respect to a recursive language. If ambiguity may arise, then the term "decidable" should be used for languages that are decidable by other kinds of Turing machine (e.g. a NDTM). In any case, this shows the fundamental importance of the Turing machines for the field of classical computation, well expressed in the following statement known as *Church-Turing thesis*:

5.1.4. *A function that is effectively calculable is a function that can be computed by a Turing machine.*

This statement, which essentially defines a computable function in terms of the Turing machine, is not a theorem, as it cannot be proved, thus remaining a thesis.[1] This said, so far no one came up with an algorithmic procedure that cannot be implemented by a Turing machine. Whether the Turing machine is an *efficient* model of computation, that is altogether another issue, as it can be extremely difficult to program a Turing machine for even very elementary functions, as Example 4.3.3 shows.

This thesis is named after A. Church, too, because it was shown by Turing (in Turing, 1937) that a Turing machine is equivalent to Church's λ-calculus in defining an effectively calculable function, i.e. Turing machines and the λ-calculus are equivalent models of computation. But the intuitive power of the Turing machine makes it an "easier" model than the other equivalent models of computation.[2] Indeed, to say of a

---

[1] From the Church-Turing thesis as formulated above, we can rigorously define a computable function as a function $f : \Sigma^* \longrightarrow \Sigma^*$ such that on every input w a Turing machine halts with only $f(w)$ on its tape. Compare this with Definition 2.1.4.7.

[2] See also Church (1936a, b). Besides the already mentioned λ-calculus, there are (many) more equivalent models of computation: e.g., register machines, Post machines, and μ-recursive functions. Incidentally, and as a justification for our focusing exclusively on Turing machines, K. Gödel considered that the Turing machine

language that it is recursive or computable is the same as saying that its elements can be *enumerated*–or, more informally, *listed*. And the easiest way to define this is by using a multi-tape Turing machine.[3]

5.1.5. (Def.) Let M_T be a k-tape Turing machine, $k \geq 1$, and let $L \subseteq \Sigma^*$ be a formal language. We say that M_T *enumerates* L if its operation satisfies the following conditions with respect to Tape 1:

1. the tape head never moves to the left, and no non-blank symbol printed on it is subsequently erased or printed over, i.e. Tape 1 is a one-way write-only tape;

2. for every $x \in L$, at some point the contents of this tape will be

$$x_1 \# x_2 \# ... \# x_n \# x \#$$

for some $n \geq 0$, $x_1, x_2, ..., x_n \in L$, $x_1, x_2, ..., x_n, x$ are all distinct, and there is nothing printed after $\#$ if L is finite.

Let us now say that a set of strings is listed in *canonical order* if shorter strings precede longer strings and strings of the same length are alphabetically ordered. Then, we have the following theorem with respect to the distinction between RELs and recursive languages:

Theorem 5.1.1. *For every language $L \subseteq \Sigma^*$, L is recursively enumerable if and only if there is a Turing machine M_T that enumerates L, and L is recursive if and only if there is a Turing machine M_T that enumerates the elements of L in canonical order.*

Proof: Left as an exercise.

Exercises

Exercise 5.1.1. Show that the set Σ^* of all strings over Σ is countable.

Exercise 5.1.2. Show that the following languages are decidable:

1. $ACPT_{FA} = \{\langle M, w \rangle \, | M$ is a FA that accepts string $w\}$.

2. $ACPT_{LBA} = \{\langle M, w \rangle \, | M$ is a LBA that accepts string $w\}$.

3. $REG_{r,w} = \{(r, w) \, | r$ is a regular expression that generates string $w\}$.

---

was sufficient to define an effectively calculable function (cf. Gödel, 1964).

[3]Recall, however, that variations such as multiple tapes do not change the computing power of the Turing machine.

4. $REG_{CFG} = \{(G, w) \,|\, G$ is a CFG that generates string $w\}$.

5. $EMPTY_{FA} = \{\langle M \rangle \,|\, M$ is a FA and $L(M) = \emptyset\}$.

Exercise 5.1.3. Prove Theorem 5.1.1.

Exercise 5.1.4. Give at least three more formulations of the Church-Turing thesis, i.e. statements equivalent to §5.1.4.

5.2. Undecidable problems and Turing-reducibility

The importance of the recursive languages for classical computing is that they mark the endpoint of the *decidable languages* and, as we shall see, of the problems solvable by a computer. In practical terms as far as decidability is concerned, there are easily formulated problems that actually have no algorithmic solution. For instance, although programs and program specifications are precisely defined mathematical objects, there is no decision procedure for the general problem of program verification.

This means that the fundamental question $x \overset{?}{\in} L$ with respect to an arbitrary string x and a language L has no conclusive answer for the languages beyond the recursive ones in the extended Chomsky hierarchy, which means that for the RELs the best scenario one may get in the case that $x \notin L$ is that a Turing machine will not answer that $x \in L$, though it is not certain whether or not it will halt. In effect, there may be input strings $x \notin L$ that may cause a Turing machine to loop forever. Formally speaking, the best we can get for RELs is *semi-decidability*.

5.2.1. (Def.) A set $S \subseteq \mathbb{N}$ is said to be *recursively enumerable* or *semi-decidable* if there is an algorithm that correctly decides when a given number $x \in S$, but the algorithm may give no answer for $x \notin S$. Formally formulated, there is a partial computable function φ such that

$$\varphi(x) = \begin{cases} 1 & \text{if } x \in S \\ \text{undefined, or does not halt} & \text{if } x \notin S \end{cases}.$$

Recall from above the definition of a computable set (cf. Def. 5.1.2).

Example 5.2.1. Consider the following set:

$$S = \{p \,|\, p \text{ is a polynomial over } x \text{ with an integral root}\}$$

We ask whether S is decidable. Given a polynomial p over x such as $2x^3 + 6x^2 - x + 5$, we ask if $p \in S$. In other words, we want to know if $x = n, n \in \mathbb{Z}$. There is indeed an algorithm to test for this decision problem: We evaluate p for the values $0, 1, -1, 2, -2, 3, ...$ one at a time successively; if for some $n \in \mathbb{Z}$ it is the case that $p = 0$, then $\chi_S(p) = 1$. Nevertheless, we have no guarantee that this algorithm will ever terminate: It will only eventually terminate if indeed $p \in S$; otherwise, it is obvious that it will run forever, because $\mathbb{Z}$ is an infinite set. Thus, S is in fact not computable, though it is recursively enumerable.[4]

Example 5.2.1 shows in a clear way that the property of being recursively enumerable may not be of much help in practical terms. The importance of these results cannot be overstated: They mark the limits of what classical computing devices can do, namely with respect to the decision problem (see above). These limits are notably illustrated by the following examples.

Example 5.2.2. *The Acceptance Problem (ACPT)* – Let the following set be given (M abbreviates M_T and TM does so for Turing machine):

$$ACPT_{TM} = \{\langle M, w\rangle \,|\, M \text{ is a TM and } M \text{ accepts } w\}$$

Although it is recursively enumerable, this set is undecidable. In effect, given input w, M can halt in either an accepting or a rejecting state, but M may loop on w, and M has no way to determine that it is looping (i.e. not halting) on a given input.

Example 5.2.3. *The Halting Problem (HALT)* – The set

$$HALT_{TM} = \{\langle M, w\rangle \,|\, M \text{ is a TM and } M \text{ halts on } w\}$$

is undecidable. This was actually one of the first decision problems to be proven undecidable, and it was so famously in Turing (1937) by means of the Turing machine. We give the sketch of a proof and leave the details as an exercise. Let $\langle M \rangle$ be the binary encoding of a TM $M_T = (Q, \Gamma, \#, \Sigma, q_0, A, \delta)$ and $w \in \{0, 1\}^+$ be some string. Assume now that there is a Turing machine H (abbreviating H_T) that solves

---

[4]S is in fact called a *Diophantine set*. Put more rigorously, it can be shown that there is a polynomial $p(n, x_1, ..., x_n)$ with integer coefficients such that the set of values of $n \in \mathbb{Z}$ for which the equation $p(n, x_1, ..., x_n) = 0$ has solution is not computable. The direct consequence of this result is that Hilbert's Tenth Problem is unsolvable. See Matiyasevich (1993) for a comprehensive elaboration on this result in the framework of Hilbert's Tenth Problem and Diophantine equations; for a discussion more immediately in the context of computability theory (typically with the restriction $n \in \mathbb{N}$), see Leary & Christiansen (2015).

HALT. H has two final states, q_Y and q_N for "Yes" and "No" answers, respectively, such that on input $(\langle M \rangle, w)$ machine H ends in state q_Y if M halts on w, and H ends in state q_N if M does not halt on w. We construct a Turing machine H' from H such that H' halts if M ends in state q_N and H' does not halt (i.e. loops forever) if M ends in state q_Y. We then construct another Turing machine H'' from H' that makes a copy of $\langle M \rangle$ and behaves like H'. We have it that H'' with input $\langle M \rangle$ runs H' with input $(\langle M \rangle, \langle M \rangle)$, and we reach a contradiction when we run H'' on input $\langle H'' \rangle$: If H'' halts, then it loops for ever; if it does not halt, then it halts.[5]

Note that in Examples 5.2.2-3 both sets $ACPT_{TM}$ and $HALT_{TM}$ are actually languages. This means that, in face of a problem requiring a "Yes/No" answer, we can formulate it in terms of whether a particular language is–or is not–recursive. Suppose now that you suspect that problem B is hard to solve and you have an unsolvable problem A formulated as a language that cannot be decided; if you can reduce A to B, then you know that B is also undecidable. On the other hand, if you know that B is decidable, then by reducing A to B you know that A is also decidable. This is known as *reducibility*.

5.2.2. (**Def.**) Given two languages A and B, we say that there is a *mapping reduction from A to B*, denoted by $A \preceq B$, if there is a computable function $f : \Sigma^* \longrightarrow \Sigma^*$ such that, for every w, we have

$$(f_{red}) \qquad w \in A \quad \text{iff} \quad f(w) \in B.$$

The function f is the *reduction from A to B*.

One can actually speak of *Turing-reducibility*:[6] it is obvious that the reduction above actually reduces questions of membership (to a lan-

---

[5]Equivalently, but perhaps more intuitively, we can think in terms of functions in the following way. Given a function $f(x)$, which we name f_x, we define the function:

$$halt(x) = \begin{cases} 1 & \text{if } f_x \text{ halts on input } x \\ 0 & \text{otherwise} \end{cases}$$

We next define a new function:

$$g(x) = \begin{cases} \text{loop forever} & \text{if } halt(x) = 1 \\ 0 & \text{otherwise} \end{cases}$$

Derive now a contradiction from defining

$$g(n) = f_n(n)$$

for n some natural number.

[6]Strictly conceived, Turing-reducibility is a generalization of mapping reducibility.

guage) in A to membership in B, it being the case, for example, that there is a total Turing machine M that is a decider for B. Then, the proofs involve combining this decider with other Turing machines, so as to form "composite" Turing machines with one tape for each of the individual machines. The basic idea is to show that language A is recursive in language B. In other words, the algorithm for deciding membership in B can be converted into an algorithm for deciding membership in A.

Theorem 5.2.1. *Let A and B be two languages. If $A \preceq B$ and B is decidable, then A is decidable.*

Proof: (Sketch) We assume that M (abbreviating M_T) is a decider for B and f is the reduction from A to B. Then, we can define a Turing machine M' such that, given input w, M' computes $f(w)$ and runs M on input w and outputs whatever is the output of M. Hence, we have $\chi_A(x) = \chi_B(f(x))$, for some string $x \in A$. **QED**

By contraposition,[7] we have the following result:

Corollary 5.2.2. *If $A \preceq B$ and A is undecidable, then B is undecidable.*

Proof: Left as an exercise.

Example 5.2.4. The *State-Entry Problem (STENTRY)*, defined as

$$STENTRY_{TM} = \{\langle M, w, q \rangle \,|\, M \text{ enters state } q \text{ on input } w\}$$

can be shown to be undecidable by reduction. We reduce HALT to STENTRY. Suppose we have an algorithm Ψ that solves the latter. Then, there is a Turing machine M (abbreviating M_T) that enters state q on input w. By Theorem 5.2.1, there is also an algorithm to solve HALT. We modify M into a Turing machine M' that on input w halts in state q if and only if M does. On input w, M halts in state q only if some transition $\delta(q_i, \sigma)$ for some state q_i and some symbol σ is undefined. In order to obtain M' we change every undefined transition to

$$\delta(q_i, \sigma) = (q, \sigma, R)$$

where q is the only final state. We run algorithm Ψ on $\langle M', w, q \rangle$: If M' enters state q, then M halts on input w; otherwise, M does not halt. But we know that there is no algorithm for (M', w, q), i.e. HALT is undecidable. Therefore, because HALT$\preceq$STENTRY, by Corollary 5.2.2, STENTRY must also be undecidable.

---

[7]I.e. the classical logical equivalence $p \to q \equiv \neg q \to \neg p$.

As seen, there is indeed an algorithm for the recursive languages. However, there is no such algorithm for the whole class of the RELs. In face of Theorems 4.4.1-2, the extended Chomsky hierarchy signifies that all languages up to and including the recursive languages are decidable, and that there are RELs that are not decidable, though they can be accepted by a Turing machine (otherwise, they would not be RELs). In effect, beyond the recursively enumerable sets, we have the *non-computable* or *undecidable* sets. In terms of the Chomsky hierarchy, we have the undecidable languages. And, impressively, the set of the languages that are not RELs is uncountable.

Theorem 5.2.3. *The set of languages over $\{0, 1\}$ that are not RELs is uncountable.*

Proof: Left as an exercise. Let $\{0, 1\}^* = S$. First, prove that $|S| = |\mathbb{N}|$. Next, prove that 2^S is uncountable (cf. Exercise 2.1.9).

On the other hand, we have the following theorem:

Theorem 5.2.4. *The set of Turing machines is countable.*

Proof: (Sketch) The set Σ^* of all strings over Σ is countable (cf. Exercise 5.1.1). Hence, we can list all the strings of Σ^*, for example, ordering them by length. For each of these strings there is an encoding $\langle M_T \rangle$ of a Turing machine, so that, if we omit all illegal encodings of Turing machines, we have a list of all Turing machines. **QED**

The result follows: There are more formal languages than Turing machines. This poses the question what the languages that are not RELs are like. Unfortunately, we have only an indirect glimpse into them.

Theorem 5.2.5. *There exists a REL L whose complement $\overline{L}$ is not recursively enumerable.*

Proof: We abbreviate M_{T_i} as M_i. By Theorem 5.2.4, given an input alphabet $\Sigma = \{a\}$, there are Turing machines $M_1, M_2, ...$ such that there is some M_i associated to each REL $L(M_i)$ over Σ. Consider now a new language L such that, for each $i \geq 1$, with respect to the string a^i we have

$$a^i \in L \quad \text{iff} \quad a^i \in L(M_i).$$

Consider now the complement of L:

$$(1) \qquad \overline{L} = \{a^i | a^i \notin L(M_i)\}$$

Both L and $\overline{L}$ are well defined, but the latter is not recursively enumerable. This can be shown by contradiction. We assume that $\overline{L}$ is recursively enumerable. Then, there must be some M_j such that:

$$(2) \qquad \overline{L} = L\left(M_j\right)$$

Let us consider now a string a^j. If $a^j \in \overline{L}$, then by (2) $a^j \in L\left(M_j\right)$ which entails by (1) that $a^j \notin \overline{L}$; if $a^j \in L$, then $a^j \notin \overline{L}$, which by (2) entails that $a^j \notin L\left(M_j\right)$, which by (1) entails that $a^j \in \overline{L}$. In either case, we reach a contradiction, so we conclude that $\overline{L}$ is not recursively enumerable. Proving that L is a REL is easy and we leave this part of the proof as an exercise. (Hint: Think universal!) **QED**

In the proof above, we remark that both L and $\overline{L}$ are well defined. However, the fact that $\overline{L}$ is not recursively enumerable shows us that there are well-defined languages that are not RELs. This, in turn, shows that there are well-defined languages for which no membership algorithm can be conceived, and thus no effective decision procedure can be obtained.

But, in fact, there are specific problems with respect to the recursive languages that are not computable in practice, either. This topic is approached in Section 5.4.

Exercises

Exercise 5.2.1. Prove the undecidability of ACPT by means of the diagonalization method.

Exercise 5.2.2. Give a full proof of the undecidability of HALT from the sketch in Example 5.2.3. (Hint: Use configurations.)

Exercise 5.2.3. Solve Exercise 2.1.1 again, now by making use of Turing machines.

Exercise 5.2.4. Show that if HALT were decidable, then every REL would be recursive.

Exercise 5.2.5. Explain why HALT is theoretically decidable for LBAs or deterministic machines with a finite memory. Explain also why only theoretically so.

Exercise 5.2.6. Show that the complement of a recursive language is recursive. (Hint: See Fig. 5.2.1, where M abbreviates M_T.)

Exercise 5.2.7. Show by combining two Turing machines M_1 and M_2 into a Turing machine M that the class of recursive languages is closed under union and intersection.

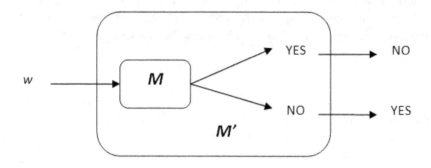

Figure 5.2.1.: A combination of Turing machines.

Exercise 5.2.8. Show by combining two Turing machines M_1 and M_2 into a Turing machine M that the class $\mathcal{REL}$ is closed under union and intersection.

Exercise 5.2.9. Show by Turing-reducibility that the following languages are undecidable:

1. $REG_{TM} = \{\langle M\rangle \,|\, M \text{ is a TM and } L(M) \text{ is regular}\}$.

2. $EMPTY_{TM} = \{\langle M\rangle \,|\, M \text{ is a TM and } L(M) = \emptyset\}$.

3. $EMPTY_{LBA} = \{\langle M\rangle \,|\, M \text{ is a LBA and } L(M) = \emptyset\}$.

4. $EQUAL_{TM} = \{\langle M_1, M_2\rangle \,|\, M_1, M_2 \text{ are TMs and } L(M_1) = L(M_2)\}$.

Exercise 5.2.10. Research into the decision problem known as *Busy Beaver* and give its main aspects, i.e. describe the problem, formalize it, and provide the details of a proof of its undecidability.

Exercise 5.2.11. Research into *Rice's theorem* and give its main points.

Exercise 5.2.12. Research into *Post's Correspondence Problem* and give its main points.

Exercise 5.2.13. Research into *Hilbert's Tenth Problem* and elaborate on the proof of its undecidability found by Y. Matiyasevich.

Exercise 5.2.14. Search in the literature for other important computational problems that have been shown unsolvable by means of Turing-reducibility.

Exercise 5.2.15. Prove (Complete the proof of) the theorems (including Theorem 5.2.5) and corollaries in this Section that were left as an exercise (with a sketchy proof, respectively).

5.3. The Chomsky hierarchy (III)

We ended last Section with an indirect glimpse into the languages beyond the RELs, i.e. the complements of RELs. As seen, the RELs are merely *Turing-recognizable*. By this it is meant that there is a Turing machine M_T that recognizes a REL L, but M_T may enter an infinite loop for strings that do not belong to L. $ACPT_{TM}$ and $HALT_{TM}$ are notorious examples of Turing-recognizable languages, and the only glimpse that we get of their complements, to wit, $\overline{ACPT_{TM}}$ and $\overline{HALT_{TM}}$, respectively, is that they are not even Turing-recognizable. If we consider the Turing-decidable languages (i.e. the recursive languages) as the border between decidability and Turing-recognizability, the extended Chomsky hierarchy can be visualized as in Figure 5.3.1. (Recall that the decidable languages include the regular languages, the CFLs, and the CSLs.)

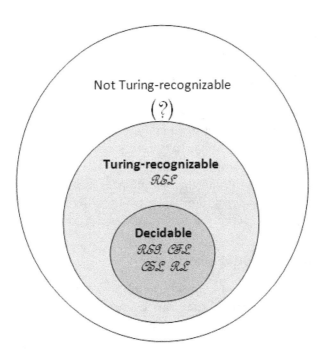

Figure 5.3.1.: The Chomsky hierarchy and beyond.

Knowledge of the material above will easily lead to the realization that just about every question of interest with respect to RELs is undecidable. Moreover, as we go up in the Chomsky hierarchy, undecidability grows. Table 5.3.1 shows the decidability properties of the language classes in the Chomsky hierarchy.

	$\mathscr{RGL}$	$\mathscr{CFL}$	$\mathscr{CSL}$	$\mathscr{REL}$
Membership	Yes	Yes	Yes	No
Finiteness	Yes	Yes	No	No
Emptiness	Yes	Yes	No	No
Inclusion	Yes	No	No	No
Equivalence	Yes	No	No	No

Table 5.3.1.: Decidability ("Yes") and undecidability ("No") of some properties of interest for the Chomsky hierarchy.

Exercises

Exercise 5.3.1. With respect to Table 5.3.1, some of the proofs of (un)decidability have already been either discussed or proposed as exercises above. Formalize the remaining decision problems in it and prove their (un)decidability.

5.4. Computational complexity

Narrowly defined, complexity theory is concerned with classifying the degree of difficulty in testing for membership in the various formal languages. Less narrowly defined, it classifies the amount of resources required to carry out a computational algorithm. This is a large field, so large indeed that a comprehensive listing of complexity classes can contain more than 400 entries. For our purposes, luckily, only a few such classes are required.

5.4.1. Computational problems

In the classical analysis of computational problems, there are resources other than time and space that can be taken into consideration, and models of computation other than the Turing machines. However, we shall concentrate on time and space resources, and our model of computation will be the Turing machine. We begin with a very general, abstract approach, and go then into more specific issues and classifications in the classical theory of computational complexity. This abstract approach is based on M. Blum's axioms for computational measures

(Blum, 1967). Although they have lost some of their original spark–due to the fact that many measures today relevant in computing theory do not satisfy them–, they will be fine for our purposes. In later Sections, further specifications are made.

The following, rather informal, definition serves our purposes well:

5.4.1. (Def.) A *computational problem* is an infinite collection of *(problem) instances* with a *solution* for every instance.

The best way to tackle a computational problem is by reducing it. This may be a reduction to a *decision problem* in which input strings–typically, but not always, over the alphabet $\Sigma = \{0, 1\}$–are problem instances.[8] Another possible reduction is to a *function problem*. Clearly, outputs in the latter reduction are more complex than the output "Yes/No" of decision problems, but function problems can be recast in terms of decision problems (and vice-versa). Other, less frequent, reductions are possible.

Example 5.4.1. Recall from Section 2.2.2 the definition of a graph and from Section 4.3.4 the notion of encoding. Given an undirected graph $\mathfrak{G}$, a Hamiltonian path in $\mathfrak{G}$ is a simple path that goes through each vertex exactly once. We want to test whether a graph $\mathfrak{G}$ contains a Hamiltonian path connecting two specified vertices, say, u and v, which constitutes a triple $(\mathfrak{G}, u, v)$. This is known as *The Hamiltonian Path Problem*, and it can be formulated in terms of a decision problem as follows with $\langle \cdot \rangle$ denoting an appropriate encoding:

$$HAMPATH = \{\langle \mathfrak{G}, u, v \rangle \mid \mathfrak{G} \text{ has a Hamiltonian path connecting } u, v\}$$

We can encode $\mathfrak{G}$ over the alphabet $\Sigma = \{0, 1\}$ by means of an adjacency matrix (cf. Exercise 2.2.8). Let $\mathfrak{G}$ be the graph of Figure 2.2.1. Then, we have the adjacency matrix

$$A_{\mathfrak{G}} = \begin{pmatrix} 0 & 1 & 1 & 1 & 0 \\ 1 & 0 & 1 & 0 & 1 \\ 1 & 1 & 0 & 1 & 0 \\ 1 & 0 & 1 & 0 & 1 \\ 0 & 1 & 0 & 1 & 0 \end{pmatrix}$$

which can be easily transformed into an array, which for our purposes constitutes a string w over the alphabet $\Sigma = \{0, 1\}$ such that $w = \langle \mathfrak{G} \rangle$.

---

[8]This *binary encoding* is especially relevant when we stipulate that the size n of the input is measured in bits, as it assures us that each character uses a constant number of bits and each integer $i > 0$ uses at most $c \log i$ bits for some constant $c > 0$. To avoid in any case is *unary encoding*, which uses the single symbol "1"; just think of representing any integer greater than, say, 20 in this system.

5.4.2. The Blum axioms and complexity measures

In practical terms, faced with a computational problem we want to know how much *effort* must be put into solving it, or what its *cost* in terms of resources is. In effect, once we determine that a problem is computable, this does not mean that we can actually compute it–efficiently, or at all. This is so because any computation takes up resources, such as (running) time and (utilized) space. Time and space might be infinite, but we are short-living and time and space have monetary costs for us; so, we require algorithms that both terminate in useful time and do not take up too much space. Thus, we need to restrict these resources appropriately. In order to do this we require a clear notion of *computational measure*; for time and space resources, the Blum axioms (Blum, 1967) provide a general approach.

5.4.2. (Def.) *The Blum axioms* – Let $M_0, M_1, ...$ be an effective enumeration of (a class) of machines. With each M_i there are associated two functions: (i) the partial recursive function $\varphi_i(n)$ for input n, and (ii) a partial recursive function $\Phi_i(n)$ such that $\Phi_i(n) = m$ is the *computational complexity of M_i on input n* if and only if the following axioms are satisfied:

- *Axiom 1:* $\varphi_i(n)$ converges if and only if $\Phi_i(n)$ converges.

- *Axiom 2:* The function

$$R(i, n, m) = \begin{cases} 1 & \text{if } \Phi_i(n) = m \\ 0 & \text{otherwise} \end{cases}$$

  is (total) recursive.

Axiom 1 can be reformulated in terms of definition, i.e. $\Phi_i(n)$ is defined if and only if $\varphi_i(n)$ is defined (i.e. M_i halts on input n); reformulated in terms of Axiom 2, we have

$$\varphi_i(n) \text{ converges iff } \exists m \left[R(i, n, m) = 1 \right].$$

Blum called the function $\Phi_i(n)$ the *step-counting function*, but it may be interpreted as counting either the number of steps or the amount of tape used by M_i given input n. So, the resources here envisaged are exclusively time and space computed as m steps or tape cells, respectively, in terms of complexity.

Blum (1967) does not specify the kind of (Turing) machine, so as to guarantee the generality of the axioms. We concentrate on two (rather general) types of Turing machine to specify complexity measures of time and space: deterministic and non-deterministic Turing machines, abbreviated as DTM and NDTM, respectively (see Section 4.3.3). We also focus on *worst-case analysis*, i.e. we are interested in longest running-time and largest storage-space requirements for inputs of length n.

5.4.3. (Def.) *Space complexity* – Let M be a Turing machine. If, for every input string of length n, M scans *at most* $S(n)$ storage tape cells, then M is said to be a *Turing machine of space complexity* $S(n)$ (or a $S(n)$ *space-bounded Turing machine*). Because every Turing machine uses at least one cell on any input, we may assume $S(n) \geq 1$ for all n. Moreover, we may assume that

$$S(n) = \max(1, \lceil S(n) \rceil)$$

where $\lceil S(n) \rceil$ denotes the ceiling for M given input n.[9] The language recognized by M is also said to be of space complexity $S(n)$.

5.4.4. (Def.) *Time complexity* – Let M be a Turing machine. If, for every input string of length n, M takes *at most* $T(n)$ steps (moves) before halting, then M is said to be a *Turing machine of time complexity* $T(n)$ (or a $T(n)$ *time-bounded Turing machine*). Because every Turing machine will require at least $n+1$ steps to read the input and certify itself that the end of the string has been reached (by reading the first blank symbol on the right of the string), we may assume $T(n) = n+1$ for all n. Moreover, we may assume that

$$T(n) = \max(n+1, \lceil T(n) \rceil)$$

where $\lceil T(n) \rceil$ denotes the ceiling for M given input n. The language recognized by M is also said to be of time complexity $T(n)$.

Example 5.4.2. Consider the language

$$L = \{wcw^R | w \in \{0,1\}^*\}$$

where c is some symbol not belonging to $\Sigma = \{0,1\}$. A Turing machine M with two tapes makes at most $n+1$ moves for an input of length n: Firstly, M copies the half of the input that is to the left of c (i.e. w) to the second tape; when M finds c, M *simultaneously* moves the head to the right on the input tape (reading w^R) and moves the head to the left on the second tape, comparing the symbols on both tapes. We say that L is of time complexity $T(n) = n+1$.

---

[9] See Exercise 2.1.1.2.

5.4.5. (Def.) Definitions 5.4.3-4 hold for DTMs.[10] We thus have the two *families* of space and time complexity classes DSPACE $(S(n))$ and DTIME $(T(n))$, respectively.

But these definitions also hold for NDTMs once we formulate some restrictions:

5.4.6. (Def.) A NDTM is of space complexity $S(n)$ if it cannot scan more than $S(n)$ tape cells, regardless of how many choices it may have. We denote this family of space complexity by NSPACE $(S(n))$. A NDTM is of time complexity $T(n)$ if it cannot make more than $T(n)$ moves, regardless of how many choices it may have. We denote this family of time complexity by NTIME $(T(n))$.

Because it is more often than not the case that we are faced with complex expressions, especially so on large inputs, we actually use what is called *big-O notation*.

5.4.7. (Def.) Consider the functions $f, g : \mathbb{N} \longrightarrow \mathbb{R}^+$, where $\mathbb{R}^+$ is the set of the positive real numbers. We say that $f(n)$ *is of order* $g(n)$, and write $f(n) = \mathscr{O}(g(n))$, if there exist $c, n_0 \in \mathbb{Z}^+$ such that, for $n \geq n_0$, c is a constant,

$$f(n) \leq cg(n).$$

When $f(n) = \mathscr{O}(g(n))$, we say that $g(n)$ is an *(asymptotic) upper bound* for $f(n)$.

Clearly, $\mathscr{O}(g(n))$ is an approximation, or estimation, of $f(n)$. In practical terms, what we do is, given a polynomial $p(x)$ of degree n, to suppress the coefficient of the highest-order term in $p(x)$ and disregard all other terms to obtain $p(x) = \mathscr{O}(x^n)$.[11]

Example 5.4.3. Given the polynomial $3x^3 + 7x^2 + x + 36$, we have

$$3x^3 + 7x^2 + x + 36 = \mathscr{O}(x^3).$$

Example 5.4.4. Consider the language $L = \{0^m 1^m | m \geq 0\}$ and a single-tape Turing machine M (abbreviating M_T). We analyze the three-stage algorithm for deciding this language given the input string $|0^k 1^k| = n$.

1. M scans across the tape to verify that the input is of the form 0^*1^*. This takes n steps.[12] M then places the tape head again at the

---

[10] With the proviso that if we use DTMs with any fixed $n \geq 1$ of tapes, we might not be able to consider all languages accepted in time $T(n)$.

[11] More correctly, we have $p(x) \in \mathscr{O}(x^n)$.

[12] We simplify here, as M actually takes $n + 1$ steps to reach the first blank symbol after the input string (cf. Def. 5.4.4).

leftmost end of the tape. This, too, takes n steps, so that in total M takes $2n = \mathcal{O}(n)$ steps.

2. M repeatedly scans across the tape, crossing off a 0 and a 1 on each scan. Each scan uses $\mathcal{O}(n)$ steps. But M crosses off two symbols on each scan, so that actually there are at most $n/2$ scans. The total time for stage 2 is thus $\frac{n}{2}\mathcal{O}(n) = \mathcal{O}(n^2)$.

3. M scans the tape only once, in order to decide whether to accept or reject. This single scan takes at most $\mathcal{O}(n)$ steps.

Hence, the total time taken by M is

$$(\maltese) \qquad \mathcal{O}(n) + \mathcal{O}(n^2) + \mathcal{O}(n) = \mathcal{O}(n^2).$$

In Example 5.4.4, we say that the Turing machine M has $\mathcal{O}(n^2)$ time complexity, or, more generally, M has polynomial time complexity. We have the equality $\maltese$, because we are concerned with upper bounds and $\mathcal{O}(n^2)$ *dominates* (over) $\mathcal{O}(n)$. In effect, for the standard functions of interest (see Table 5.4.2) we have, for $k, m \in \mathbb{N}$,

$$\mathcal{O}(\log n) \subset \mathcal{O}(n) \subset \mathcal{O}(n \log n) \subset \mathcal{O}\left(n^k\right) \subset \mathcal{O}(2^n)$$

and

$$\mathcal{O}\left(n^k\right) \subset \mathcal{O}\left(n^{k+1}\right) \subset \mathcal{O}\left(n^{k+2}\right) \subset \ldots \subset \mathcal{O}\left(n^{k+(m-1)}\right) \subset \mathcal{O}\left(n^{k+m}\right).$$

Thus, if given some function $f(n)$ we have $f = \mathcal{O}(n^2)$, then $f = \mathcal{O}(n^3)$, too, as $\mathcal{O}(n^3)$ is still an upper bound on f, but $f \neq \mathcal{O}(n)$.

5.4.8. (Def.) A Turing machine M has *polynomial-time complexity* if there exists a polynomial function $p(n) = \mathcal{O}(n^k)$, $k \in \mathbb{N}$, such that $T(x) \leq p(n)$ for $n = 0, 1, \ldots$. M has *polynomial-space complexity* if there is a polynomial function $p(n) = \mathcal{O}(n^k)$, $k \in \mathbb{N}$, such that $S(x) \leq p(n)$ for $n = 0, 1, \ldots$. M has *exponential-time complexity* if there is an exponential function $ex(n) = \mathcal{O}\left(2^{n^k}\right)$, $k \in \mathbb{N}$, such that $T(x) \leq ex(n)$ for $n = 0, 1, \ldots$. M has *exponential-space complexity* if there is an exponential function $ex(n) = \mathcal{O}\left(2^{n^k}\right)$, $k \in \mathbb{N}$, such that $S(x) \leq ex(n)$ for $n = 0, 1, \ldots$.

When we speak of computational complexity, we are actually referring to rates of growth of a function given an input n. To really appreciate the difference between a polynomial and an exponential function in terms of resource expenditure or requirements, check Table 5.4.1. Many interesting computational problems can be solved in polynomial time. Exponential-time algorithms are typically associated to *brute-force*

n	$\log n$	n	$n \log n$	n^2	n^3	2^n
5	3	5	15	25	125	32
10	4	10	40	100	10^3	10^3
100	7	100	700	10^4	10^6	10^{30}
1000	10	1000	10^4	10^6	10^9	10^{300}

Table 5.4.1.: Rates of growth of some standard functions.

search, i.e. an exhaustive search of the solution space, but this can often be replaced by an algorithm running in polynomial time. However, for many problems there has been found as yet no polynomial-time algorithm, whether because the problem has not been fully grasped or for other reasons. Therefore, familiarity with the classes of both polynomial- and exponential-time running algorithms is essential.

5.4.3. Complexity classes

5.4.9. (Def.) We now define the complexity classes with respect to time and space complexity:[13]

1. The complexity class **P** contains all languages that are decidable by a DTM with polynomial-time complexity, i.e.

$$\mathbf{P} = \bigcup_{k \in \mathbb{N}} \mathrm{DTIME}\left(n^k\right).$$

2. The complexity class **PSPACE** contains all languages that are decidable by a DTM with polynomial-space complexity, i.e.

$$\mathbf{PSPACE} = \bigcup_{k \in \mathbb{N}} \mathrm{DSPACE}\left(n^k\right).$$

3. The complexity class **NP** contains all languages that are decidable by a NDTM with polynomial-time complexity, i.e.

$$\mathbf{NP} = \bigcup_{k \in \mathbb{N}} \mathrm{NTIME}\left(n^k\right).$$

---

[13] Although we denote classes elsewhere in this book by means of formal script font (e.g., $\mathscr{C}$, $\mathscr{L}$), it is usual to denote the complexity classes by bold fonts. We keep to this usage.

4. The complexity class **NPSPACE** contains all languages that are decidable by a NDTM with polynomial-space complexity, i.e.

$$\textbf{NPSPACE} = \bigcup_{k \in \mathbb{N}} \text{NSPACE}\left(n^k\right).$$

5. The complexity class **EXPTIME** contains all languages that are decidable by a DTM with exponential-time complexity, i.e.

$$\textbf{EXPTIME} = \bigcup_{k \in \mathbb{N}} \text{DTIME}\left(2^{n^k}\right).$$

6. The complexity class **EXPSPACE** contains all the languages that are decidable by a DTM with exponential-space complexity, i.e.

$$\textbf{EXPSPACE} = \bigcup_{k \in \mathbb{N}} \text{DSPACE}\left(2^{n^k}\right).$$

7. The complexity class **NEXPTIME** contains all the languages that are decidable by a NDTM with exponential-time complexity, i.e.

$$\textbf{NEXPTIME} = \bigcup_{k \in \mathbb{N}} \text{NTIME}\left(2^{n^k}\right).$$

8. The complexity class **NEXPSPACE** contains all the languages that are decidable by a NDTM with exponential-space complexity, i.e.

$$\textbf{NEXPSPACE} = \bigcup_{k \in \mathbb{N}} \text{NSPACE}\left(2^{n^k}\right).$$

Given this classification, we say that a computational problem is in a specific complexity class if, given an appropriate encoding of instances of the problem, the encoded language of Yes-instances–i.e., encoded instances for which an algorithm halts and outputs "Yes"–is a member of this class.

With respect to Definition 5.4.9, we have the following important remarks:

5.4.10. In fact,

$$\textbf{PSPACE} = \textbf{NPSPACE}$$

by *Savitch's theorem*, which states that for any function $f : \mathbb{N} \longrightarrow \mathbb{R}^+$ with $f(n) \geq n$,

$$\text{NSPACE}\left(f(n)\right) \subseteq \text{DSPACE}\left(f^2(n)\right).$$

In other words, a DTM can simulate a NDTM without requiring much more space. Thus we also have:

$$\mathbf{EXPSPACE} = \mathbf{NEXPSPACE}$$

5.4.11. The question whether the complexity class **P** equals the complexity class **NP**, written $\mathbf{P} \overset{?}{=} \mathbf{NP}$, is considered to be the most important open problem in theoretical computer science. (We shall have more to say on this.)

5.4.12. As seen above (Table 5.4.1), there are standard functions whose rate of growth is sublinear, i.e. far slower compared to polynomial or exponential growth rates. These functions can also be associated to tape space (but not moves[14]) of Turing machines, so that we have the following additional complexity classes:

1. The complexity class **L** contains all the languages that are decidable by a DTM with logarithmic-space complexity, i.e.

$$\mathbf{L} = \mathrm{DSPACE}\,(\log n)\,.$$

2. The complexity class **NL** contains all the languages that are decidable by a NDTM with logarithmic-space complexity, i.e.

$$\mathbf{NL} = \mathrm{NSPACE}\,(\log n)\,.$$

5.4.13. Just as in the case of the **P** and **NP** complexity classes, we have the open problem $\mathbf{L} \overset{?}{=} \mathbf{NL}$. As a matter of fact, we have the hierarchy of complexity classes shown in Figure 5.4.1, which depicts not only the relative sizes of each class, but also the open problems in the theory of complexity. Additionally, this Figure shows the tractability status of the computational problems of the different complexity classes.

5.4.14. (Def.) A computational problem is said to be *tractable* if it can be solved in practice. Otherwise, it is said to be *intractable*.

This is a rather vague definition, but the topic of computational tractability is a field of open questions. Nevertheless, some basic "guidelines" can be given.

Because time is the resource most often considered we concentrate now on the classes **P** and **NP**. Note that these two classes are directly

---

[14]Because a sublinear bound does not allow a Turing machine to read the input. This poses problems for space resources, too, but these can be remediated by considering two tapes, a read-only input tape and another read-and-write tape, with only the latter contributing to the space complexity of the machine.

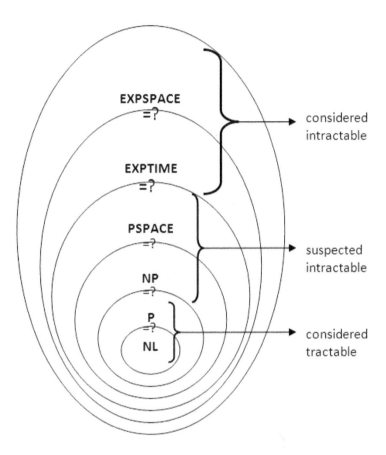

Figure 5.4.1.: The hierarchy of complexity classes with corresponding
tractability status.

associated with tractable and intractable problems, respectively (see Fig. 5.4.1), as we can say that a tractable problem is one that can be solved in *polynomial time*, hence a problem in class **P**; but also in **NP**, which actually stands for *non-deterministic polynomial time*, as this class corresponds to the problems that can be decided by a NDTM in polynomial time, *if* **P** $=$ **NP**. An intractable problem is one that requires super-polynomial time to be solved. This distinction between tractable $=$ polynomial-time and intractable $=$ super-polynomial-time is known as the *Cook-Karp thesis*. But if **P** $\neq$ **NP**, then **NP**-*hard* problems are intractable. This introduces some further fundamental specifications to the classes **P** and **NP**, of which we begin by giving notable examples.

Example 5.4.5. The following are (instances of) problems that are in the class **P**:

The 2-SAT Problem – Given a formula ϕ that is a conjunction of disjunctions of exactly two variables, is ϕ satisfiable?

The Path Problem – Given a digraph $\vec{\mathfrak{G}}$, is there a directed path in $\vec{\mathfrak{G}}$ from vertices u to v?

The Shortest Path Problem – Given a graph $\mathfrak{G}$, is there a path in $\mathfrak{G}$ from vertices u and v that uses the fewest edges?

The Relative Primes Problem – We say that two numbers a and b are relative primes if $\gcd(a, b) = 1$. Given two numbers x and y, are they relative primes?

5.4.4. The Cook-Levin theorem and polynomial-time reducibility

As seen above (cf. Section 5.2), once we have determined that a decision problem is in a certain complexity class, we can reduce other problems to this one, so that they are also in this class. This is particularly relevant when we are concerned only with time complexity, as we are then most often faced with problems that are either in **P** or in **NP**. Recall that if a problem A is reducible to a problem B, we write "$A \preceq B$" and read informally "A is no harder than B" or "B is at least as hard as A." We can actually further specify this "hardness reduction" as polynomial-time reducibility as follows:

5.4.15. (Def.) *Polynomial-time reducibility* – Let A and B be two decision problems and let function f be defined as in Definition 5.2.2. To condition f_{red} stated in Definition 5.2.2 add the condition:

$$(f_P) \qquad f \text{ can be computed in polynomial time}$$

Then, if conditions f_{red} and f_P are both satisfied, we say that A can be *polynomial-time reducible* to B and we write "$A \preceq_P B$".

We state the following theorem in terms of languages for the sake of generality.

Theorem 5.4.1. *Let L_1 and L_2 be languages. If $L_1 \preceq_P L_2$ and $L_2 \in \mathbf{P}$, then $L_1 \in \mathbf{P}$.*

Proof: Let f be the polynomial-time reduction from L_1 to L_2, so that we have $L_1 \preceq_P L_2$. Then, there is a polynomial-time algorithm M_1 deciding L_1 such that, given a polynomial-time algorithm M_2 deciding L_2, on a given input w, M_1 (i) computes $f(w)$, and (ii) runs M_2 on input $f(w)$ and outputs the same as M_2. Hence, by condition f_{red} in Definition 5.2.2, M_2 accepts $f(w)$ whenever $w \in L_1$. Because M_2 computes $f(w)$ in polynomial time, $|f(w)|$ is bounded by a polynomial function of $|w|$, and $L_2 \in \mathbf{P}$. Moreover, stages (i) and (ii) constitute the polynomial-time algorithm M_1 that requires the number of steps to compute $f(w)$ plus the number of steps needed by M_2 on input $f(w)$, so that in fact M_1 is a composition of polynomials. As a composition of polynomials is also a polynomial, we have $L_1 \in \mathbf{P}$. **QED**

5.4.16. (Def.) A language L is said to be **NP**-*complete*, or a member of the class **NPC** if (i) $L \in \mathbf{NP}$, and (ii) for every $L_i \in \mathbf{NP}$ it is the case that $L_i \preceq_P L$.

Informally, a problem is **NP**-complete if it is one of the hardest **NP** problems.

Example 5.4.6. The following are (instances of) problems in the class **NPC**:[15]

The Satisfiability Problem (SAT) – See Definition 2.2.14 and also below.[16]

The k-SAT Problem – Given a formula ϕ that is a conjunction of disjunctions of $k \geq 3$ variables, is ϕ satisfiable?

The Circuit Satisfiability Problem – Given a Boolean combinatorial circuit C, is C satisfiable?

The Hamiltonian Path Problem – See Example 5.4.1 above.

The Subgraph Isomorphism Problem – Given two graphs $\mathfrak{G}_1$ and $\mathfrak{G}_2$, is $\mathfrak{G}_1$ isomorphic to a subgraph of $\mathfrak{G}_2$?

---

[15]See Garey & Johnson (1979 or later editions) for an extensive listing and account of problems in the class **NPC**.

[16]This was actually the first problem found to be **NP**-complete, being as such the one problem to which all **NP** problems can be reduced. Because this problem is at the very core of classical computation we elaborate on it in detail below.

The Vertex Cover Problem – Given an undirected graph $\mathfrak{G} = (V, E)$, a vertex cover is a set $V' \subseteq V$ such that if $(u, v) \in E$, then $u \in V'$ or $v \in V'$, or both. The size of a vertex cover is the number of vertices that are its members. We want to find a vertex cover of (minimum) size k in $\mathfrak{G}$.

The Graph Colorability Problem – Given an undirected graph $\mathfrak{G}$, what is the minimum number k of colors required to color it in a way that no adjacent vertices have the same color?

The Hamiltonian Cycle Problem – Given a graph $\mathfrak{G} = (V, E)$, is there a Hamiltonian cycle–i.e. a simple cycle that contains each $v_i \in V$–in $\mathfrak{G}$?

The Clique Problem – Given an undirected graph $\mathfrak{G}$, is there a clique (i.e. a complete subgraph) of $\mathfrak{G}$ of size k?

The Subset-Sum Problem – Given a set $S \subseteq \mathbb{N}$, we wish to know whether there is a subset S' whose elements sum to $t \in \mathbb{N}$ (t is called a *target*).

The Traveling Salesman Problem (TSP) – Is there a route of length at most k passing through n places?

The Graph Isomorphism Problem – Are two given graphs $\mathfrak{G}_1$ and $\mathfrak{G}_2$ isomorphic?

Theorem 5.4.2. *If $L_1 \in$ **NPC** and $L_1 \preceq_P L_2$, for $L_2 \in$ **NP**, then $L_2 \in$ **NPC**.*

Proof: If L_1 is **NP**-complete, then every other language $L \in$ **NP** is polynomial-time reducible to L_1. In turn, L_1 is polynomial-time reducible to L_2. Hence, by composition of polynomial-time reductions, every language in **NP** is polynomial-time reducible to L_2. **QED**

Theorem 5.4.2 entails that once we have found a **NP**-complete problem, then we can prove that other problems belong to the **NPC** class by means of polynomial-time reduction. In fact, we have one such problem, the Satisfiability Problem, or SAT.

5.4.17. (Def.) The language

$$SAT = \{\langle \phi \rangle \,|\, \phi \text{ is satisfiable}\}$$

for a given formula ϕ and $\langle \phi \rangle$ an adequate encoding thereof, is called the *(Boolean) satisfiability problem*, or, abbreviated, *SAT*.

We now give the adequate encoding $\langle \phi \rangle$:

5.4.18. (Def.) An instance of SAT is a formula $\phi = \phi(x_1, ..., x_n)$ composed of

1. $x_1, ..., x_n$ Boolean variables;

2. k Boolean connectives $\neg, \wedge, \vee$.

Recall Definition 2.2.14: We say that a Boolean expression $\phi(x_1, ..., x_n)$ is satisfiable if and only if there is at least one assignment of truth values to the variables $x_1, ..., x_n$ of ϕ such that we have $f^n(\phi) = 1$. In logical jargon, we say that there is a *model* for ϕ and denote this by $\models_\mathcal{M} \phi$. SAT is thus formulated as a logical problem as the language

$$SAT = \{\phi | \models_\mathcal{M} \phi\}$$

where the symbol $\models$ denotes (semantical) logical consequence.[17]

Interestingly enough, SAT was the very first problem to be proven to be **NP**-complete, namely in Cook (1971).[18]

Theorem 5.4.3. *(Cook-Levin theorem) SAT is* **NP***-complete.*

Proof: The proof of this theorem, which requires contents from Section 2.2.1.2, is quite fastidious, and thus we give here only the most important aspects thereof, leaving as an exercise the research into its details. We divide the proof into two parts for convenience.

Part I – Recall Definition 5.4.16. This definition dictates that the first step in the proof of this theorem is to show that SAT is in the class **NP**. Let us consider a Boolean formula in the form

$$\phi = \bigwedge_i \left(\bigvee_j L_{ij} \right).$$

This is an abbreviation of a conjunctive normal form (CNF). Recall that a formula in CNF is a series of conjunctions of disjunctions of (negated) atoms. An example of a formula in this form is

$$\phi = (x_1 \vee x_3 \vee \neg x_4) \wedge \neg x_2 \wedge (\neg x_1 \vee x_2).$$

Because these are Boolean variables, it is easy to devise a deterministic algorithm: We take all the possible truth-value assignments of the variables $x_1, ..., x_n$ and evaluate ϕ for each of the assignments. As there are 2^n different assignments, this exhaustive algorithm is of exponential-time complexity, i.e. is in the **EXPTIME** class. However, we can improve on this by means of a non-deterministic polynomial-time algorithm that

---

[17]See Augusto (2020c) for a comprehensive elaboration on logical consequence.
[18]Later on, in 1973, and independently, also by L. Levin.

guesses a truth-value assignment to ϕ and returns "accept" if the assignment satisfies ϕ. Hence, SAT is a **NP** problem.

Part II – Now, the fastidious part is showing that any **NP** problem is polynomial-time reducible to SAT, i.e. SAT is a **NP**-complete problem. We give the essentials of this proof, which requires knowledge of the Turing machine (see Section 4.3).

Let L be any language in the **NP** class. We aim to show that

$$L \preceq_P SAT.$$

We consider a non-deterministic Turing machine M_T that decides L in time n^k for some constant k; we thus have $L = L(M_T)$. (We abbreviate M_T as M.) The alphabet of L is $\Sigma = \{\neg, \wedge, \vee, x, 0, 1\}$, possibly with parentheses. For convenience, we shall write $\overline{x}$ instead of $\neg x$. Recall from Definition 5.2.2 that $L \preceq SAT$ means that $w \in L$ if and only if $f(w) \in SAT$. We aim to show that we can construct a function

$$f_L : \Sigma_L^* \longrightarrow CNF_L$$

such that (i) for every $w \in \Sigma^*$, w is accepted by M if and only if $f_L(w) = \phi \in CNF_L$, ϕ is a (Boolean) formula in CNF, is satisfiable, and (ii) the corresponding function $g_M : \Sigma^* \to \{\neg, \wedge, x, 1\}^*$,

$$g_M(w) = \phi \in L$$

is computable in polynomial time.

Part (i) is the fastidious one; (ii) is easily verifiable. The idea of the proof is based on the fact that there will be satisfying assignments of $f_L(w)$ if and only if there are accepting configurations of M on w, so that in fact the reduction of L to SAT is carried out via what we can call "computation histories." In order to achieve this objective we have both to describe the computations of M by Boolean variables and to express accepting states of M on w by Boolean formulas.

But first of all, we need a *tableau* for M, i.e. a $n^k \times n^k$ table each row of which is one of the n^k configurations $C_i = Q \cup \Gamma \cup \{\$\}$, $\$$ is a delimiter symbol, of a branch of the computation of M on w for $|w| = n$ (cf. Fig. 5.4.2). Let C_1 be the start configuration. Let each cell (i, j) of the $(n^k)^2$ cells of the tableau have its contents represented by $|C|$ Boolean variables of ϕ

$$\{x_{i,j,\sigma} | \sigma \in C\}$$

indicating that cell (i, j) contains σ if $x_{i,j,\sigma} = 1$. Given $1 \leq i, j \leq n^k$, there will be $|C| \cdot (n^k)^2$ Boolean variables.

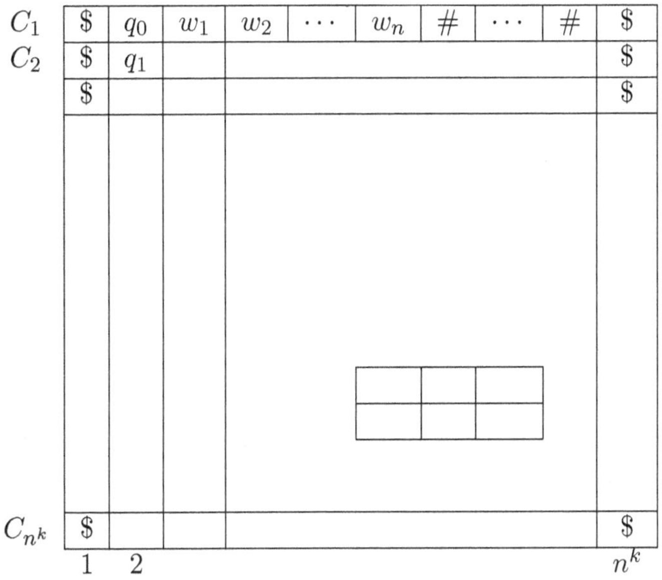

C_1	\$	q_0	w_1	w_2	$\cdots$	w_n	#	$\cdots$	#	\$
C_2	\$	q_1								\$
	\$									\$
C_{n^k}	\$									\$
	1	2							n^k	

Figure 5.4.2.: A tableau for the Turing machine M.

A tableau is said to be an *accepting tableau* if there is a row that is an accepting configuration $C_{p(|w|)=n^k}$, and $f_L(w)$ is satisfiable if and only if there is a "computation history" (a computation branch) of consecutive configurations of M

$$C_1, C_2, ..., C_{n^k}$$

where two configurations are said to be consecutive if we have $C_{i-1} \vdash_M C_i$ (or $C = C'$). In order to produce an accepting tableau for ϕ we have to produce the corresponding CNF of ϕ:

$$CNF(\phi) = \phi_{cell} \wedge \phi_{start} \wedge \phi_{move} \wedge \phi_{accept}$$

The first thing to consider in this correspondence between the tableau and $CNF(\phi)$ is to make sure that for each assignment there must be exactly one symbol $\sigma \in C$ such that $x_{i,j,\sigma} = 1$. This is expressible in Boolean terms as follows:

$$\phi_{cell} = \bigwedge_{\substack{1 \leq i \\ j \leq n^k}} \left[\left(\bigvee_{\sigma \in C} x_{i,j,\sigma} \right) \wedge \left(\bigwedge_{\substack{\sigma, \tau \in C \\ \sigma \neq \tau}} (\overline{x}_{i,j,\sigma} \vee \overline{x}_{i,j,\tau}) \right) \right]$$

277

where $\left(\bigvee_{\sigma \in C} x_{i,j,\sigma}\right)$ means that at least for one of the variables it is the case that $x_{i,j,\sigma} = 1$ *and* $\bigwedge_{\sigma,\tau \in C; \sigma \neq \tau} \left(\overline{x}_{i,j,\sigma} \vee \overline{x}_{i,j,\tau}\right)$ expresses the fact that for no more than one variable it is the case that $x_{i,j,\sigma} = 1$.

The formula ϕ_{start} guarantees that the first row of the tableau is the starting configuration. This it expresses as:

$$\phi_{start} = x_{1,1,\$} \wedge x_{1,2,q_0} \wedge x_{1,3,w_1} \wedge x_{1,4,w_2} \wedge \dots$$

$$\wedge x_{1,n+2,w_n} \wedge x_{1,n+3,\#} \wedge \dots$$

$$\wedge x_{1,n^k-1,\#} \wedge x_{1,n^k,\$}$$

We now require a formula that guarantees that there occurs an accepting configuration in the tableau. This is the formula

$$\phi_{accept} = \bigvee_{\substack{1 \leq i \\ j \leq n^k}} x_{i,j,q_a}$$

where q_a denotes the accepting state. Obviously, if for some cell (i, j) we have a variable x_{i,j,q_a} such that $x_{i,j,q_a} = 1$, then we have an accepting configuration.

We spoke above of a "computation history." This entails that in the sequence of consecutive configurations of M

$$C_1, C_2, \dots, C_{n^k}$$

we have it that C_{i+1} follows *legally* from C_i. In terms of the tableau for M, this means that each 2×3 *window* of cells (see center of the tableau in Fig. 5.4.2) strictly follows–or does not violate–the transition function of M. In order to verify that each row of the tableau corresponds to a configuration that preserves this legality we have the formula

$$\phi_{move} = \bigwedge_{\substack{1 \leq i < n^k \\ 1 < j < n^k}} \mathcal{W}_{i,j}$$

where $\mathcal{W}_{i,j}$ denotes the valid 2×3 window with top-middle cell at (i, j) and

$$\mathcal{W}_{i,j} =$$

$$\bigvee_{(a_1,\dots,a_6) \in Val} \left(x_{i,j',a_1} \wedge x_{i,j,a_2} \wedge x_{i,j'',a_3} \wedge x_{i+1,j',a_4} \wedge x_{i+1,j,a_5} \wedge x_{i+1,j'',a_6}\right)$$

278

where Val is the set of 6-tuples of valid assignments to the cells of $\mathcal{W}$, and $j' = j - 1, j'' = j + 1$.

This done, we now have to prove that each of the four formulas above can be expressed by a formula of size $\mathcal{O}\left(n^{2k}\right)$ and can be constructed in polynomial time from w. That is, we have to show that the "computation history" above can be abbreviated as

$$C_1 \vdash^*_M C_{n^k}$$

for $n^k = p\left(|w|\right)$ for a given formula w. (This is left as an exercise.) **QED**

Figure 5.4.3 shows some fundamental polynomial-time reductions. Notice the central position of SAT, but also the transitivity of polynomial-time reducibility, i.e. if $L_1 \preceq_P L_2$ and $L_2 \preceq_P L_3$, then $L_1 \preceq_P L_3$.

Example 5.4.7. We show in general traits how to reduce the Vertex Cover Problem to the Clique Problem. Let $(\mathfrak{G}, k)$ be an instance of the former, for $\mathfrak{G} = (V, E)$. We construct the complement of $\mathfrak{G}$, denoted by $\overline{\mathfrak{G}}$, such that $V_{\overline{\mathfrak{G}}} = V_{\mathfrak{G}}$, but the edge $(u, v) \in \overline{\mathfrak{G}}$ if and only if $(u, v) \notin \mathfrak{G}$. Where k is the integer parameter for the Vertex Cover Problem, we now define the integer parameter for the Clique Problem as $n - k$. Then–and the reduction consists in this–, $\overline{\mathfrak{G}}$ has a clique of size at least $n - k$ if and only if $\mathfrak{G}$ has a vertex cover of size at most k. Moreover, the construction for the Clique problem runs in polynomial time, so that this is a polynomial-time reduction.

Theorem 5.4.4. *If L is a **NP**-complete language and $L \in$ **P**, then* **P = NP**.

Proof: Follows directly from the definition of polynomial-time reducibility. **QED**

5.4.19. (Def.) A language L is said to be **NP**-*hard* if for every $L_i \in$ **NP** we have $L_i \preceq_P L$, but L need not be a member of the class **NP**.

Informally, a problem is **NP**-hard if it is at least as hard as all the **NP** problems.

Example 5.4.8. The following are **NP**-hard problems:
The Halting Problem (Not **NP**-complete)
The Circuit Satisfiability Problem (**NP**-complete)
The Clique Problem (**NP**-complete)
The Vertex Cover Problem (**NP**-complete)
The Traveling Salesman Problem (**NP**-complete)

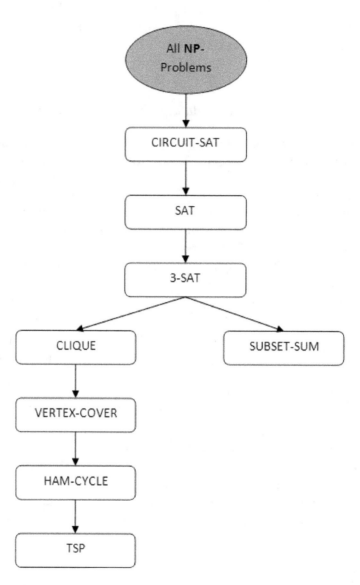

Figure 5.4.3.: Typical structure of **NP**-completeness proofs by polynomial-time reductions.

The Subset-Sum Problem (**NP**-complete)

Above, we remarked that if $\mathbf{P} \neq \mathbf{NP}$, then **NP**-*hard* problems are intractable. Indeed, if $\mathbf{P} \neq \mathbf{NP}$, we actually have

$$\mathbf{NPC} = \mathbf{NP} \cap \mathbf{NP}\text{-hard}$$

and

$$\mathbf{P} \cap \mathbf{NPC} = \emptyset.$$

On the other hand, if $\mathbf{P} = \mathbf{NP}$, then

$$(\mathbf{NPC} = \mathbf{NP} = \mathbf{P}) \subset \mathbf{NP}\text{-hard}.$$

The real impact of $\mathbf{P} \overset{?}{=} \mathbf{NP}$ becomes clearer when we define $\mathbf{P}$ as the class of problems that can be *solved* in polynomial time (i.e. quickly), and $\mathbf{NP}$ as the class of problems for which a solution, if one has been found, can be *verified* in polynomial time.[19] The crux posed by problems in $\mathbf{NP}$ is that there is no known efficient way to find a solution for them in the first place.

However, polynomial time other than $\mathcal{O}\left(n^2\right), \mathcal{O}\left(n^3\right)$, and $\mathcal{O}\left(n^4\right)$ is not necessarily synonymous with *quickly*, or even efficiently computable at all. For instance, an input as low as $n = 100$ will be uncomputable in practice if raised to the power of, say, 15. On the other hand, exponential time algorithms are efficient for very low inputs.

Exercises

Exercise 5.4.1. Show that DTIME, DSPACE, NTIME, and NSPACE satisfy the Blum axioms.

Exercise 5.4.2. Show that $p\left(n\right) = \mathcal{O}\left(n^k\right)$ for $p\left(n\right) = a_0 + a_1 n + a_2 n^2 + ... + a_k n^k$.

Exercise 5.4.3. With respect to Example 5.4.4:

---

[19]For which we need a *verifier*, an algorithm Ψ that uses additional information–a *certificate*, or *proof*, of membership, denoted by, say, c–so that a language L is defined as

$$L = \{w | \Psi \text{ accepts } z = e\left(wc\right) = \langle w, c \rangle \text{ for some string } c\}.$$

A verifier Ψ is a *polynomial-time verifier* if there is a polynomial $p\left(n\right)$ such that the number of moves of Ψ is no greater than $p\left(|n|\right)$, where $n = |w|$. For instance, suppose that we have the following sequence $c = \langle v_1, v_2, ..., v_n \rangle$ of $|V| = n$ vertices that has been given as a solution to an instance of the Hamiltonian Cycle Problem. Then, one can verify in polynomial time that $(v_i, v_{i+1}) \in E$ for $i = 1, 2, ..., n - 1$ and also that $(v_n, v_1) \in E$.

5. Computability and complexity

1. Find a Turing machine with time complexity lower than $\mathcal{O}\left(n^2\right)$.

2. Show that no single-tape Turing machine can decide L more quickly than in time $\mathcal{O}\left(n \log n\right)$.

Exercise 5.4.4. Given a FA $M = (Q, \Sigma, q_0, A, \delta)$, Algorithm 4.2 has time complexity for $n = |Q|$ and $k = |\Sigma|$ (choose the correct answer, if any):

1. $\mathcal{O}\left(kn \log n\right)$.

2. $\mathcal{O}\left(n \log n\right)$.

3. $\mathcal{O}\left(kn^2\right)$.

Exercise 5.4.5. Prove the following theorem:

Theorem 5.4.5. *For $T\left(n\right) \geq n$, every $T\left(n\right)$ time multi-tape Turing machine has an equivalent $\mathcal{O}\left(T^2\left(n\right)\right)$ time single-tape Turing machine.*

Exercise 5.4.6. Prove the following theorem:

Theorem 5.4.6. *For $T\left(n\right) \geq n$, every $T\left(n\right)$ time non-deterministic single-tape Turing machine has an equivalent $2^{\mathcal{O}\left(T\left(n\right)\right)}$ time deterministic single-tape Turing machine.*

Exercise 5.4.7. Formulate the problems of Examples 5.4.5-6 as languages. Explain in a detailed way why these problems are in the classes **P**, **NP**, or **NPC**.

Exercise 5.4.8. SAT can be solved with a linear-space algorithm, but it cannot even be solved by a polynomial-time algorithm, as it is a **NP**-complete problem. Provide an account of this by appealing to the Turing machine.

Exercise 5.4.9. Give an informal account of the following facts:

1. **P⊆PSPACE**.

2. **NP⊆NPSPACE**.

3. **NP⊆PSPACE**.

Exercise 5.4.10. Show that if $L \in$ **P**, L is a language, then $\overline{L} \in$ **P**.

Exercise 5.4.11. Show that the relation $\preceq_P$ on the set of languages is transitive.

Exercise 5.4.12. Devise an algorithm to solve the Clique Problem.

Exercise 5.4.13. Show that **NP** is closed under union, intersection, concatenation, and Kleene star.

Exercise 5.4.14. Show that the Vertex Cover Problem is **NP**-hard.

Exercise 5.4.15. Show, by giving an example, that the Vertex Cover Problem can be reduced to the Subset-Sum Problem.

Exercise 5.4.16. With respect to Part II of the proof above of Theorem 5.4.3:

1. Provide the details of the construction and verification of the set *Val*.

2. Prove (ii).

Exercise 5.4.17. Give the complete proof of Theorem 5.4.4.

Exercise 5.4.18. Show that the *general SAT*, i.e. SAT for Boolean formulas not necessarily in CNF, is **NP**-complete.

Exercise 5.4.19. It can be shown that CIRCUIT-SAT$\preceq_P$SAT (cf. Fig. 5.4.3). Research into the CIRCUIT-SAT and:

1. Give the essentials of the straightforward proof that this is an **NP**-complete problem.

2. Give the proof that CIRCUIT-SAT$\preceq_P$SAT.

Exercise 5.4.20. Prove that 3-SAT is **NP**-complete by the reduction

$$SAT \preceq_P 3\text{-}SAT.$$

Exercise 5.4.21. Prove the following statements:

1. 2-SAT$\in$**P**.

2. DNF-SAT$\in$**P**.

3. 3-SAT is **NP**-complete.

4. k-SAT, $k \geq 3$, is **NP**-complete.

Exercise 5.4.22. If DNF-SAT$\in$**P**, but (CNF-)SAT is **NP**-complete, why is the Boolean satisfiability problem not typically formulated in terms of DNFs?

Exercise 5.4.23. The language

$$HORN\text{-}SAT = \{\phi| \models_\mathcal{M} \phi, \phi \text{ is a Horn formula}\}$$

for a Horn formula a CNF formula whose clauses have at most one positive literal, is called the *satisfiability problem for Horn formulas*, or, abbreviated, *HORN-SAT*. Research into the result

$$HORN\text{-}SAT \in \mathbf{P}.$$

Exercise 5.4.24. Recall the definition of a quantified Boolean formula (QBF; cf. Def. 2.2.8). The language

$$QBF\text{-}SAT = \{\phi| \models_\mathcal{M} \phi, \phi \text{ is a QBF}\}$$

is called the *satisfiability problem for QBFs*, or, abbreviated, *QBF-SAT*. Research into the result that QBF-SAT is **PSPACE**-complete.

Exercise 5.4.25. Research into the *maximum satisfiability problem*, abbreviated MAX-SAT:

1. Give a formal definition of this problem and its complexity class.

2. Is MAX-SAT a decision problem?

5.5. The Chomsky hierarchy (IV)

Above in this Chapter, we concentrated our discussion mostly on recursive languages and RELs. We now revisit the Chomsky hierarchy and provide complexity results for the other languages in this hierarchy. Note, however, that these results are not yet well understood, not the least because the complexity classes are themselves far from clearly grasped. For instance, when we consider the family of classes DTIME (n^k), $k = 1, 2, ...$, we are actually considering an infinite number of properly nested complexity classes.

Theorem 5.5.1. *Every regular language is a member of DTIME(n).*

Proof: Left as an exercise.

Theorem 5.5.2. *Every regular language is a member of* **P**.

Proof: Left as an exercise.

Theorem 5.5.3. *Every CFL is a member of* **P**.

Proof: (Sketch) Let a CFL L be generated by a CFG G in Chomsky normal form. Given a string w, in order to test membership of w to $L(G)$ we consider whether every variable in G generates a substring of w. We apply the *CYK Algorithm*, which consists in filling in a triangular table with ij entries such that only the cells for $i \leq j$ are filled in with the collection of variables generating the substrings. Given a string $|w| = n$ such that $w = w_1w_2...w_n$, we begin at the bottom of the table for substrings of length $\ell = 1$, next move one row up for substrings of length $\ell = 2$, and so on up to $\ell = n$. For example, for a string $|w| = 5$, we have the following table:

$V_{1,5}$				
$V_{1,4}$	$V_{2,5}$			
$V_{1,3}$	$V_{2,4}$	$V_{3,5}$		
$V_{1,2}$	$V_{2,3}$	$V_{3,4}$	$V_{4,5}$	
$V_{1,1}$	$V_{2,2}$	$V_{3,3}$	$V_{4,4}$	$V_{5,5}$
w_1	w_2	w_3	w_4	w_5

Let us now denote by $V_{i,i}$ the set of variables $V = \{S, A, B, ...\}$ such that $S, A, B, ... \rightarrow w_i$ is a production rule of G. Then, the algorithm consists in comparing at most n pairs of previously computed sets

$$(V_{i,i}, V_{i+1,j}), (V_{i,i+1}, V_{i+2,j}), ..., (V_{i,j-1}, V_{j,j}).$$

The algorithm terminates in an accepting state if and only if $S \in V_{1,n}$; otherwise, the algorithm ends in a rejecting state. It can be shown that the running time by a Turing machine simulation of the CYK algorithm is $\mathcal{O}(n^3)$.[20] **QED**

---

[20]See, e.g., Younger (1967). D. Younger is one of the three inventors of this algorithm, the other two being J. Cocke and T. Kasami.

Example 5.5.1. The CFG of Example 3.3.6 can be converted into a CFG in ChNF with the following production set:

$$P = \left\{ \begin{array}{c} S \rightarrow CF \\ A \rightarrow BE \\ B \rightarrow DB \mid c \\ C \rightarrow a \\ D \rightarrow b \\ E \rightarrow DC \\ F \rightarrow AB \end{array} \right\}$$

For string $acbabc$, we have the following table for its substrings:

acbabc					
acbab	cbabc				
acba	cbab	babc			
acb	cba	bab	abc		
ac	cb	ba	ab	bc	
a	c	b	a	b	c

Application of the CYK algorithm gives us the following table, where empty cells should be considered as containing $\emptyset$:

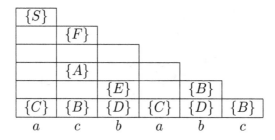

It can be easily verified that the algorithm terminates in an accepting state.

Exercises

Exercise 5.5.1. Formulate the CYK algorithm in pseudo-code.

Exercise 5.5.2. Prove (Complete the proof of) the theorems in this Section that were left as an exercise (with a sketchy proof, respectively).

Exercise 5.5.3. Prove the following statements for a CFG G whose total length of production bodies is n:

1. It takes time $\mathscr{O}(n)$ to determine whether a CFL $L = \emptyset$.

2. It takes time $\mathscr{O}(n^2)$ to find the equivalent G' in ChNF.

References

Anderson, J. A. (2006). *Automata theory with modern applications*. Cambridge, etc.: Cambridge University Press.

Arden, D. N. (1961). Delayed-logic and finite-state machines. *Proceedings of the 2nd Annual Symposium on Switching Circuit Theory and Logical Design (SWCT 1961)*, 133-151.

Augusto, L. M. (2018). *Computational logic. Vol. 1: Classical deductive computing with classical logic*. London: College Publications.

Augusto, L. M. (2019). *Formal logic: Classical problems and proofs*. London: College Publications.

Augusto, L. M. (2020a). *Computational logic. Vol. 1: Classical deductive computing with classical logic*. 2nd ed. London: College Publications.

Augusto, L. M. (2020b). *Many-valued logics. A mathematical and computational introduction*. 2nd ed. London: College Publications.

Augusto, L. M. (2020c). *Logical consequences. Theory and applications: An introduction*. 2nd ed. London: College Publications.

Augusto, L. M. (2020d). Toward a general theory of knowledge. *Journal of Knowledge Structures & Systems, 1*(1), 63-97.

Bar-Hillel, Y., Perles, M., & Shamir, E. (1961). On formal properties of simple phrase structure grammars. *Zeitschrift für Phonetik, Sprachwissenschaft und Kommunikationsforschung, 14*(2), 143-172.

Bloch, E. D. (2011). *Proofs and fundamentals: A first course in abstract mathematics*. 2nd ed. New York, etc.: Springer.

Blum, M. (1967). A machine-independent theory of the complexity of recursive functions. *Journal of the Association for Computing Machinery, 14*(2), 322-336.

Bridges, D. S. (1994). *Computability. A mathematical sketchbook*. New York, etc.: Springer.

Chomsky, N. (1956). Three models for the description of language. *IRE Transactions on Information Theory, 2*(3), 113-124.

Chomsky, N. (1957). *Syntactic structures*. The Hague & Paris: Muton.

Chomsky, N. (1959). On certain formal properties of grammars. *Information and Control, 2*(2), 113-124.

Chomsky, N. (1962). Context-free grammars and pushdown storage. *MIT Quarterly Progress Reports, 65,* 187-194.

Church, A. (1936a). A note on the Entscheidungsproblem. *Journal of Symbolic Logic, 1*(1), 40-41.

Church, A. (1936b). An unsolvable problem of elementary number theory. *American Journal of Mathematics, 58*(2), 345-363.

Cook, S. A. (1971). The complexity of theorem proving procedures. *Proceedings of the 3rd Annual ACM Symposium of Theory of Computing,* 151-158.

Cooper, S. B. (2003). *Computability theory.* Boca Raton, etc.: CRC Press.

Cooper, K. D. & Torczon, L. (2012). *Engineering a compiler.* 2nd ed. Amsterdam, etc.: Morgan Kaufmann.

Cormen, T. H., Leiserson, C. E., Rivest, R. L., & Stein, C. (2009). *Introduction to algorithms.* 3rd ed. Cambridge, MA & London, UK: MIT Press.

Crama, Y. & Hammer, P. L. (2011). *Boolean functions: Theory, algorithms and applications.* Cambridge, etc.: Cambridge University Press.

Crochemore, M., Hancart, C., & Lecroq, T. (2007). *Algorithms on strings.* Cambridge, etc.: Cambridge University Press.

Davis, M. D. & Weyuker, E. J. (1983). *Computability, complexity, and languages. Fundamentals of theoretical computer science.* Orlando, etc.: Academic Press.

Du, D.-Z. & Ko, K.-I. (2001). *Problem solving in automata, languages, and complexity.* New York, etc.: John Wiley & Sons.

Fogel, L. J., Owens, A. J., & Walsh, M. J. (1966). *Artificial intelligence through simulated evolution.* New York, NY: John Wiley & Sons.

Gallier, J. (2011). *Discrete mathematics.* New York, etc.: Springer.

Garey, M. R. & Johnson, D. S. (1979). *Computers and intractability: A guide to the theory of NP-completeness.* New York: W. H. Freeman and Company.

Gödel, K. (1964). Postscriptum to Gödel (1934). In *Collected works I* (pp. 369-371). Oxford: Oxford University Press, 1986.

Gopalakrishnan, G. (2006). *Computation engineering. Applied automata theory and logic.* New York: Springer.

Grune, D. & Jacobs, C. J. H. (2010). *Parsing techniques: A practical guide.* 2nd ed. New York, NY: Springer.

Hausser, R. (2014). *Foundations of computational linguistics. Human-computer communication in natural language.* 3rd ed. Heidelberg, etc.: Springer.

Hilbert, D. & Ackermann, W. (1928). *Grundzüge der theoretischen Logik.* Berlin: Springer.

Holland, J. H. (1975). *Adaptation in natural and artificial systems.* Ann Arbor, MI: University of Michigan Press.

Hopcroft, J. E & Ullman, J. (1979). *Introduction to automata theory, languages, and computation.* 1st ed. Reading, MA, etc.: Addison-Wesley.

Hopcroft, J. E., Motwani, R., & Ullman, J. (2013). *Introduction to automata theory, languages, and computation.* 3rd ed. Boston, etc.: Pearson.

Khoussainov, B. & Nerode, N. (2001). *Automata theory and its applications.* New York: Springer.

Kleene, S. C. (1938). On notation for ordinal numbers. *Journal of Symbolic Logic, 3*(4), 150-155.

Kleene, S. C. (1956). Representation of events in nerve nets and finite automata. In C. E. Shannon & J. McCarthy (eds.), *Automata studies* (pp. 3-42). Princeton: Princeton University Press.

Kohavi, Z. & Jha, N. (2010). *Switching and finite automata theory.* 3rd ed. Cambridge, etc.: Cambridge University Press.

Leary, C. C. & Kristiansen, L. (2015). *A friendly introduction to mathematical logic.* 2nd ed. Geneseo, NY: Milne Library.

Lovelace, A. (1843). Notes on L. Menabrea's "Sketch of the Analytical Engine invented by Charles Babbage, Esq." *Taylor's Scientific Memoirs*, vol. 3. London: J. E. & R. Taylor.

Makinson, D. (2008). *Sets, logic, and maths for computing.* London: Springer.

Matiyasevich, Y. V. (1993). *Hilbert's Tenth Problem.* Cambridge, MA: MIT Press.

McCulloch, W. S. & Pitts, W. (1943). A logical calculus of the ideas immanent in nervous activity. *Bulletin of Mathematical Biophysics, 5,* 115-133.

Mealy, G. H. (1955). A method for synthesizing sequential circuits. *Bell System Technical Journal, 34*(5), 1045-1079.

Moore, E. F. (1956). Gedanken-experiments on sequential machines. *Automata Studies, Annals of Mathematical Studies, 34,* 129-153.

Nerode, A. (1958). Linear automaton transformations. *Proceedings of the AMS, 9*(4), 541-544.

Oettinger, A. G. (1961). Automatic syntactic analysis and the pushdown store. In R. Jakobson (ed.), *Structure of language and its mathematical aspects* (pp. 104-139). *Proceedings of Smposia in Applied Mathematics, 12.* Providence, RI: American Mathematical Society.

Ogden, W. (1968). A helpful result for proving inherent ambiguity. *Mathematical Systems Theory, 2,* 191-194.

Rabin, M. O. & Scott, D. (1959). Finite automata and their decision problems. *IBM Journal, 3*(2), 115-125.

Reghizzi, S. C., Breveglieri, L., & Morzenti, A. (2019). *Formal languages and compilation.* 3rd ed. London: Springer.

Révész, G. E. (1991). *Introduction to formal languages.* Minneola, NY: Dover.

Rumelhart, D. E., McClelland, J. L., & the PDP Research Group (1988). *Parallel distributed processing. Explorations in the microstructure of cognition. Vol. 1: Foundations.* Cambridge, MA & London, UK: The MIT Press.

Sakarovitch, J. (2009). *Elements of automata theory.* Cambridge: Cambridge University Press.

Scott, M. L. (2009). *Programming language pragmatics.* 3rd ed. Amsterdam, etc.: Morgan Kaufmann.

Sebesta, R. W. (2012). *Concepts of programming languages.* 10th ed. Boston, etc.: Pearson.

Sippu, S. & Soisalon-Soininen, E. (1990). *Parsing theory. Vol. II: LR(k) and LL(k) parsing.* Berlin, Heidelberg: Springer.

Turing, A. M. (1937). On computable numbers, with an application to the Entscheidungsproblem. *Proceedings of the London Mathematical Society, Series 2, 42*(1), 230-265.

Turing, A. M. (1950). Computing machinery and intelligence. *Mind, 59*(236), 433-460.

von Neumann, J. (1945). *First draft of a report on the EVDAC.* Technical report. University of Pennsylvania. (Reprinted in B. Randell (ed.), *The origins of digital computers. Selected papers* (pp. 383-392). 3rd ed. Berlin, etc.: Springer. 1982.)

Younger, D. H. (1967). Recognition and parsing of context-free languages in time n^3. *Information and Control, 10*(2), 189-208.

Zadeh, L. A. (1965). Fuzzy sets. *Information and Control, 8*(3), 338-353.

Index

Index